Nature and Nurture in Personality and Psychopathology

Psychiatry and clinical psychology have long been divided about the roles of nature and nurture in the pathways to psychopathology. Some clinicians offer treatment almost entirely based on neuroscience. Some psychologists offer psychotherapies almost entirely based on the impact of environmental stressors. Paris argues for a balanced middle ground between nature and nurture in human development. This book reviews and integrates research showing that the key to understanding the development of mental disorders lies in interactions between genes and environment. It explores why personality is a key determinant of how people respond to stress, functioning as a kind of psychological immune system. This model represents a shift from overly simple and reductionistic constructs, based primarily on biological risks or on psychosocial risks in development. Instead, it offers a complex and multivariate approach that encourages a broader approach to treatment.

This book is essential for all mental health clinicians who are interested in understanding the roles of nature and nurture in the development of psychopathology.

Joel Paris, MD, is a research associate at the Sir Mortimer B. Davis Jewish General Hospital in Montreal, Canada, and emeritus professor of Psychiatry at McGill University. He is the author of 25 books and over 200 scientific papers. His main area of research has been borderline personality disorder.

Nature and Nurture in Personality and Psychopathology
A Guide for Clinicians

Joel Paris

NEW YORK AND LONDON

First published 2022
by Routledge
605 Third Avenue, New York, NY 10158

and by Routledge
4 Park Square, Milton Park, Abingdon, Oxon, OX14 4RN

Routledge is an imprint of the Taylor & Francis Group, an informa business

© 2022 Joel Paris

The right of Joel Paris to be identified as author of this work has been asserted in accordance with sections 77 and 78 of the Copyright, Designs and Patents Act 1988.

All rights reserved. No part of this book may be reprinted or reproduced or utilised in any form or by any electronic, mechanical, or other means, now known or hereafter invented, including photocopying and recording, or in any information storage or retrieval system, without permission in writing from the publishers.

Trademark notice: Product or corporate names may be trademarks or registered trademarks, and are used only for identification and explanation without intent to infringe.

Library of Congress Cataloguing-in-Publication Data
Names: Paris, Joel, 1940- author.
Title: Nature and nurture in personality and psychopathology: a guide for clinicians / Joel Paris, Emeritus Professor of Psychiatry, McGill University.
Description: New York, NY: Routledge, 2022. | Includes bibliographical references and index. |
Identifiers: LCCN 2021043082 (print) | LCCN 2021043083 (ebook) | ISBN 9780367741389 (hardback) | ISBN 9780367741365 (paperback) | ISBN 9781003156215 (ebook)
Subjects: LCSH: Nature and nurture. | Personality. | Psychology, Pathological. | Mental illness--Genetic aspects.
Classification: LCC BF341.P27 2022 (print) | LCC BF341 (ebook) | DDC 155.2/34--dc23
LC record available at https://lccn.loc.gov/2021043082
LC ebook record available at https://lccn.loc.gov/2021043083

ISBN: 978-0-367-74138-9 (hbk)
ISBN: 978-0-367-74136-5 (pbk)
ISBN: 978-1-003-15621-5 (ebk)

DOI: 10.4324/9781003156215

Typeset in Bembo
by MPS Limited, Dehradun

Contents

	Introduction	1
1	Defining and Measuring Psychopathology	10
2	Personality and Psychopathology	24
3	What Genes Can and Cannot Tell Us	37
4	Neuroscience: Triumphs and Limitations	47
5	Childhood Adversities and Adult Functioning	56
6	Resilience: Surviving a Bad Childhood	71
7	Nature–Nurture Interactions	82
8	Problems with Causality	93
9	Implications for Psychotherapy	104
10	Implications for Prevention and Management	112
	References	126
	Index	146

Introduction

Mental health clinicians treat psychopathology. If they carry out psychotherapy, they also aim to modify personality traits. This book will show that the development of both psychopathology and personality has similar roots. It will guide clinicians to research that sheds light on their origins and demonstrate the need for a complex, interactional, multivariate, and biopsychosocial model.

Psychopathology is characterized by abnormal thoughts, behaviors, and experiences. But there are problems with almost any definition of "abnormality", and with the boundaries of what we call "mental disorders". Both these terms turn out to be rather tricky. Neither *Diagnostic and Statistical Manual of Mental Disorders (DSM)-5* (American Psychiatric Association, 2013) nor the *International Classification of Diseases*, 11th edition (World Health Organization, 2018) has been able to define mental disorders in a way that everyone can agree on. Allen Frances (2014) once stated that he has never seen a valid distinction between what is normal and what is abnormal in psychiatry. One reason is that definitions can be, at least in part, culturally determined.

Wakefield (2007) made an attempt to work around these problems by defining mental disorders in an evolutionary framework. He used the term *harmful dysfunction*, i.e., conditions that interfere with survival and/or reproduction. But we are still left with the problem of precisely defining the words "harmful" and "dysfunction".

My conclusion is that we have to accept that psychopathology has fuzzy edges. Thus, thoughts, emotions, and behaviors vary continuously, without any definite boundary from disorder. That is why this book will use the term"psychopathology", consistent with seeing mental disorders as transdiagnostic, and as quantitative rather than qualitative.

Personality is a key concept for understanding the individual differences between people in thoughts, behaviors, and emotions that remain fairly stable over time. Personality trait profiles help account for responses to stress and for vulnerability for psychopathology, functioning as a kind of *psychological immune system* (Millon and Davis, 1996). These traits reflect genetically shaped temperamental biases that are also shaped by life experiences. Their origins and role in development overlap with psychopathology.

DOI: 10.4324/9781003156215-101

Nature and Nurture

Traditionally, psychological differences between people have been understood as largely due to *nature* (i.e. genes) or to nurture (i.e. life experiences). Yet neither inborn traits nor life experiences can, by themselves, account for psychological development. This book will review a broad range of research supporting the view that development requires an integrative approach. This interactive model has been called biopsychosocial (Engel, 1980), or, more precisely, *gene-environment interplay* (Rutter, 2012). The causal pathways that emerge from the model are complex, but offer the best explanation of why people differ in vulnerability or in resilience to psychopathology. Similar conclusions apply to the pathways shaping personality, whose structure also reflects an interplay between genes and the environment.

Supported by a large body of data, this book will show that *interactions* between genes and the environment are the main basis of individual differences in traits and in vulnerability to mental disorders. Thus, genes can shape the environment and the environment can modify the activity of genes. This point of view explains why risk factors affect different people in a different way, and why no single factor or set of risk factors is strongly predictive of psychological outcomes. I will also show how personality acts as a modulator of gene–environment interplay, serving as a system that governs the processing of life events.

Finally, I will show how these complexities can be usefully applied to planning and carrying out interventions in clinical practice. The roles of nature and nurture in psychological treatment have long been the subject of controversy. Nature tends to be favored by physicians, particularly when their practice focuses on neuroscience and medication. Nurture tends to be favored by clinicians who practice psychotherapy, as well as by social scientists.

Some dismiss the nature–nurture controversy as an anachronism. Even so, it remains alive and well. One might think that most clinicians understand that neither nature nor nurture is sufficient, on their own, to account for psychological development, or to be the primary basis of psychological treatment. Yet this is often not the case. While almost all clinicians pay lip service to an interactive approach, mental health practice tends to be based on theories that favor one, and not the other. This book will show how simplistic and linear models, however appealing, lead to serious pitfalls. For this reason, disputes over the roles of nature and nurture are not just academic. The models that clinicians use influence how they manage patients. When theory is too narrow, treatment may not be effective.

How I Came to Embrace Nature–Nurture Integration

I have been a psychiatrist for 50 years. Several prior interests led me to choose this profession. One concerned the origins of human nature. As an undergraduate in psychology, I witnessed some of the early steps in the development of a discipline then called physiological psychology, which later evolved into neuroscience. I chose a medical school (McGill University) that was a pioneer in that kind of research. Sixty years later, I still work at McGill.

My second interest was in psychotherapy, using evidence-based methods supported by research to help troubled people. Even as a student, I rejected dogma and hoped to make talking therapy scientific. But psychotherapy was just beginning to rely on data rather than on clinical opinion.

Third, I entered psychiatry with the hope of integrating biological, psychological, and social models of psychopathology. Then, after practicing and teaching for a decade, I developed a sub-specialty in personality disorders. This is a domain in which both nature and nurture play a major role, but in which psychotherapy is the most evidence-based form of treatment.

I had to learn that standing on the middle ground of a sharp controversy can be perilous. Nonetheless, I have retained my reputation among students and colleagues as a skeptic.

For example, while neuroscience has made great scientific strides, seeing it as the only basis for psychopathology is not supported by evidence and can be a liability in clinical work. As a young psychiatrist, I was a witness to the golden age of psychopharmacology, in which once incurable patients with severe mental disorders began to be treated successfully. What I did not anticipate was the present mode of psychiatric practice, in which almost *all* patients are treated with drugs, and in which evidence-based psychotherapy has been replaced by 15-minute checkups focusing almost entirely on symptoms described in a manual, with clinicians making minimal inquiries as to what is going on in the lives of their patients.

As a resident in psychiatry, I was trained in the then-dominant psychodynamic model that focused on the impact of childhood experiences on adult functioning. But, like many others in my generation, I found this approach to be both limited and misleading. Clinicians always need to know about the past and to validate patients' life stories. But the problems for which people come for help lie in the present, and they require the teaching of skills to manage current problems. That approach makes more sense: instead, trying to change personality, we can help our patients learn how to modify traits and to work with the ones they already have.

These days, psychiatrists do much less psychotherapy, most of which is now provided by clinical psychologists (or social workers). Most therapists today use models based on cognitive behavior therapy (CBT), a treatment method that has strong empirical support. Unfortunately, psychotherapies of all kinds have never been easily available or affordable. Talking therapy is expensive, and making referrals for this kind of treatment is often impractical. I have been fortunate to work in a public health care system that aims to make treatment affordable, but the demand for therapy has always greatly exceeded the supply. That is why my clinical work has focused on briefer, more targeted forms of psychotherapy.

At mid-career, I looked back on my work as a therapist, and did not think I was doing enough for my patients. With this in mind, with the help of colleagues, I retrained myself as a researcher. My focus, both in research and practice, was on borderline personality disorder (BPD). This form of psychopathology cannot be fully explained either by neuroscience or by life adversities. Both play a role. In spite of its reputation for being linked to childhood trauma, BPD is most likely to develop in people who are emotionally sensitive but have not had sufficient validation for their feelings (Linehan, 1993). And like other mental disorders, BPD is partially heritable, and requires a model based on gene–environment interactions (Paris, 2020a). It is a complex condition that requires a complex model.

In many ways, BPD is a good model for understanding the nature–nurture interactions in all forms of psychopathology. In BPD patients, the genetic component consists of personality traits that lead to emotion dysregulation after exposure to adverse life events. The environmental component may involve traumatic events, but more often reflects a failure of emotional support from significant others, leaving people at the mercy of their own emotions. Patients can fall into a spiral in which adversity makes them dysregulated while dysregulation leads to further adversity. This scenario describes an interactive model in which heritable traits of emotional dysregulation are amplified by an invalidating environment that fails to provide recognition of emotions and the skills to master them.

BPD is hardly the only category of psychopathology that demands nature–nurture integration. Interactive models are needed to account for the causes of most of the problems that clinicians treat. This integrative approach to etiology and treatment was introduced decades ago into psychiatry as a *biopsychosocial model* (BPS; Engel, 1980).

Yet while the empirical literature on psychopathology is rich, it is unfortunately rare for research to assess the effects of nature and nurture in the same study. Where this strategy has been attempted, as in the famous but still controversial studies of Caspi et al. (2002, 2003), it suggests that temperamental vulnerability as reflected in genetic variations generally interacts with life stressors.

However, as this book will show, single genes are rarely the cause of psychopathology. Moreover, adverse life events are also complex variables that need to be unpacked. Thus, neither measures of the genome as a whole, nor broad constructs of the environment such as "trauma" or "maltreatment" are sufficient to predict the development of psychopathology. Whether theories are based on nature, nurture, or both, we need to be suspicious of simplifications. Both genetic predispositions and environmental stressors contribute to a highly complex web of interactions that shape psychological outcomes.

The Dimensions of Psychopathology

This book differs from a previous volume, *Nature and Nurture in Mental Disorders*", now published in a revised edition (Paris, 2020b). Since I wrote that book for the publishers of the 5th edition of the (*DSM*-5; American Psychiatric Association, 2013), I adopted a categorical approach to classification that is the basis of that highly influential manual. My book described how a gene–environment interactive model can be applied to the various categories of psychopathology listed in diagnostic manuals. Thus, I applied a system that has served as a common language for psychiatry and clinical psychology for over four decades. For each group of mental disorders, I showed that they could be best understood through the lens of an interactive model.

This book will not repeat what I said in that previous volume. Instead, here, I will examine psychopathology as a whole, describing symptomatic outcomes in terms of transdiagnostic *dimensions*. That term refers to an approach in which self-reports or observations of thoughts, emotions, and behaviors are given quantitative scores. Doing so demonstrates that mental symptoms lie on a continuum with normality. This model is also useful in showing how personality traits are linked to psychopathology, influencing how life adversities are processed, and shaping both vulnerability and resilience.

In this book, therefore, I have not made great use of the *DSM*-5 classification. The reason is that there are many serious problems with a categorical approach to diagnosis. One is that these models fail to capture continuous variations in symptoms, and yield a vast and problematic overlap between diagnoses.

Like the rest of medicine, psychiatry uses a system in which each disorder is defined and separately categorized on the basis of its clinical presentation. But unlike the rest of medicine, psychiatry lacks the biomarkers and endophenotypes that can distinguish these conditions or explain their origins. Even when medical conditions are poorly understood, definitions may not be entirely dependent on clinical symptoms. For example, even though we do not know what causes multiple sclerosis, a disease that greatly varies in its symptomatic presentation, we can rely on data from spinal taps and brain scans to make a firm diagnosis.

This is clearly not the case for the diagnoses in *DSM*-5. When one relies entirely on symptom-based algorithms, categories of disorder inevitably suffer from overlap. The editors of *DSM*-5 had originally hoped to develop a different system based not on symptoms, but on stable dimensions that describe traits. But the evidence was insufficient to make such a radical change. Moreover, doing so would have separated psychiatry from medicine. That is why, at our present state of knowledge, we have little choice but to make diagnoses using rules set down in a manual. There are 265 categories in *DSM*-5. But we need not believe that all these diagnoses are valid, or that they will still be used 50 years from now.

There are alternatives to *DSM*-5, but they have many of the same limitations. The International Classification of Diseases (ICD-11; World Health Organization, 2018) is not that different from *DSM*-5 (except for taking a dimensional approach to personality disorders), and it suffers from the same problems. The ICD-11 categories are based on symptoms that are common in many domains of psychopathology, so the more symptoms you have, the more diagnoses will be made.

The Research Domain Criteria (RDoC; Cuthbert and Insel, 2013) promoted by the National Institute of Mental Health offers another alternative that claims to be more scientific than DSM. But while it uses a matrix that was intended to be biopsychosocial, RDoC was designed by brain researchers, and is almost entirely based on data from neuroscience. Unfortunately, the science it depends on can only be described as preliminary and is nowhere near ready for clinical application.

At our current state of knowledge, none of these competing classification systems is really adequate. That is why this book will explore the value of dimensional and transdiagnostic models. Chapter 1 will describe some of the most promising of these systems in the current literature. But we need to keep in mind that we do not know enough to develop a fully valid model.

Nature, Nurture, and Personality

Personality traits are dispositions in thought, emotion, and behavior that can be understood as an amalgam of temperament and experience (Rutter, 1987). Infants are born with temperamental characteristics, some of which show stability over time, and some of which change over time. When temperament is extreme, it tends to be more stable (Kagan, 2010). Over the course of childhood, these patterns become recognizable and come to shape individual differences. Personality traits can, however, be modified to some extent by positive or negative life experiences.

Psychopathology cannot be considered separate from personality. Mental disorders and personality traits share many key features, have overlapping relationships with genetic and neurobiological variations, and are modified by the same environmental stressors. Moreover, without considering individual differences in traits that determine how people respond to adverse life events, one cannot understand why some develop symptoms, but most do not.

This book will therefore present a critique of the current focus on the role of trauma in the development of psychopathology. This domain requires a more nuanced perspective. Since traumatic experiences tend to be dramatic, it has long been tempting to attribute psychopathology in adulthood to maltreatment in childhood. However, most early adversities have limited long-term effects when they are single and time-limited, but become most pathogenic when multiple and repeated, and become associated with a cumulative impact (Rutter, 1991).

Over two decades ago, I wrote a book called *Myths of Childhood* (Paris, 2000). In that volume, the myths I focused on were that personality traits and mental disorders are mainly shaped by early childhood adversities, and that effective psychotherapy requires the reconstruction of these experiences. These ideas are much too broad, and they bend too far in favoring nurture over nature. While research certaiinly shows *correlations* between childhood events and adult functioning, these relationships are not necessarily *causal*.

That does not mean that childhood adversities are not important in development. But what research continues to support is the view that risk factors in childhood can best be understood in the context of gene–environment interactions. Moreover, the most important adversities in development are not necessarily based on dramatic events that can be termed as "traumatic", but derive from *multiple* negative experiences that are *consistent* and *cumulative* over time.

Research has also become more specific about the mechanisms behind these interactions. For example, we now have a large body of research on the problem of *emotion regulation* (Gross, 2015). Managing emotions depends on temperament, and also requires a mastery of skills that can be modeled and taught. While best studied in personality disorders, emotional dysregulation is implicated in a broad range of psychopathology. Some children have heritable temperamental profiles that make emotions easier to master. Others have temperamental qualities that make doing so more difficult. This can lead to vicious circles in which a difficult temperament creates interpersonal problems, and in which interpersonal conflicts amplify the problematic effects of temperament.

Emotional neglect in childhood is highly correlated with psychopathology (Parker, 1983). The concept of emotional neglect refers to the failure of parents to understand a child's emotions. It is also a more subtle risk factor: it is not an episode, but a long-lasting pattern. It helps explain, above and beyond genetics, why the outcome of traumatic events is so variable (Stoltenborgh et al., 2013).

Yet none of these environmental risk factors is likely to lead to psychopathology without a significant degree of genetic vulnerability. The long-term impact of either neglect or trauma depends on inborn *temperament*, shaping the personality traits that process life events (Plomin, 2018). Temperament is also reflected in the concept of "differential sensitivity to the environment", which describes how children can respond so differently to the same adversities (Belsky and Pluess, 2009).

Finally, while there is a large body of research on childhood maltreatment (i.e. abuse and/or neglect), it does not find highly consistent relationships with adult symptoms. When the evidence is exposed to close critical scrutiny, only a *minority* of those exposed will suffer long-term sequelae (Hailes et al., 2019). This is largely due to individual differences in temperament and personality.

In summary, we need to explain why some children are vulnerable to adverse life events while others are resilient. Does the explanation lie in nature or in nurture? The answer to that question is, once again, both. Although each child begins life with a unique and heritable temperament, personality traits in adults are shaped by a multitude of life experiences. Yet only the most severe adversities can override the inborn resilience that most people have (Rutter, 2012). Thus, individual differences in how experiences are processed are the result of interactions between genes and environment. In other words, nature and nurture each play a role, and Rutter's term "interplay" captures the way that they influence each other in the course of psychological development.

Integrating Nature and Nurture in Clinical Practice

The models of psychopathology and personality that clinicians use influence what they do with patients. If your model is based entirely on genetics and neuroscience, you will probably take less account of life histories. The result is an exclusive focus on symptoms, failing to consider the mental processes that underlie them, or to provide patients with a sense of agency. That is what many contemporary psychiatrists do when they only offer medication as treatment.

A parallel problem can occur in the practice of psychotherapy, particularly when clinicians use a model based on trauma and adversity. That approach fails to account for individual differences in the response to life events. The result can lead to promoting a narrative of victimhood, and a failure to encourage agency. Therapists need to modify these narratives, declining to blame families. Instead, they can teach patients to think interactively about the temperaments that shape their problems, and to be proactive in finding a way to deal with them effectively.

It is, however, difficult for most people to think interactively. They tend to prefer models in which a single variable explains almost everything. It is all too tempting to ignore the complex multivariate nature of psychology, and to apply simple, linear explanations. The most common bias in human thought is to be either–or, dividing all phenomena into categories. In the well-known words of the American journalist HL Mencken: "For every complex problem there is an answer that is clear, simple, and wrong".

This book aims to help clinicians to embrace the complexity that emerges from scientific research. Both clinicians and researchers have often gone wrong in attributing causality to correlations between single variables and single outcomes. That kind of error fails to account for why adverse life experiences have high base rates, but are associated with hugely variable outcomes.

Studying psychological development in the context of nature–nurture interactions also requires a more sophisticated approach to the complexities of genetics and neuroscience. It means avoiding over-simplified concepts of nature, such as beliefs that single genes can shape phenomena as complex as human behavior, or that personality traits can be located in a specific area of the brain. It also means avoiding over-simplified concepts of nurture, such as overall measures of maltreatment or trauma, as opposed to multiple measures locating adversity in the larger context of family and community.

Even so, it tends to be more comfortable to believe that complex outcomes can emerge from single causes. As a result, the history of nature and nurture has seen radical swings in intellectual fashion, in which either genes or environment become the main focus of research and practice. Even today, few studies are published that measure genes and environment in the same population. By and large, neurobiology and developmental psychopathology do not attract the same investigators. Moreover, research on interactions between genes and environment requires interdisciplinary teams and is therefore expensive. Even so, that is the best way to discover how nature and nurture are bound together. Such research needs to be based on models that consider interactions between multiple variables, whether biological or psychosocial.

The world in which we live is enormously multivariate. Univariate thinking sometimes provides an illusory way to "connect the dots". Scientific thinking requires a more sophisticated approach that embraces complexity. It is time to study psychological development in a way that acknowledges the roles of nature and nurture.

Acknowledgment

David Goldbloom read an earlier version of this book and provided detailed and much-needed feedback. Sarah Gore at Routledge helped me focus on the issues highlighted in the title of this book. Roman Kotov and Thomas Achenbach provded permission to reprint three figures describing dimensional systems of psychopathology.

1 Defining and Measuring Psychopathology

Separating Normal from Abnormal

Psychopathology refers to behaviors, emotions, and thinking patterns that are associated with significant psychological impairment. Yet like many other scientific terms in psychology, psychopathology has fuzzy boundaries. It can be very difficult to separate what is abnormal from what is normal (Frances, 2013). At what point do symptomatic responses to the challenges people face in the course of a human life merit formal diagnoses?

It is easy to forget that in the course of a normal life, most of us have periods of significant suffering. Grief is a good example—it produces dysphoria and affects functioning while it lasts, but is not the same thing as depression, and need not be considered an illness (Wakefield, 2012). Many of the symptoms that clinicians see, such as anxiety and depression, can be viewed as exaggerations of potentially adaptive responses to the environment (Nesse, 2019). And some are just part of the human condition.

Quite a few experts, inside and outside of psychiatry, see current diagnostic systems, whether based on the *DSM*-5 (American Psychiatric Association, 2013), or the International Classification of Diseases (World Health Organization, 2018), as suffering from serious problems. I agree. When we divide psychopathology into categories, mental disorders lack specificity (i.e. they overlap with each other). Moreover, diagnoses have no validating biological markers like those found in most medical conditions.

While most academics understand these problems, clinicians – and many of the patients they treat – sometimes seem to be "in love" with categorical diagnoses. The main reason is these categories provide hope that suffering can be understood and treated. But while that is often the case, many of the diagnoses we use are not scientifically valid. They may be given to patients on the basis of a rapid evaluation, and suffer from an *availability bias*, i.e. using whatever category most easily comes to mind, or from a *confirmation bias*, i.e. actively looking to confirm a diagnosis and then "finding" it (Kahnemann, 2011).

Working for two hospitals, I carry out about 500 consultations a year. I am constantly amazed at the level of confidence that people have in the

DOI: 10.4324/9781003156215-1

diagnoses they have received from other professionals. Many are relieved to be told about the name of their condition, assume that the category is well researched, and believe they can benefit from a known method of treatment. Thus, patients proudly announce: "I have been diagnosed with x" as if they had been placed in a category as valid as tuberculosis or heart failure. In some cases, as in psychoses, a certain level of certainty is justified. But, all too often, patients only show some of the features of these constructs. And since diagnosis often serves, for better or worse, as a guide to therapy, treatment choices may also be problematic.

The root of the problem is that diagnoses in psychiatry are almost entirely symptomatic. Until we know more about the causes of psychopathology, we have little choice but to classify patients on the basis of symptoms. Yet doing so can only be, at best, an approximation. (Note that general medicine has its own purely symptomatic labels, such as irritable bowel syndrome or migraine.)

Diagnosis can be a valuable exercise if it provides some measure of guidance for treatment choices. That can often be the case for the most severe mental disorders, such as schizophrenia, bipolarity, or melancholic depression. But even when labels are useful, we need not *believe* in the reality of current diagnoses. It would be better if we admitted how imprecise they are, and to avoid attributing them the level of validity one finds in other medical specialities. Diagnoses can best be seen as a language: a convenient way to summarize and communicate basic information about patients.

There has been no lack of criticism of psychiatric diagnosis over the years. Unfortunately, much of it has been aimed at the wrong targets. The idea that mental illness is a myth, or a social construct, is absurd. But its popularity can be explained in several ways. One is that being mentally ill carries a stigma. Moreover, people are so afraid of mental illness that they want to deny its existence. Still another is that the treatment of psychopathology can be difficult and uncertain.

Some advocates of "anti-psychiatry" (e.g. Whitaker, 2002) seem to believe that even the most severe mental disorders are variations on normality that may not even require medical treatment. This view can only be described as irresponsible. I invite those who say such things to spend an evening in a psychiatric emergency room to see just how sick psychiatric patients can be. The more severe mental disorders are still not well understood, but are as valid as most conditions in neurology and internal medicine.

A famous study by Rosenhan (1973), published in the prestigious journal *Science*, has long been used to debunk psychiatric diagnosis. Its method was to send eight volunteers to pretend to be psychotic (describing auditory hallucinations) in emergency rooms. The reported results were that these pseudo-patients were admitted to hospital and treated. This finding is still touted as showing that psychiatrists cannot tell the difference between sane and insane people. Actually, all this study actually showed was that patients can fool physicians by faking an illness. Quite a few are known to fake physical illness in the same way.

The real story behind the study is even darker. As Cahalan (2019) showed in a book-length investigation, Rosenhan was a fraudster who invented most of the data he reported. There were at most two people (including Rosenhan himself) who did the pretending. The others were imaginary.

This is not the first or the last example of fraud in science. But an uncritical response to Rosenhan's paper did incalculable damage to the treatment of patients with serious psychopathology. Even today, this study is quoted in psychology textbooks. It plays much the same role in mental health research as the false claims published in *Lancet* some years ago claiming that vaccines cause autism.

The critics of psychiatric diagnoses have often misdirected their commentaries by focusing on the most severe (and scientifically valid) categories of illness. Schizophrenia and bipolar disorders are clearly diseases of the brain. The critics would have done better to focus on the conditions that are most common in community populations. But these are the categories that lack well-defined boundaries, and that are all too often over-diagnosed. The list includes major depression, so-called "bipolar spectrum" disorders, attention-deficit hyperactivity disorder, post-traumatic stress disorder, autism spectrum disorder, as well as (I am sorry to say) my own area of personality disorders (Paris, 2020a). It is not that the problems these labels describe are imaginary – they most definitely are real. It is the way disorders are classified that is problematic. We do not know enough to do that properly. An unjustified certainty about classification can lead to bad or unnecessary treatment.

For all these reasons, there still is a fundamental difference between psychopathology and diseases in medicine. Yet many leading researchers disagree with that conclusion (Insel and Qurion, 2005). The current climate of opinion rejects any separation between the realm of the mental and the realm of the physical. In one sense, I agree – like almost everyone who have been trained in scientific medicine, I reject any kind of dualism between mind and body. But the difference is that mental health care is about dysfunctional people, not dysfunctional organs. Of course, disorders of the mind do produced changes in the brain. But they may require methods of treatment that are not necessarily medical, and that take psychosocial issues and life histories into account. Even in medicine, there is a need for humanistic models that aim to understand patients, and not just their diseases.

History provides a perspective on these issues. Psychiatry began in the 19th century as a sub-specialty of neurology. But in the 20th century, partly due to the rise of psychotherapy, it became a specialty on its own. Insel and Quirion (2005) argued that this separation was a mistake. They followed the mantra that *all* mental disorders are brain disorders, and that psychiatry should become a sub specialty of neurology defined by the clinical application of neuroscience.

I do not agree, and shudder to think what kind of treatment mentally ill patients would get if neurologists took over their care. The world view of these two specialities is very different, and pathology that primarily affects the mind (thoughts, emotions, and behaviors) belongs to a different conceptual universe from diseases that primarily affect sensorimotor systems. Mental illnesses are not associated with lesions or biomarkers, and although they may be eventually identified, I doubt that any will be found soon. That is what makes psychopathology very different – albeit much more mysterious – than general medicine.

Categories and Dimensions of Psychopathology

As discussed in the Introduction, this book will preferentially use the term *psychopathology* to describe the domain of mental disorders. This term allows for a quantitative and dimensional alternative to current systems that use qualitative categories.

Categorical systems do reflect the way that people naturally think, and have long been the basis of medical diagnosis. It is a defensible approach for schizophrenia and bipolar disorder. Yet, at this point, we just do not know enough about other forms of psychopathology to uncritically adopt a categorical approach to diagnosis. It is possible that categories will become more useful in the future when we actually understand the etiology of severe mental disorders. However, current diagnoses fail to do justice to the problems we see in the clinic, which tend to center around common disorders with symptoms of depression and/or anxiety. These clinical features strongly overlap, and are often associated with other categories, such as substance abuse. The result is that it is not uncommon for patients to be given 3, 4, or 5 diagnoses. That kind of diagnostic practice is not coherent, and it is not a useful guide to management.

At our current level of knowledge, there are advantages to using dimensions that are "transdiagnostic" and apply a quantitative approach. That cannot be done by following a *DSM* manual and counting up symptoms. The problem is that we do not know the weight of each feature in relation to the diagnosis. To deal with this problem, we need *psychometrics,* a method pioneered by research psychologists. Based on self-report drawn from questionnaires, or by structured clinical observations, psychopathology can be described with scores that are subject to the statistical methods of factor analysis. Doing so creates a set of continuously variable and scorable dimensions.

The search for a better system is driven by the weaknesses of the one we are currently using. After 40 years, the most important diagnoses in *DSM*-5 still lack reliability, with major depression doing no better than a low reliability (kappa coefficient of 0.2 between clinicians) in a field trial (Regier et al., 2013). As any researcher will tell you, one cannot have validity without reliability.

Yet there are advantages and disadvantages to seeing psychopathology as a set of continuously varying dimensions or as a set of categories. The most severe disorders do seem to fit into a categorical medical model of classification. But the lack of validity for most current diagnoses is notable. Many, if not most, of the conditions that clinicians see are not separate diseases, but descriptions of characteristic symptoms that group together into syndromes.

A good example is major depression, which is not necessarily that "major". The bar for diagnosis is set very low, and anyone who has symptoms for two weeks or more can receive it. Moreover, clinical depression describes a clinical picture that can derive from very different etiological pathways, and which takes different forms that require different methods of treatment (Parker, 2007). There are severe forms of depression that should be treated as life-threatening illnesses that require urgent medical treatment. However, the mild and moderate forms of depression that clinicians see might make more sense as a dimensional score, as opposed to a category that leads many clinicians to automatically conclude that medication is required for every patient, a view that is not supported by good evidence.

We may still need to retain categories that describe disorders which, even if they have fuzzy boundaries, have unique clinical features that can guide therapy. This applies to classical cases of schizophrenia or bipolar disorder, whose etiology reflects a large biological component (Zwicker et al., 2018). We may also want to retain categories of disorder that have important psychosocial causes, such as anorexia nervosa (Zipfel et al., 2015) or borderline personality disorder (Paris, 2020b), and which also point to prescribing specific treatment methods.

Yet, as knowledgeable clinicians recognize, the way that disorders are described in current manuals is at best approximate, and at worst unsatisfactory. Only the most severe disorders can be diagnosed in the same way as medical conditions, and even then, they either lack biomarkers, or have markers more closely related to traits than to categories of illness. For example, even the highly researched categories of bipolar disorder and schizophrenia tend to overlap, and seem to be associated with a common genetic predisposition (Zwicker et al., 2018). And most categories are highly "comorbid" with several other disorders, which is to say they lack definite boundaries. We cannot even begin to talk about psychopathology without a good system to measure it.

I view psychopathology as *both* dimensional and categorical. (Thinking in two ways at once can be considered parallel to the conclusion that mental illness reflects both nature and nurture.) In medicine, even when a dimensional score (blood pressure of 140/90) is used to as a cut-off to define pathology, physicians still treat hypertension as a category.

The problem is that while too many forms of psychopathology do not easily fit into categories, most people, including mental health professionals, find it easier to think in these terms (Minda, 2020). That is how the human mind works. This preference may explain why the less definitive term "mental disorder" has usually been preferred over "mental illness" in psychiatry. This usage reflects our reluctance to call our diagnoses "illnesses" until we understand their causes.

Moreover, the *overall* definition of mental disorder in current manuals is unnervingly vague (Frances, 2013). Wakefield (2007, p.149), usefully defined this term as "a *harmful dysfunction*, where "harmful" is a value term, referring to conditions judged negative by sociocultural standards, and "dysfunction" is a scientific factual term, referring to failure of biologically designed functioning". This may well be the best we can do for now, but Wakefield's definition has its own problems. It is not always clear what is biologically designed and what is not, nor it is always clear what is dysfunctional and what is not (Kennair, 2003).

For all these reasons, the focus of this book will be on the dimensions of psychopathology, except in cases where research yields strong findings that are specific to a category. And as we will see, psychopathology as a whole has some general characteristics that can be found in all mental disorders (Caspi et al., 2014).

I am aware that this solution is not quite satisfactory. We might eventually find a way to square this circle. But currently, we do not have enough evidence to fully support any system of classification. It will take many decades before research comes up with satisfactory answers. In the meantime, we have two choices. While awaiting a better system, we can continue to use the *DSM* manual, while being careful not to "believe" in it. Alternatively, we can explore a model that aims to address some of the limitations of the current system by describing the dimensions of psychopathology. Or we can do *both*.

I, therefore, suggest that we imitate other domains of science, applying either dimensional or categorical approaches when they best fit observations. To consider a well-known example, physicists use quantum mechanics to describe the same phenomena in terms of waves or particles, depending on context. Biologists who define species also know that their boundaries can be fuzzy, and that evolution from other species reflects quantitative changes that became qualitative over time. That is why classification in biology can be fuzzy, but is still useful as a guide to evolutionary change.

The RDoC Model of Psychopathology

Given that the last four decades of research has failed to validate *DSM*-5 categories (or those listed in the various editions of the International Classification of Diseases; ICD), we need a viable alternative. One competitor that offers a dimensional system of diagnosis to replace *DSM*-5 is the *Research*

Domain Criteria (RDoC) developed by the National Institute of Mental Health (Cuthbert and Insel, 2013). This system is unique in that it aims to be based on neuroscience, most particularly research on neural connectivity.

The developers of the RDoC system aimed to advance translational research, i.e. to apply the findings of neuroscience to the classification of psychopathology. The idea was to replace categories with a matrix that lists various levels at which multiple domains of psychopathology can be measured. The seven levels or units of analysis outlined in RDoC are genes, molecules, cells, circuits, physiology, behavior, and self-reports. Its five broad domains/constructs are:

1. negative valence systems (acute threat, potential threat, sustained threat, loss, and frustrative non-reward)
2. positive valence systems (approach motivation, initial responsiveness to reward, sustained responsiveness to reward, reward learning, and habit)
3. cognitive systems (attention, perception, working memory, declarative memory, language behavior, and cognitive control)
4. systems for social processes (affiliation/attachment, social communication, perception/understanding of self, and perception/understanding of others);
5. arousal/modulatory systems (arousal, biological rhythms, and sleep-wake).

These domains are derived from research in cognitive neuroscience. But their relevance to clinical practice is uncertain. Moreover, the body of research that RDoC hopes to build on is at a very early stage of development. Nonetheless, a decision was made to require using this model in future NIMH grant applications, a ruling that I consider to be an abuse of power. Using RDoC routinely would be based on theory without practice, so that doing so is seriously premature. The decision to prioritize the system for grants also blocks research on other subjects, such as the treatment of common disorders, even if they have more immediate clinical applications. Finally, it is hard to see how these five domains alone can account for the great variety of clinical symptoms associated with common mental disorders such as anxiety or depression as well as severe mental disorders.

The current state of research in cognitive neuroscience is just not sufficiently mature to account for the complex phenomena that constitute psychopathology. Moreover, the domains of RDoC have a limited correspondence to those derived from other disciplines including the social sciences. RDoC is not a biopsychosocial model. It can only be called a "bio-bio-bio model". In short, the system is much too dependent on current trends in neuroscience, and on what its developers believe to be well-established brain mechanisms. It describes a hierarchy of risk factors for psychopathology, but the emphasis is clearly on changes at the level of neurons and circuitry. While one cannot deny that brain activity is based on how it is wired, our ability to measure neuroconnectivity is very limited.

Moreover, RDoC marginalizes the psychosocial aspects of psychiatry (Paris and Kirmayer, 2016). Psychological factors are defined vaguely, in a way that seriously fail to acknowledge their lack of firm support in empirical research favoring what Insel and Quirion (2005) called "the clinical application of neuroscience". Adopting the RDoC model would be a large step backward, offering a reductionistic approach that focuses on phenomena at the level of molecules and cells, while ignoring the emergent properties of mind that reflect the functioning of the brain as a whole. One cannot fully understand complex mental systems by reducing them in this way. Any replacement for current models needs to pay respect to all levels of analysis.

The Hierarchical Taxonomy of Psychopathology

I will now discuss another system, the *Hierarchical Taxonomy of Psychopathology* (HiTOP; Kotov et al., 2017), which I find to be more on the right track. HiToP is an attempt to develop a fully dimensional model of mental illness. But instead of being based on neuroscience, it derives its domains from the factor analysis of symptoms. In other words, it focuses on the same level as *DSM* and ICD, because symptoms are phenomena we know how to measure.

Decades ago, Krueger (1999) showed that most diagnoses in the *DSM* system are based on overlapping symptomatology, and can be described by scores on two or three broad dimensions. Today, Krueger, along with Kotov, and many others in the HITOP consortium, and actively promoting research into such a system, The HiTOP model (Kotov et al., 2017) slices the pie into smaller pieces, but has the advantage of developing a hierarchy, from an overall "p-factor" to more specific domains of psychopathology, going all the way down to clinical symptoms and maladaptive traits.

Like *DSM*, the HiTOP system sticks to observable phenomena and eschews speculation about etiology until more is known. The model is summarized in a diagram (see Figure 1.1).

Let us have a look, moving down the hierarchy from the top.

p-Factor

HiTOP is unique in describing a high-level spectrum that lies behind all forms of psychopathology ("p-factor"), based on data showing that all mental disorders are associated with a common vulnerability (Caspi et al., 2014; Selzam et al., 2018). In other words, above and beyond specific predispositions, people can be predisposed to develop *some* form of psychopathology. A high p-factor has also been shown to be associated with a thinner cerebral cortex (Romerr et al., 2021).

The p-factor is a relatively new idea for the science of classification. While it is not entirely clear what it measures, a recent review by Smith et al. (2020) concluded that it likely reflects levels of functional impairment.

18 *Defining and Measuring Psychopathology*

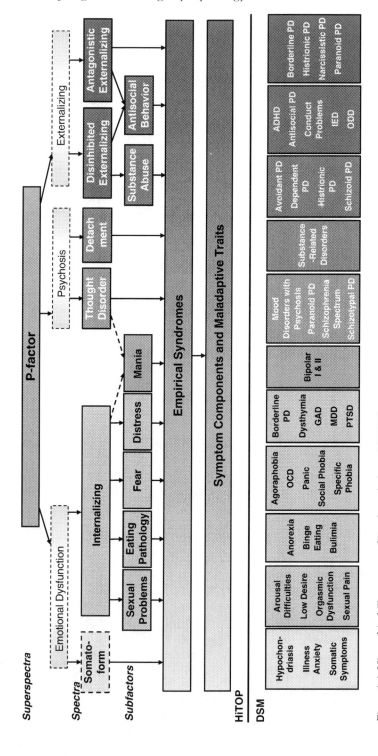

Figure 1.1 Hierarchical Taxonomy of Psychopathology (HiTOP).

Source: From a review paper in *World Psychiatry* by Kotov et al. 2020.

Super-spectra

The second level of the HiToP hierarchy is described by six "super-spectra": internalizing (or negative affectivity), thought disorder (or psychoticism), disinhibited externalizing, antagonistic externalizing, detachment, and somatoform. Many of these higher-level spectra have long been recognized. The most consistent support from research has been for spectra described as externalizing, internalizing, or thought disorder.

Decades ago, Achenbach (1966) described most symptoms in children as falling into either an internalizing or an externalizing spectrum. This schema is outlined in Figure 1.2.

The Child Behavior Checklist (Achenbach and McConaughy, 1997), which measures these dimensions, is still widely used in clinical settings. Its dimensions can also be identified in adults, where they account for overlap between a wide range of mental disorders (Krueger and Markon, 2006).

An *internalizing* spectrum describes psychopathology marked by inner suffering, and it is closely related to the personality domain of neuroticism, to be discussed in more detail in Chapter 2. This domain of psychopathology includes anxiety disorders, PTSD, and depression.

The two *externalizing* spectra capture features of behavioral disorders such as substance use, oppositional defiant disorder (ODD), conduct disorder, adult antisocial behavior, and attention-deficit-hyperactivity disorder (ADHD).

A dimension of *thought disorder* aims to capture psychotic phenomena. This broad construct may be valuable given that psychosis is another domain marked by comorbidity between current diagnostic categories.

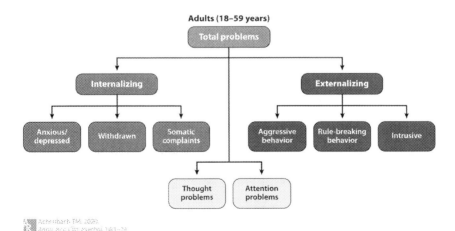

Figure 1.2 Hierarchy of Empirically Derived Achenbach System of Empirically Based Assessment (ASBEA) problem scales for ages 18–59.

Source: Drawn from Achenbach, 2020.

As we move down the hierarchy, the next levels are sub-factors, followed by empirical syndromes. next lowest level describes symptom components and maladaptive traits. At the very bottom, we may describe syndromes that correspond to *DSM* categories.

HiTOP, as one might expect in any new system, has a number of limitations. Like *DSM*, it is not based on etiological pathways. Since HiToP scores depend on either clinical observation or self-report, the system does not always cut psychopathology at its joints, or adequately account for changes over time (Achenbach, 2020). It also has a long way to go in developing reliable measures of its constructs, although some preliminary work in that direction has begun (Ruggero et al., 2019). Even so, this model may offer a good start on the way to developing a valid classification of psychopathology.

There are still other approaches to a dimensional classification of psychopathology. One is *network theory* (Borsboom et al., 2019; McNally, 2021). This model sees disorders as "nodes" of interaction between continuously scored measures of symptoms. Theorists taking this view (e.g. McNally, 2016) reject both categories and dimensions in favor of a system of "network analysis", in which mental disorders are considered to be more or less identical to their symptoms, or to the causal relationships between mutually reinforcing symptoms. But this is not a model that can lead us to etiological factors.

At our current state of knowledge, we just do not know enough to develop a consistently valid dimensional model. It is possible, however, that some of these models could turn out to be more closely related to risk factors than *DSM*-5 or ICD-11.

Another possible reason for optimism is that, as the next chapter will show, the structures of psychopathology and personality run in parallel. Current personality theory favors dimensional systems such as the Five Factor Model (FFM; Costa and Widiger, 2013), describing trait domains that are also quantitative rather than qualitative. Notably, many of the supporters of dimensional models were involved in the development of a similar system for classifying personality disorders. This is the "Alternative Model of Personality Disorders" (AMPD, Krueger and Markon, 2014), which can now be found in Section III of the *DSM*-5 (and could eventually replace the categories of personality disorder listed in Section II of that manual). When one applies factor analysis to all features of psychopathology, the dimensions that emerge seem to overlap with personality traits (Jang, 2013; Widiger et al., 2019). Moreover, the AMPD has created a measure called "Levels of Personality Functioning" that cuts across all categories and that resembles the p-factor (Kreuger and Markon, 2014).

Dimensional approaches to diagnosis add something that has been missing from classification (more reliably measured constructs) and subtract something that is not needed (massive comorbidity). While awaiting more research, we can benefit from both perspectives. Whether or not dimensional systems, in their present form, or in future revisions, can entirely replace categorical diagnosis remains to be seen. However well rooted they are in research on dimensions of psychopathology, they are mainly based on observable data, and do not explain much about the etiology and course of mental disorders.

The greatest strength of dimensional systems is that they address some of the limitations of current models by viewing all psychopathology as a spectrum. Doing so simplifies classification by eliminating confusing multiple diagnoses, which have, rather misleadingly, been called "comorbidities". (Comorbidity is little but an artefact of a system in which the same symptoms are found in multiple disorder – a better term might be "co-occurrence".)

A dimensional system of psychopathology is also consistent with models that reflect highly complex interactions. As we will see, it is hopeless to look for a gene "for" any diagnosis, or a life event related to any category. Dimensions might turn out to be more closely related to biological markers, although this has not yet been demonstrated. Currently, neither genetic variance, neurotransmitters, nor the findings of brain imaging run in parallel to diagnostic categories (Hyman, 2010). Instead, pathological traits reflect broad risk factors that cut across many current diagnoses.

Are any of these models ready for clinical application? Over the past few years, RDoC has not been widely used in research outside neuroscience and cognitive science. But HiTOP is more relevant to clinical issues, and has gained significant support from researchers (its consortium now includes 150 academics). Over the last few years, the *Journal of Abnormal Psychology* has organized its published papers under *DSM*-free headings such as "Transdiagnostic Research", "Internalizing Disorders" and "Externalizing Disorders".

While research into the system is in its very early stages, other lines of evidence suggest that psychopathology may have a dimensional structure that overlaps with measures of personality traits (Krueger et al., 2020), a finding that supports the central role of personality in the development of psychopathology. Individual differences in trait profiles map into the overall risk for mental disorders, helping to explain why some people develop one kind of disorder while others develop an entirely different type when exposed to same stressors (Kotov et al., 2010; Conway et al., 2019).

This dimensional point of view is consistent with a predisposition-stress model of psychopathology (Monroe and Simons, 1991), with a biopsychosocial model (Engel, 1980), with the concept that individuals vary in their sensitivity to the environment (Belsky and Pluess, 2009). It is also consistent in principle with Network Analysis of the most prominent symptoms of psychopathology (McNally, 2021).

A special section of the journal *World Psychiatry* in February 2021 was devoted to the HiToP model. The lead article by Leahy et al. (2021) described the benefits of a hierarchical dimensional system, followed by eight commentaries. One was by Thomas Achenbach, who pioneered this approach more than 50 years ago. But Achenbach (2020) was careful to point out problems that must be resolved before adopting such a system. One is that it is not entirely clear how to conceptualize the meaning of a p-factor. Another is the need for a confirmatory factor analysis to support claims of superiority to other systems. Still another is that classifications are used for different purposes: we have little or no data on how such a system would work in clinical practice.

Zimmerman (2012) echoes that concern, suggesting that clinicians will not accept a new system until it can be clearly shown that it benefits patients. This is the ultimate test of any classification—no matter how well domains can be separated by factor analysis, we need to base our understanding of psychopathology around etiology and treatment.

The Future of Dimensional Models

I admit to having long been reluctant to get on board with dimensionality. Some of my hesitation derived from doubt about the ultimate validity of scoring self-report questionnaires filled in by patients, or about relying on structured interviews to guide clinician ratings. I have also been concerned about the clinical utility of replacing categories, which are closer to way most clinicians think, with scores that they don't necessarily find informative and user-friendly.

Nobody wants a system that is overly academic and abstract. Our minds are programmed to deal more easily with qualitative than with quantitative information. But we need to learn how to think in more than one way at the same time.

One of the main advantages of conceptualizing psychopathology in a dimensional mode is that quantitative diagnosis of multiple dimensions solves an important problem: e.g. the tendency of mental disorders to be highly comorbid, and the constant proliferation of categories in successive editions of diagnostic manuals. One result is that patients received different diagnoses from different professionals for the same symptoms.

The *DSM* system is cross-sectional and describes current symptoms, but tells us little about etiology or pathogenesis. (That is, of course, because we *know* little or nothing.) In that respect, dimensional systems have few advantages over categories. But if symptoms and traits could be shown to be strongly correlated with biological markers and/or psychosocial risk factors (Conway et al., 2020), this approach could have positive value for research.

The push for dimensionality has been particularly intense in my own area of research, personality disorder (PD). This is a domain where normal personality and psychopathology meet. There are ten categories of PD in Section II of *DSM*-5, but most experts agree that many could be dropped. They have not been well researched, and they have unacceptably high levels of overlap with each other (Paris, 2015a).

To this, end, the "hybrid system" or AMPD in *DSM*-5 (Krueger and Markon, 2014), defines smaller number of PD categories derived from dimensional trait ratings. In 2013, for lack of strong empirical support for radical change, the AMPD was put in Section III of the manual (disorders that require more research), but since then, the data behind it has become more convincing. The AMPD is consistent with the FFM in its measurement of traits, but it differs in that it is designed to convert its dimensions into user-friendly categories. It is possible that a hybrid system for psychopathology as a whole would add something important to dimensional models, allowing them to gain clinical favor by being linked to reasonably valid categories.

ICD-11 (World Health Organization, 2018), the official international system for the diagnosis of mental disorders, has now been revised, with official use beginning in 2022. In most respects, this edition makes no radical break with categorical models. But it has adopted a more radical system for personality disorders, with an aim to avoid using categories. However, due to objections from researchers (like me) who have devoted their careers to studying a borderline category, a separate algorithm was added to recognize a "borderline pattern". Even so, the AMPD model, which derives its categories from trait dimensions could be a preferable option.

I felt better about these problems after consulting a colleague, Mark Zimmerman of Brown University. Mark has made unique contributions to the scientific study of categorical diagnosis and to research on personality disorders--conducting large-scale studies in his clinic without ever applying for a grant. Although Mark's research has been mostly on categories, he was a co-author on the Kotov et al. (2017) paper. When I asked him about this apparent discrepancy, he explained that he is happy to think dimensionally when doing so is more useful, but to be categorical when that approach works better.

I am again reminded of the wave-particle duality of quantum mechanics, in which concepts that are incompatible in macroscopic physics turn out to be the most precise way to study a sub-atomic world. Many other concepts in science, including the boundaries between life and non-life, have an intrinsic duality. Psychology, which studies some of the most complex phenomena in the universe, should not be ashamed to embrace multiple points of view.

2 Personality and Psychopathology

Temperament and Personality

Personality is a term that describes individual differences in patterns of thinking, feeling, and behaving that are consistent over time. Trait psychology has developed a large literature in which personality is usually measured as *traits*, using quantitative self-report data on standard questionnaires (Costa and Widiger, 2013). For example, some people are more extraverted, while others are more introverted. People can also be more or less neurotic (easily distressed). These characteristics can be measured by self-report but there are also systems in which traits can be assessed using clinical evaluation (Krueger and Markon, 2014).

Humans are not the only species to have personalities – animals have them too (Weinstein et al., 2008). Personality traits can be thought of as alternative evolutionary strategies designed by natural selection to cope with variable environmental challenges (Beck and Freeman, 2015). For example, in some situations it is better to be fearless and worry-free, while in others it is better to be cautious and worried.

This view of individual differences as embedded in temperament and personality is part of a set of ideas that characterize *evolutionary psychology* (Buss, 2019). In this model, one needs to ask not just how cognition, emotions, and behavior function, but why they emerged from natural selection, and how they promote survival and reproduction (Schakelford, 2013). This attention to *ultimate* causes is part of what the ethologist Niko Tinbergen called "four questions" that any biological theory must address (Nesse, 2019). These questions concern causation, development, evolution, and survival value.

Personality is a complex construct with complex origins. It is the outcome of a series of interactions between nature and nurture; Rutter (1987) described personality as an "amalgam" of temperament and experience. To consider one example, while individual differences in temperament are heritable, they can also differ in response to whether their environment is more positive or negative. These interactions shape a "life history strategy" that chooses the timing of reproduction to make it is most likely to be successful (Belsky, 2007).

DOI: 10.4324/9781003156215-2

Temperament refers to heritable variations in behavior that can be observed at birth or during infancy. A note of caution: if you look up temperament research on the web, you will find a lot of articles on traits, because some researchers (e.g. Cloninger, 1994) have incorrectly used the term "temperament" to describe personality in adults. Temperament is what we are born with, while personality also reflects the outcome of experience.

Temperament does not always remain stable with time, particularly in infancy. It is affected by context and can look different in different circumstances. In this way, temperament bends the twig but does not determine the final shape of the tree. With this in mind, Kagan (1994) described a "temperamenal bias" (instead of direct causality). Thus, temperament shapes personality but does not fully determine it. But if these characteristics remains stable at school-age, they are likely to be present for decades to come, and remain fairly stable over the course of a life span (Costa and Widiger, 2013). It should be acknowledged that there is room for some degree of adjustment in trait profiles. On the other hand, introverts do not become extraverts, and neurotic people do not become fearless.

The construct of temperament goes back to the Roman physician Galen, who described four types: *sanguine, choleric, melancholic,* and (Eysenck, 1982; Kagan, 1994). In some ways, this ancient system is not entirely different from the models we used today. For example, sanguine people have low neuroticism, while melancholic people score high on this trait.

Temperament can be observed very early in life. Some children are more excitable and active, while others are less reactive and tend to withdraw (Belsky et al., 2020). If we are born with high extraversion and neuroticism, the chances are that these features will still be apparent as we mature. The outcome is often dependent on what Chess and Thomas (1999) called "goodness of fit", i.e. how well families meet the needs of different children. (It has often been said that parents who have one child believe in nurture, but those with two children come to believe in nature.) Fortunately, most variations in temperament fall within a normal range, and these characteristics early in life do not necessarily predict later psychopathology.

But there is an important exception. When temperament is extreme, it can be a risk factor for psychopathology. For example, overactive children are difficult for families to control, while underactive children find it hard to connect with peers. These temperamental variations undergo interaction with the environment, leading either to vicious circles when environmental factors are problematic, or positive changes when the environment is supportive. In this way, an extreme temperament can shape the life of a child for many years to come.

Researchers measure temperament by systematically observing infants, and then classifying these patterns. However, the classification of temperament can be confusing, and there are many systems described in the literature that are not quite interchangeable.

One of the earliest studies of temperament was conducted by Chess and Thomas (1984), who described nine aspects: activity, regularity, initial reaction, adaptability, intensity, mood, distractibility, persistence, and sensitivity. Scores on all these aspects can be grouped into three overall patterns: *easy, difficult,* and *slow to warm up.* One hundred and thirty three children from the sample were followed up regularly until they reached adulthood. The difficult children often had more psychological problems later in life.

Mary Rothbart was one of the most influential researchers on childhood temperament (Rothbart 1991). Her six temperamental types, based on factor analysis of observational data, emphasize differences in emotional reactions. They are:

1. non-aggressive negative affect (fear and sadness);
2. aggressive negative affect (frustration and social anger);
3. effortful control (activation and attentional control);
4. extraversion/surgency (sociability, high-intensity pleasure, and positive affect);
5. orienting sensitivity (general and affective perceptual sensitivity and associative sensitivity); and
6. affiliation (emotional empathy and empathetic guilt).

In a book-length review of the literature, Rothbart (2011) examined longitudinal data showing that temperamental fear can be a precursor of internalizing disorders (e.g. anxiety and depression), while temperamental impulsivity can be a risk factor for externalizing disorders (e.g. antisocial behavior). Rothbart pointed out how fearful children elicit responses from others (overprotection) that amplify their temperament, and that impulsive children also elicit responses (rejection and anger) that tend to reinforce their inborn nature, leading to a vicious circle. But this research focused on continuities between infancy and early childhood (Rothbart, 2011), and did not follow cohorts into adulthood. Other researchers have simplified Rothbart's profile into three super-factors: *Positive Emotionality, Negative Emotionality, and Constraint.* These patterns are easy to remember and are sometimes called the "Big Three" (Tellegen and Waller, 2008).

The reason why no single classification dominates temperament research may have to do with the method of *factor analysis* used to describe larger patterns of variation. This complex statistical procedure can be open to different interpretations. Moreover, similar dimensions appear in a wide range of schemata, but have different names. What most agree on is that the best way to measure temperament is through direct observation of infants by trained raters (Saudino, 2005). Measurements of temperament later in childhood have often depended on parent or teacher ratings, which may be a less accurate measurement.

Again, the extreme ranges of temperaments are most likely to have effects on adult personality and functioning. The Harvard psychologist

Jerome Kagan (2010) was one of the leaders in this line of research. His work focused on infants who were either "high-reactive" or "low-reactive". Those who were high-reactive tended to show greater anxiety and withdrawal in the face of unfamiliar stimuli, a characteristic he called "behavioral inhibition". The more severe this kind of temperament was, the more likely it was to be observable on follow-up into adolescence. Thus, Kagan (2010) reported that a significant minority of these children who had shown behavioral inhibition in infancy were still clinically anxious at age 13, although a majority of them did "grow out" of earlier problems. In contrast, children who were unusually low on this characteristic were somewhat more likely to develop the impulsive symptoms of conduct disorder.

The Dunedin study is one of the most famous research projects in the history of developmental psychopathology. Its findings are nicely summarized in a book by Belsky et al. (2020). A birth cohort of over 1000 children born in the 1970s in a medium-sized city in New Zealand was observed at age three, and then followed up over several decades.

These researchers described five types of temperament: well-adjusted, confident, reserved, under-controlled, and inhibited. In children who were neither under-controlled nor inhibited, early temperament had only minor effects on adult outcome. In contrast, the more extreme temperaments had major effects on later functioning, particularly in children who were either highly impulsive or highly anxious. While the majority of children did not show extreme patterns, temperament may still "bend the twig".

These effects are consistent with the strong evidence that both temperament and personality are partially heritable (Kagan, 1994; Jang, 2020). Based on observations of twins in infancy or early childhood, and depending on the trait, 20–60% of temperamental variations can be accounted for by heritability, depending on what is being measured (Saudino, 2005). These estimates demonstrated significant genetic effects but still leave room for a major contribution from the environment.

The stability of temperament increases over the course of childhood (Caspi et al., 2005). Kagan (2010) described it as a "thread" that shapes development but that can undergo modification by the environment. When he followed samples into early adolescence, most had developed in the direction of greater normality. In the Dunedin study, (Belsky et al., 2020), longitudinal data also showed that the most extreme temperaments are the most stable. For example, although effect sizes were small, a highly impulsive temperament at age 3 statistically predicted antisocial behavior at age 18 (Caspi et al., 1996).

In summary, the outcome of early temperament is not strictly determined. Statistically informed readers will know that one can find significant correlations in cohorts even when they do not apply to most people in the sample, given that significant findings can be driven by sub-groups who lie at the extreme of a distribution.

Measuring Personality Traits

Personality traits have a large research literature, and are usually measured from scores on self-report questionnaires. Scoring them quantitatively as continuous variables allows investigators and clinicians to consider them as *dimensions* rather than categories.

Many models of personality structure have been developed over the years. A century ago, the Swiss psychoanalyst Carl Jung (1921) described three dimensions: sensation, intuition, and extraversion-introversion. Only the last of these domains has passed the test of time and can still be found in modern concepts. This trait is related to either a need for high stimulation (extraversion) or for low stimulation (introversion).

The British psychologist Hans Eysenck (1982) also described three dimensions of personality: extraversion-introversion, neuroticism, and psychoticism. Neuroticism is the most important, and can be found in all current trait models, even when a different terminology is used. It describes how easily people get upset, as well as how long it takes them to calm down. Psychoticism, on the other hand, is a misnomer, as it has nothing to do with psychosis, and is a measure of impulsivity vs. self-control.

When one does factor analysis of questionnaire data, one can be either a splitter or a lumper. The American psychologist Raymond Cattell (1946) was clearly a splitter: his system required as many as 16 personality factors. One hears little of that model these days, probably because it is too complicated.

The American psychologist Auke Tellegen was more of a lumper. He developed a four-factor model (Tellegen and Waller, 2008) that has had some currency in research, mainly at his own university in Minnesota. The four broad factors (which can be divided into 11 sub-factors) are Positive Emotional Temperament, Negative Emotional Temperament, Constraint, and Absorption.

However, all these systems have now been replaced by the dominance of the Five Factor Model (FFM; Costa and Widiger, 2013). A consensus among most trait psychologists has emerged that this is the best validated and most widely researched system. These "Big Five" factors are Openness to Experience, Conscientiousness, Extraversion, Agreeableness, and Neuroticism. (I have placed them in this order because they can be easily remembered using the acronym "OCEAN".) Each of these dimensions has a polar opposite: Cautiousness, Impulsivity, Introversion, Disagreeableness, and Emotional Stability. The Big Five can then be sub-divided into "facets" that describe a larger but narrower range of characteristics. There is also a six-factor (HEXACO) model, but it is not widely used in research (Widiger, 2017).

The origins of the FFM lie with the idea, first proposed in the 19th century by Francis Galton, of a "lexical" approach. That involves listing all the adjectives in the dictionary describing personality characteristics, and carrying out factor analysis of questionnaire data to reduce them to a manageable number (Goldberg, 1990).

The leaders of FFM research in the following decades have been Paul Costa and Robert McCrae, who developed a standard self-report measure of the Big Five: the NEO Personality Inventory Revised (NEO-PI-R; Costa and Widiger, 2013). The current generation of researchers is led by Thomas Widiger, who was the editor of a large Handbook on the FFM (Widiger, 2017).

Since the FFM provides quantitative data, the model has been particularly useful in research on personality disorders (Costa and Widiger, 2013). As we will see, a parallel dimensional framework has also been developed for psychopathology as a whole.

Some research has been done to determine whether the FFM is equally valid in other cultures (Terracciano and McCrae, 2006). It shows that at least three of the five factors (neuroticism, agreeableness, and conscientiousness) can be found across the world, while extraversion and openness show more cultural variation.

Neuroticism accounts for symptoms seen in many different forms of psychopathology. This dimension is strongly related to major depression, anxiety, and post-traumatic stress disorder. People who have strong and prolonged emotional reactions to stressors can be at risk for all of these conditions.

Yet not everyone with high neuroticism develops a mental disorder. Being easily upset or worried is not always irrational or dysfunctional. From an evolutionary perspective, neuroticism can be adaptive because it makes people quicker to see danger in their environment. Many people do not develop psychopathology in spite of high neuroticism, and may have benefited from a benign environment. In contrast, those who do develop symptoms may have been exposed to more stressors.

The other four dimensions of the FFM are not as closely linked to a vulnerability to pathology. Extraversion and introversion represent different strategies in social life, connecting more or less easily with other people. Such variations are not by themselves risk factors for psychological symptoms. But extremes on this dimension, particularly when combined with neuroticism, can lead to vicious cycles, especially if these traits are amplified by an unsupportive environment. Although different societies can value them differently, there is plenty of room in the world for both extraverts and introverts.

Conscientiousness is usually a good thing, unless it is extreme. It is a predictor of success in many domains of life. Kern et al. (2009) studied subjects drawn from the Terman Life Course Study of children with unusually high intelligence, who were followed into old age. In spite of their unusually high IQ, none of these children ever became famous. But low scores on the dimension of conscientiousness were associated with less career success, as well as a shorter life span. If subjects were also high in Neuroticism, they were prone to develop anxiety or depression, probably because of the difficulty in meeting their own high standards.

Agreeableness is a strong predictor of success in interpersonal relationships. Caspi et al. (1987), using longitudinal data, found that children who are irritable and conflictual are more likely to have unstable relationships and careers in adulthood. On the other hand, being overly agreeable can be problematic when other people take advantage of this trait.

The last of the Big Five factors, Openness to Experience, does not have a consistent relationship to any form of psychopathology, and is more related to curiosity and creativity (Costa and Widiger, 2013). For that reason, clinicians only need to think about the other dimensions of the FFM.

Personality Profiles Related to Psychopathology

Personality and psychopathology are not separate domains, but overlapping measures of individual differences that are also interactive. Personality traits have a hierarchical dimensional structure that can be used to score overall levels of psychopathology, cutting across diagnostic categories while defining broad dimensions that reflect strengths and vulnerabilities (Conway et al., 2019).

The relationship of personality to psychopathology can be described in a number of ways (Widiger, 2011). First, a *vulnerability or predisposition model*, sees maladaptive personality traits as predispositions to psychopathology. Second, in a *complication or scar model*, personality traits are exaggerated and made dysfunctional by psychopathology. Third, a *spectrum or co-aggregation model* sees personality and psychopathology as overlapping. Fourth, a *pathoplasty model* focuses on how personality can complicate the development of symptoms.

While each of these points of view has some degree of validity, this chapter will give more weight to the spectrum model. In that view, personality traits, by mediating and processing the effects of the environment, help to explain why psychopathology is associated with different symptoms in different people.

Moreover, there may be a genetic link between the predispositions for psychopathology and personality trait profiles. Behavioral genetic studies have established the heritability of traits and of almost all mental disorders (Plomin, 2018). That method does this by comparing concordance rates in monozygotic and dizygotic twins, and by converting that difference into a percentage: what it shows about the roles of genes and environment will be discussed in more detail in Chapter 3.

Personality traits, however measured, are about 40–50% heritable (Widiger, 2011; Plomin, 2018). Much the same level of heritability applies to most of the categories of mental disorders (Paris, 2020d).

There are important overlaps between personality trait models and hierarchical models of psychopathology such as HiToP (Forbes et al., 2017). Widiger et al. (2019) have usefully described these relationships. One major area is that personality trait profiles are strong predictors of the vulnerability to mental disorders. A related issue is that since personality changes with time, treatment for problematic traits might precede the development of diagnosable symptoms. As Widiger et al. (p. 84) conclude:

> There are multiple ways in which personality and psychopathology can be related to one another. Personality and psychopathology can influence the presentation or appearance of one another (pathoplastic relationships); they can share a common, underlying etiology (spectrum relationships); and each can have a causal role in the development or etiology of the other…It is evident that the relationship of personality to personality disorder is largely a spectrum relationship…and the same is perhaps largely true for personality and psychopathology.

Moreover, the domains of mental functioning may all be related to each other. In a recent article, Littlefield et al. (2021) reported significant overlaps between a "General Factor of Personality" (describing the adaptive or maladaptive aspects of all factors in the FFM), the p-factor, and intelligence. The authors concluded that factor analysis tends to create artificial boundaries between domains that overlap. However, this study is also an example of another problem. While the sample was large ($n = 489$), it consisted entirely of undergraduate students, a convenient choice for many professors. As one anthropologist (Henrich, 2020) has pointed out, the populations that are easiest to recruit for research tend to come from unrepresentative, or "WEIRD" societies, i.e. Western, educated, industrialized, rich and democratic. If subjects are students, they are even more unusual. For that reason, a common failing of psychological research is its use of samples of convenience as opposed to community or clinical populations.

Nonetheless, the relationship between personality and psychopathology is becoming an important topic for investigation. A special issue of the Journal of Research in Personality (November 2019), edited by several members of the HiToP consortium, was devoted to this issue. Essentially, the theme was that *extremes* on any of the FFM domains carry a risk for psychopathology. Some have even suggested that the main difference between a trait and a symptom is time scale (Torgersen, 2011; De Young et al., 2020). But as we will see in Chapter 6, research on resilience shows that personality profiles can also be protective against psychopathology.

Neuroticism is the most important personality trait domain for the understanding of psychopathology. Widiger and Oltmanns (2017, p. 144) describe this domain as "the trait disposition to experience negative affects, including anger, anxiety, self-consciousness, irritability, emotional instability, and depression. Persons with elevated levels of neuroticism respond poorly to environmental stress, interpret ordinary situations as threatening, and can experience minor frustrations as hopelessly overwhelming".

Gender differences on the FFM show that women are, compared to men, more neurotic, more extraverted, more agreeable, and more conscientious (Costa and Widiger, 2013). These characteristics seem designed for effective parenting. However, a higher level of neuroticism helps to explain why women are more likely to develop internalizing disorders, while men are more likely to develop externalizing disorders.

Neuroticism can also present differently depending on interactions with other traits (as well as with environmental challenges). Widiger (2011, p. 103) offers a good example of how a range of trait profiles can affect symptom presentations in eating disorders:

> ...anorexia and bulimia tend to emerge during adolescence (driven in part perhaps by high levels of neuroticism). Persons with a preoccupation with weight loss who go on to develop anorexia are most likely characterized in part by high premorbid conscientiousness.....Persons high in conscientiousness have high levels of self-discipline, competence, and achievement-striving, precisely the attributes that would be necessary to be so successful in weight loss. In contrast, persons low in conscientiousness would be prone to the impulsive dyscontrol characteristic of binge eating and bulimia.

In other forms of psychopathology, high levels of scores on conscientiousness can also be associated with obsessive–compulsive disorder, while low levels are associated with substance use and a wide range of disorders marked by impulsivity. While people who are conscientious are more likely to succeed in life (Duckworth et al., 2019), this domain works best when it lies close to a golden mean.

Agreeableness follows the same pattern. To be overly agreeable can fail to protect people against those who misuse their dominance, while to be insufficiently agreeable interferes with social networks and intimacy (Graziano and Tobin, 2009).

Within normal limits, neither extraversion nor introversion need create serious problems. But high extraversion, if associated with low conscientiousness, can lead to pathology marked by high impulsivity, while high introversion, particularly when accompanied by neuroticism, tends to be associated with internalizing disorders (Krueger and Tackett, 2003).

In summary, personality profiles provide a framework for psychopathology that avoids the confusing comorbidity that so often characterizes categorical diagnosis. As Torgersen (2011) has suggested, personality and psychopathology overlap with each other and are not necessarily distinct phenomena.

Personality and Personality Disorders

Personality disorders lie at the interface of traits and severe psychopathology, and they are exemplars of that relationship. Moreover, while

PDs long been familiar as categorical diagnoses, they can also be understood in terms of trait dimensions.

PDs are defined in *DSM*-5 as long-term patterns of behavior and inner experiences that begin by late adolescence or early adulthood and cause distress or problems in functioning. The ICD-11 definition is fairly similar. PDs are patterns, not episodes, and are not necessarily based on symptoms. Instead, they describe some of the same higher-level phenomena as dimensional systems of psychopathology.

Categorical diagnosis of PDs has been problematic. Only two of the *DSM*-5 categories (borderline and antisocial) have a large research literature, and these diagnoses are also more likely to be used by clinicians. About half of the total PD population have to be diagnosed as "unspecified" because they do not fit any of the other categories (Zimmerman et al., 2005). As a researcher in this domain, I feel quite comfortable dropping most of the categories still listed in *DSM*-5, and about replacing them with dimensional scores.

That is the approach taken in ICD-11 (World Health Organization, 2018), in which PDs have been almost entirely dimensionalized. The new system describes five dimensions that track several aspects of the FFM, as well as HiToP, but are more related to clinical presentations. The first, Negative Affectivity, resembles Neuroticism or an internalizing pattern. The second, Detachment, resembles Introversion. The third, Disinhibition, reflects impulsivity or low conscientiousness. The fourth, Dissociality, describes an antisocial pattern, associated with low Agreeableness and an externalizing pattern. The fifth, Anankastia, describes a compulsive or overconscientious pattern. PDs can then be coded as a profile, along with measures of their severity. Since these traits are designed to be rated by clinicians, they would need training to do so reliably. But given the complexity of this task, it may be doubtful that most would achieve good reliability.

DSM-5 had hoped to begin a process of dimensionalization of all psychopathology, and made PD into a test case. Since research on this system was just beginning in 2013, the model was placed, most likely temporarily, in Section III of *DSM*-5, reserved for diagnostic concepts that require further research. it is now called the Alternative Model of Personality Disorders (AMPD; Krueger and Markon, 2014). The revised manual (American Psychiatric Association, 2013) differs from ICD-11 in building up 5 categories of PD from trait profiles. (Those who do not fit any of these categories are classified as unspecified.) It has therefore been described as a "hybrid model". Over the last decade, the proponents of this system have published hundreds of papers. Thus far, the system has not often been used in clinics, but that could change if it were moved into the main section of the manual.

Forensic psychiatrists did not protest the elimination of what ICD-10 had called dissocial personality (corresponding to *DSM*-5's antisocial category). Perhaps they are comfortable with the venerable but extensively researched construct of psychopathy, which is diagnosed with a widely used checklist (Patrick, 2018), even if the diagnosis is not listed in ICD-11. However, researchers who study BPD did protest, with the result that this category was more or less reinstated with criteria similar to those of *DSM*-5, as a "borderline pattern qualifier". This allows researchers to continue investigating BPD, and it allows clinicians to continue to diagnose the disorder. This decision provided continuity with thousands of published research papers. Moreover, why pick on BPD? Similar problems (fuzzy boundaries and high levels of comorbidity) apply to all categories in the ICD manual.

There are also gaps between professional affiliations, as well as between research and practice. The personality disorder research community is dominated by trait psychologists, who prefer trait profiles to categories. Resistance to dimensions is more common among physicians, deriving from medicine's traditional preference for categorical diagnoses that can guide the choice of specific treatments.

Conceiving mental disorders as categories also aims to separate severe dysfunction from normal variants. It is consistent with a dichotomous procedure of clinical decision-making in practice in which treatment decisions are based on the presence or absence of a defined illness. Yet in principle, the symptoms of any mental disorder, including schizophrenia, bipolar disorder, or melancholic depression can be scored dimensionally. Physicians already do this, as when measures of blood pressure are converted to the categories of hypertension, using established cut-offs.

There are several unsolved problems in the use of trait dimensions to describe PDs. One is that most current PD categories overlap because they share a common profile on the FFM: high levels of neuroticism, low levels of conscientiousness, and low levels of agreeableness (Trull and Widiger, 2013). While analysis of trait facets might account more precisely for symptoms, we do not know if that approach would be too complex for clinical utility. However, there is a meaningful correspondence between the dimensions of psychopathology described by HiToP, the FFM, and the hybrid system of PD diagnosis in *DSM*-5 (see Figure 2.1).

A second problem is that the question of whether there is always a correspondence between personality traits measured by self-report and manual-based evaluations by clinical observers. One might also ask whether either of these methods, especially responses to questionnaires, is the last word in psychometrics.

A third problem is that while some PDs are readily mapped by dimensional methods, this may not be the case for the most symptomatic of all PDs, the borderline type. These patients show a mixture of internalizing and externalizing symptoms that cut across dimensions of personality and psychopathology (Paris, 2005). One could say BPD is a disorder that includes a bit of everything. That conclusion is confirmed by a large-scale survey that found a strong relationship between BPD and the p-factor (Gluschkoff et al., 2021).

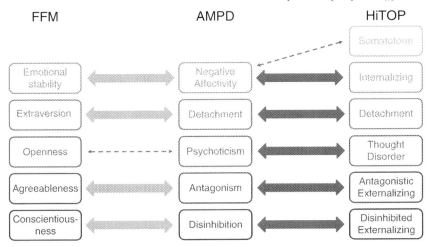

Figure 2.1 Comparison of the Five Factor Model of Personality (FFM), the Alternate Model of Personality disorders (AMPD), and the Hierarchical Taxonomy of Psychopathology (HiTOP).

Source: drawn from Kotov et al., in press.

A fourth problem is that not all people who have the features of a PD are sufficiently distressed to seek help. Consider, for example, narcissistic PD, a condition that has been retained in the AMPD, but that typically does more harm to others than to those who meet criteria for the diagnosis (Campbell and Miller, 2011). While we want to avoid unnecessarily expanding the definition of psychopathology, the presence of these traits in prominent political figures has been irresistible to clinicians familiar with the narcissistic pattern of grandiosity and low empathy. One could consider another example: people with compulsive traits are more likely to think that everyone else is just plain sloppy.

A fifth problem is that some PDs, particularly BPD, can be associated with dramatic symptoms that go beyond trait dimensions. Patients who can be characterized by extreme levels of traits, without many symptoms, most easily fit dimensional theory. In contrast, patients with active and distressing symptoms require a somewhat different model. Thus, while many features of BPD are rooted in underlying traits of affective instability and impulsivity (Crowell et al., 2009), these dimensions do not fully account for other features of the disorder, such as self-harm, chronic suicidality, chaotic relationships, or micro-psychotic phenomena. Moreover, the fact that about 10% of BPD patients eventually die by suicide (Paris, 2021) suggests the need for a model that goes beyond personality traits as defined by the FFM.

Finally, the unique trajectory over time of PDs in general, and of BPD in particular, is that while dysfunctional traits tend to remain stable, symptoms tend to remit (Zanarini, 2018). This is consistent with the idea that PD is an amalgam of traits and symptoms. Much the same conclusion could apply to common disorders such as depression and anxiety. It is just a little more obvious in patients who have personality disorders.

In summary, personality and psychopathology are closely related but not identical. But there is a great need for clinicians to be more aware of the importance of personality traits. Otherwise, as one can already observe in contemporary practice, symptoms become the only focus. And that can lead to a rigid *DSM*-based practice in which every symptom is treated with drugs, and psychotherapy is not provided.

3 What Genes Can and Cannot Tell Us

Reading the Genome: Advances and Disappointments

Genetics is one of the hottest areas of research in biology. Nearly all aspects of life are at least partially heritable. For nearly a century, it has been known that psychopathology has a genetic component, which is particularly large in severe mental disorders. After the human genome was sequenced 20 years ago, many had hopes for this new research method, with the idea of applying genetics to the etiology and treatment of psychopathology (Arribas-Avilon et al., 2019).

The expectation was that scientists would find a single gene, or set of genes, that determine heritability. This hope was based on the assumption that the genome has a gene "for" every trait or disorder. That is one reason why many experts estimated the total number on the genome must be about 100,000. Actually, the number of genes in humans later turned out to be less than 20,000, no more than in many plants and animals.

We now understand that almost all genetic effects reflect complex interactions between multiple sites on the genome. The genes that are involved in any trait number in the hundreds or the thousands. In addition, each gene can be turned on, turned off, or made to take on a different task. Finally, the effects of genes can be modified by epigenetic "dimmer switches" located at non-coding sites on the genome (Plomin, 2018).

A related hope was that genetics could be the basis for the cure of diseases, either by editing the genome, or by offering "personalized medicine" based on individual differences in sequences (Kandel, 2018). In the current age of Clustered Regularly Interspaced Short Palindromic Repeats (CRISPR), DNA that bacteria use to kill viruses can be edited to change the genome (Bak et al., 2018). That might be a reasonable expectation for classical Mendelian diseases like sickle-cell anemia. But it is *not* reasonable for disorders that have a complex inheritance, involving hundreds of interactions.

Research on the whole genome shows that even when one considers large numbers of alleles, each accounts for only a small part of the variance in any outcome. That conclusion emerges from genome-wide association studies (GWAS; Tam et al., 2019), in which the entire genome is

DOI: 10.4324/9781003156215-3

sequenced to determine whether any combination of alleles is associated with a given outcome. Clearly, complex inheritance is much more complex than we realized. The same conclusions apply to virtually every condition seen by mental health professionals (Paris, 2021).

Around the time when the genome was decoded, I was asked to head a committee searching for the best candidate for an endowed chair in schizophrenia. The family providing the donation had lost a son to medical complications associated with that illness. They were persuaded (in part by the social climate) to consult a genetics professor, who assured them that science was on the cusp of a breakthrough which could lead to a cure.

Many members of the committee seemed to think so too. A brain-imaging researcher was of a different opinion about how a breakthrough would be achieved, but also believed that if mental disorders are brain disorders, we can find out how to treat them by discovering abnormalities in neuro-connectivity. This belief that the cure for mental illness is "just around the corner", and that it will come from genetics and neuroscience, has long been promoted (Insel and Quirion, 2005) and remains very much with us. Yet the corner remains stubbornly out of sight.

Our search committee included a geneticist from another city, known for his work in discovering a recessive gene on chromosome 7 associated with cystic fibrosis. But we now know that many other mutations can be associated with that illness, and that they interact with the main gene (Cutting, 2015). Today, the treatment of cystic fibrosis remains difficult but benefits most from improvements in the technology of ventilators (rather than from advances in genomics).

In the end, I was outvoted by the committee, and a research neurologist who specialized in brain diseases with a complex inheritance was chosen for the job. Unfortunately, he knew little about schizophrenia, which he saw only as a genetic puzzle to be unraveled. Little or no progress in research emerged over the years after he was hired. I was not surprised, and the outcome confirmed my view that understanding the origins of psychosis is a task not for a decade, but for a century.

We have learned a lot about the genome since then. But these advances are associated with a great disappointment. Almost all categories of mental disorders developed for the *DSM* manuals lack genetic or biological markers. The idea was that even if psychopathology lacks a Mendelian pattern of heredity, the heritable basis of illness might be explained by just a few alleles. This led to a futile search over many years for "candidate genes" associated with major mental disorders. But the idea that bipolar disorder or schizophrenia can be accounted in this way turned out to be mistaken. The hope that we could cure these conditions based on knowledge of their genetic origins also turned out to be an illusion.

As has long been known, it is hard for scientists to give up their paradigms. Some have suggested that genes are more closely related to *endophenotypes*, i.e. processes associated with psychopathology that are closer to genetic origins than symptoms (Gottesman and Gould, 2003). However, only minor progress has been made in defining and measuring such processes, not to speak of targeting them in treatment.

The failure of the dream that GWAS would cut this Gordian knot has been humbling. What the line of research actually shows is that very large numbers of genes, each with a small effect, interact with each other (and with environmental factors) to shape variations that lead to psychopathology (Paris, 2020a). These findings demonstrate that the effects of genes on the mind are mind-bogglingly complex. The problem of understanding these relationships is not likely to be solved any time soon, and may never achieve precision.

We know from twin studies (and other sources of evidence) that most forms of psychopathology are about 50% heritable. But the gap between these highly replicable findings from behavior genetics and the failure to identify specific genes associated with mental illness has been called the problem of "missing heritability" (Manolio et al., 2009). The search for what is missing continues, and researchers are in no way ready to give up.

The latest wrinkle in the story is that the effect sizes that emerge from GWAS, however weak, can be added up. That procedure yields a *polygenic risk score* (PRS; Dudbridge, 2013), the sum of effect sizes of all alleles associated with risk for a given outcome. Even so, PRS scores do not generally account for more than 5% of the variance in either mental disorders or personality traits (Bogdan et al., 2018). For that reason, these scores are not useful in making predictions. Even so, we hear a great deal about the idea that once genes for mental disorders are identified, patients can be offered personalized medicine. Thus far, that possibility remains very distant.

Alternatively, missing heritability can be seen as a signal to change our point of view. The problem could be rooted in the difficulty changing from linear associations to multivariate models of psychopathology. If the origins of mental disorders had turned out to be as simple as had been hoped, we would already be editing the genes of patients. But the pathways to psychopathology are as complex as the neural networks that govern them. One again, keep in mind that the complexity of the human brain is greater than anything else in the known universe.

In summary, genetic variations have major effects on psychological development and the risk for psychopathology. But that does not mean that single genes are associated with specific disorders or behaviors. We now understand the genes are not, as once thought, beads on a chromosomal string. They consist of sites on the genome that are widely spread out and not always precisely locatable. Genes carry out multiple functions, and their effects can be turned on or off by epigenetic markers (Dupre, 2012). Thus, the fact that genomic studies have thus far not been able to clearly elucidate the origins of mental disorders is not because we lack a better method. More likely, the problem is that research has not given sufficient attention to gene-environment interplay. As long as the search is limited to the genome itself, it will not explain the sources of psychopathology.

It is also notable that a risk for developing psychopathology is not always evident in early childhood. As we have seen, temperament bends the twig but does not determine the shape of the tree. Some genetic effects appear later in development.

Many of the effects of heritable risks first appear in adolescence. This is the age of onset for many mental disorders that carry over into adult life (Ullsperger and Nikolas, 2017), and that both sexes tend to develop more symptoms around the onset of puberty. This suggests an important, however delayed, role for hormones as a trigger for psychopathology.

There are notable differences between males and females in the development of psychopathology. Rutter et al. (2003), noted that some problems show a male excess, particularly in relation to neurodevelopmental impairment and aggressive behavior, while a female excess applies to emotional disorders. This parallels observations that men are much more likely to develop antisocial behavior, often linked to substance abuse, and also have a somewhat higher rate of schizophrenia. In contrast, females are more likely to develop depression (as well as anxiety and eating disorders) which tend to appear after puberty and can continue well into the young adult years.

Lessons from Behavior Genetics

Behavior genetics has been, and continues to be, the best way to quantify the influence of genetic and environmental factors on personality and psychopathology (Jang, 2020). Even though the search for genetic markers for psychopathology has not been very successful, we can still estimate the heritability of many outcomes of interest, including psychopathology and personality.

Behavior genetics usually uses twin samples to measure heritability. As discussed in Chapter 2, the calculation of a coefficient of heritability is made from differences in concordance for traits between monozygotic (MZ) and dizygotic (DZ) twins, expressed as a percentage for heritable effects.

Given the power of this method, researchers have recruited twin cohorts from the community all over the world. One of the richest sources of data has been the Virginia Twin Study of Adolescent Behavioral Development, led by Kenneth Kendler (at Virginia Commonwealth University), which recruited 2762 families. Hundreds of published papers have emerged from this project, and many of its most clinically relevant results were summarized in a book (Kendler and Prescott, 2007). Kendler, one of the most productive and influential researchers in contemporary psychiatry, has also been involved in large-scale twin studies in Sweden and other European sites (Kendler et al., 2020).

Robert Plomin, an American psychologist who works in the UK, has also been a leader in behavior genetics for several decades, and can be considered one of the founders of the field. Plomin has recruited large twin samples in the US and the UK, and has written a number of books for the educated public on the implications of his research (Plomin, 2018). In my own country (Canada), the British Columbia Twin Project has been the largest research program, focusing on the heritability of personality traits (Jang, 2013, 2020).

Keep in mind that the percentage of heritability of any trait does not apply to individuals. Rather, it is an average across a population. Thus, the same outcomes could be derived from either higher or lower heritability in different people. It is also worth noting that results may not be the same in all samples. For example, IQ is more heritable in people who benefit from a highly favorable environment, and less heritable in people in whom the environment seriously interferes with development, flattening the curve of variability (Plomin, 2018).

The twin method requires an "equal environments assumption", i.e. that twins, whether MZ of DZ, have been raised in the same family in much the same way (Uher and Zwicker, 2017). This assumption has been questioned but has been generally supported by a large-scale meta-analysis (Polderman et al., 2015). Also, while twins raised together sometimes try to minimize their differences, they usually become more similar over time (Plomin, 2018).

Twin research would be even more common if it were not so expensive. Large community samples are needed to compare MZ and DZ twins for levels of concordance. While fewer studies have made use of other samples, such as adoptees, twins separated at birth, or siblings, the results are very similar (Jang, 2020).

The findings of twin research can be summarized by what Turkheimer (2000) called "the three laws of behavior genetics". These are:

1. all human behavioural traits are heritable;
2. the effects of being raised in the same family are smaller than the effect of genes;
3. a substantial portion of the variation in complex human behavioural traits is not accounted for by the effects of genes *or* families.

In an update on this literature, Plomin et al. (2016) came to much the same conclusions, listing the "top-ten" findings of behavior genetics. The most important are that all psychological traits show significant and substantial genetic influence, that no traits are 100% heritable, and that heritability is associated with large numbers of genes, each with a small effect.

In summary, behavior genetics provides stronger evidence for the heritability of traits, for both personality and psychopathology, than any other research method, including GWAS. However, the failure of genetic associations to fully account for gene–environment interactions shows that they are only the first step on the way to a more sophisticated approach.

Again, keep in mind that the method measures group (not individual) differences). In a review of progress in behavior genetics since the genome was sequenced, Harden (2021) noted that as social conditions have improved, we have learned that genetics is far from deterministic. When the environment changes, it can raise the bar for an outcome for everyone, so that genes become more (rather than less) important in determining individual differences. For example, educational attainment is related to a shared environment that families use to promote the advancement of their children. Harden recommends that genetics should now be incorporated more routinely in psychological research, pointing out (p. 85) that "advances in genotyping technology, open science practices, massive sample sizes, and large-scale international collaborations have finally begun to yield replicable knowledge about specific genes associated with human psychology and behavior. This knowledge can most readily be put to use by psychological researchers in the form of polygenic scores". Even so, we now know that PRS data explain only a small proportion of the variance in outcome. These scores are a good beginning, but they do not solve the problem of missing heritability.

Behavior Genetics and the Environment

The findings of behavior genetics challenge many long-held ideas in psychology. It was long believed that personality traits and mental disorders are mainly determined by family environment. But while the data show that nearly half of the variance affecting underlying personality and psychopathology can be attributed to heritable factors, this leaves only half of the variance that can be attributed to the environment. The problem is that it does not necessarily tell us precisely which environmental risks are crucial.

By comparing children brought up in the same family, behavior genetics can be used to determine whether environmental factors derive from growing up in the same family (Plomin, 2018). The method allows researchers to test the hypothesis that children become more similar if they have the same parents. This is done by partitioning the variance into *shared* and *non-shared* components, with the shared component reflecting whether people grow up in the same family.

The results of these analyses came as a major surprise to many researchers and clinicians. Most of the environmental portion of the variance affecting psychopathology and personality is *non-shared*, and little variance is related to growing up in the same family. This finding is so counter-intuitive that it is often challenged or dismissed. Moreover, when we are measuring outcomes that seem likely to be influenced by rearing, we assume that the family environment *must* play a role. For example, it is known that suicidality runs in families. Yet a recent study in Sweden (Kendler et al., 2020) that examined suicide attempts and death by suicide found a strong heritable component (close to half the variance). Moreover, the environmental component in suicidality was *not* associated with having a parent with a history of this behavior, a finding that does not support direct parent–child transmission.

Clearly, the sources of environmental variance affecting psychopathology are not, as many of us would have thought, *mainly* derived from experiences in rearing. In this way, twin research contradicts the long-held belief that the most important environmental factors affecting personality and psychopathology come from rearing and experiences in families. Another way of understanding this conclusion is that living in the same family does not make twins more similar, above and beyond shared heredity. That leaves us with a residual domain that is rooted in a broader non-shared environment. These data seem to upend decades of assumptions in developmental psychopathology. Moreover, children from the same family can be remarkably different. It has often been said that parents with one child believe in environment, but that parents with two children believe in genes.

Quite a few suggestions have been offered about the possible meaning of non-shared environment. It could derive from differences in experiences within the family that are unique to one child, the effects of life experiences outside the family, or simply reflect measurement error (Jang, 2020). Turkheimer and Waldron (2000) reviewed this literature, and they noted that *no* measurements of extra-familial experiences have been found to account for non-shared environment. This failure of confirmation of common beliefs remains the same today. We are, therefore, left to speculate what the actual pathways might be.

One is that within the family, even if the equal environments assumption is supported, experiences are not identical. Moreover, life experiences *outside* the family are not strictly determined, and can sometimes be random. Another possibility is that neural development, both during fetal life and childhood, has a component of randomness (Mitchell, 2018). Thus, neurons proliferate and grow without being given precise directions as to where to make connections). For this reason, neural development is a complex process and monozygotic wins do not have identical brain structures. As Eagelman (2020) points out, the newborn brain in humans is largely unfinished in structure and function, and is strongly shaped by factors that influence how it ends up being wired. This developmental factor is not accounted for by any behavioral genetics research program.

Finally, as Jang (2020) notes, the influence of family environment is very difficult to measure, and crucial details may be lost in twin research. Psychological development is an extremely complex process, and researchers may not always be looking in the right place. With support from most experts, I find it difficult to believe that highly dysfunctional families with pathological rearing practices lack the ability to harm children. I suspect that one source of the paradox of finding little effect for shared environment is that there is a wide range of effects from nurture that are absorbed by resilience and the psychological immune system. For this reason, it usually takes a *high* level of adversity to trigger psychopathology. Conversely, children with high genetic vulnerability may develop abnormally when exposed to lower levels of environmental adversity.

Thus, shared environmental effects may be more influential in extreme situations (such as in abusive parenting). If those who are easily triggered by adversity are more affected by a dysfunctional family environment, this relationship may not be apparent if it is only true for a minority. Since twin studies are conducted in normal non-clinical populations and report mean differences, they may miss outliers in which extremity plays a major role in risk.

While Plomin (2011) is definitive about the lack of evidence for an effect of family life on adult outcomes, I find his views too rigid. But he does list some alternate explanations for the prominence of nonshared environment. Plomin echoes Jang in noting that lack of support for shared effects could reflect errors of measurement. Plomin also raises the possibility that prenatal factors may contribute to nonshared effects. For example, twins differ in size and may not have equal access to nutrients from the placenta. This effect has not been well researched.

Environmental effects can also be different at different stages of development. It is also well-known that genes have stronger effects as people grow older (Eaton et al., 2012). Moreover, Burt (2011) carried out a meta-analysis suggesting that shared environment, even though not dominant over the life span, plays a larger role in adolescence, particularly in relation to the risk for psychopathology.

Finally, if some effects on development are random and unpredictable, non-shared environment could also reflect sheer luck (Kagan, 2010; Rutter, 2012). While we sometimes think that the course of life is determined, there are good reasons to believe that it is not. (This point of view assumes that many life events are random and/or that human beings have free will.)

Any or all of these mechanisms could be operative. But the data still seem to suggest that families are less responsible for psychological problems in their children than most clinicians think. Harris (2009), in a widely read book, used behavior genetic data to support the counter-intuitive hypothesis that peer groups may be more important than families in psychological development. Kagan (2010), rejecting this conclusion, suggested that we are not looking hard enough to confirm the role of families (and social class) in the risk for psychopathology. But without the grounding of biomarkers or endophenotypes that could validate the outcome measures used in developmental psychopathology, it is hard to be sure.

In short, we cannot conclude family functioning has *no* effect on children. Taking an interactive point of view, family dysfunction is not necessarily a cause of psychopathology *by itself*, but it raises risk for those who are vulnerable for other reasons. This concept has been called "differential susceptibility to the environment", i.e. that some children, for better or worse, respond more strongly to what happens in their family and social environment (Belsky and Pluess, 2009). The correlations we see between adversity and outcome (in research that does not measure heritability) could well be driven by this subgroup.

Moreover, we are limited by the concepts and measures we use to describe risks as well as those we use to determine the outcome of adversity. As Kagan (2010) notes, when we use words like "trauma" or "dysfunction", not every observer is talking about the same thing, or is even on the same page. As the next chapter will show, all kinds of life events, ranging from frank abuse to emotional neglect have been called "traumatic". But each type of adversity has different effects on development.

My conclusion is that an interpretation of behavior genetics as proving that parents do not matter is doubtful. As Kaufman (2019) points out:

> ...for traits like IQ that are only about 50% heritable, even if there are no effects of the so-called "shared environment", parents may nonetheless be an important part of the so-called "non-shared environment", as long as the effects they have on their children tend to make them different from each other. This may seem counter-intuitive – surely given that children in the same family have the same parents, then parents must be part of the shared environment – but that is not true because of the technical meaning of "shared environment" in the models used to estimate heritability. Again, only forces that make children in the same family more similar to each other count as "shared environment", so the present state of scientific knowledge means that parents may be important in influencing their children to become more unique.

Finally, the effects of parenting depend on goodness-of-fit with the temperament of children. These interactions are unique to individuals, and may therefore end up falling within the domain of the non-shared environment. Moreover, family dysfunction makes the greatest difference when it is extreme. That may be what behavior genetics misses when it depends on data from samples of normal twins.

Epigenetics

We now know that the environment has an effect on the functioning of the genome (O'Donnell and Meany, 2020). Epigenetic research shows that life experiences, while not changing the genome itself, can produce changes in genetic switches. These effects are due to chemical changes (methyl groups or histones) that can either turn genes on and off, or act as a dimmer switch. Such changes can be passed on to future generations: in a study of those who survived the 1944–45 Dutch famine, epigenetic markers affecting the activity of genes were found in the grandchildren of those who had been exposed to severe hunger early in pregnancy (Hejmans et al., 2008).

A team led by my McGill University colleague Michael Meaney carried out a widely quoted study of epigenetic effects in rats (Weaver et al., 2004). Higher rates of licking and grooming of pups by the mother in the early weeks of life were protective against later exposure to stress, and these protective factors persisted into adulthood. This research group also studied humans who suffered death by suicide, and they found that people who reported childhood abuse had a lower expression of glucocorticoid receptors in the hippocampus, a change known to be linked to lower resistance to stress (O'Donnell and Meaney, 2020). The mechanism involves changes in gene expression related to environmental adversity.

The McGill research group also found that people who had died by suicide, and who had previously reported childhood abuse, had less expression of hippocampal glucocorticoid receptors than non-abused suicide victims or non-suicidal subjects (O'Donnell and Meaney., 2020). However, note that this study, unlike the one in rats, was not longitudinal, but depended on the validity of childhood memories.

As Dupre (2012) has pointed out, genomes are not static, but are in a constant state of change and flow as the organism faces new challenges. However, there are limitations to the degree of change. First, epigenetics does not account for individual differences in reactivity to an adverse environment. Second, the measures of adversity used in most studies are broad and lack specificity. Nonetheless, the importance of epigenetics lies in its description of a mechanism by which genes are regulated by the environment, something that was not considered possible in the earlier years of genomic research.

In short, research on epigenetics is a large step in the right direction. But it remains to be seen whether this measure of gene–environment interaction can become a predictive tool. Epigenetic studies have aroused great interest, but the breadth of applicability of these mechanisms remains unknown. I once heard a neuroscientist at a conference thank Michael Meaney for "bringing us to pay attention to the environment". But some of us have been paying attention all along. We only need a better theoretical model to account for these effects.

Conclusions

In summary, since the human genome was mapped, scientists have hoped that research can identify which genes are responsible for mental illness. But very few diseases are governed by a single gene. These Mendelian disorders are the exception, and most forms of pathology emerge from *complex inheritance*, in which many genes interact each other, and with environmental triggers. In this model, while genes remain a crucial influence, the key pathways to psychopathology are almost all based on interactions. Some of these interactions will be between multiple genes. Others will be interactions between genes and environment. The effects of genes can be entirely different in the context of different life experiences and social contexts. This helps explain why heredity does not necessarily determine how children develop into adults. In fact, there is little determinism in psychological development. As in any complex system, individual differences in the functioning of the human mind can never be entirely predictable.

4 Neuroscience: Triumphs and Limitations

The Current Status of Neuroscience

Neuroscience has become a dominant paradigm in psychiatry, and it is also influential in many domains of psychology. Yet we have to ask how close the correspondence is between what we can currently measure about the brain, and how people think, feel, and behave.

This chapter will present a sympathetic but critical review of progress in neuroscience relevant to psychopathology and personality. I have been interested since my student days in the link between biology and the mind. The field of neuroscience was then called "physiological psychology". But at that time, little was known about how the brain works. Researchers could only hypothesize about the precise role of neurotransmitters. For example, one of my teachers was studying the hippocampus, but its role in memory was still a matter for speculation.

Since then, basic research moved forward by leaps and bounds. We can now measure interactions between dozens of neurotransmitters. We can now localize, at least partially, the role of specific brain regions. But while neuroscience has greatly illuminated the functioning of neurons and neural circuity, it is very far from explaining the mind or the roots of human behavior.

One issue here is whether one can explain complex phenomena by reducing them to a simpler level of analysis That method, in which complex phenomena are understood by reducing them to simpler levels, has long been adopted by science and medicine. The results in medicine have given many of us additional years (if not decades) of life. A good deal of progress has derived from linking biology to chemistry. Biochemistry has made modern medical treatment, much of which can be studied at a molecular level, possible. In most domains of science, from particle physics to genetics, focusing analysis to a more fundamental level does tend to lead to progress. Some of the most dramatic examples include Mendeleev's periodic table, quantum physics, and the structure of DNA.

Psychiatry has attempted to repeat this success by establishing strong links with neuroscience. Most of the academic leaders in the discipline are now brain researchers who are rarely active clinicians. Those of us who are

DOI: 10.4324/9781003156215-4

interested in studying mental phenomena at a mental level have been relegated to a minority position. As one of my colleagues quipped, many of today's academic leaders in psychiatry know more about ions than about people.

In the USA, the National Institute of Mental Health (NIMH) has promoted a strongly reductionist agenda, and its leadership is drawn from the ranks of neuroscientists. In line with that point of view, NIMH has developed its own classification system of psychopathology, the Research Domain Criteria (RDoC; Cuthbert and Insel, 2013). As discussed in Chapter 1, RDoC claims to reflect advances in neuroscience, but is so far from this goal that it can only be called "a bridge too far" (Paris and Kirmayer, 2016). Frances (2014) has described the RDoC system as "oversold", and he pointed out that while the NIMH generously funds brain research, it does almost nothing to support investigations that could have practical value for treating the sickest patients. Psychiatry may be making a bad bet if it believes that most of its problems can be solved by research on brain connectivity.

Neuroscience has advanced greatly at the level of basic research. We definitely know much more about the brain than we did when I was a student. Yet the potential for understanding psychopathology at a neural level, like the long-expected breakthroughs from reading the genome, has proved elusive. Repeated promises of progress in clinical applications of new knowledge have not been redeemed. Reducing mental processes to a cellular level has not helped the work of clinicians. It does not tell us how to diagnose, treat, or prevent manage psychopathology.

Biological psychiatry in current practice consists largely of drug prescriptions, most of which do not out-perform the agents we have 50 years ago. In spite of these limitations, psychiatric drugs are generally effective for severe mental illness (Paris, 2010). I was privileged to live through the psychopharmacology revolution years as a student. (As an undergraduate, I also had the opportunity to visit mental hospitals prior to the introduction of antipsychotic drugs.) Yet ironically, the most dramatic advances in drug therapy have not been based on basic science, but on serendipitous discoveries. In spite of great progress in neuroscience, the biological treatment of patients with severe mental disorders has not undergone radical change in the last 50 years. If we still only had the drugs that were available in 1970, we would see more side effects, but hardly any change in the efficacy of biological treatment for severe psychopathology. Finally, in common mental disorders, such as depression and anxiety, drugs do not out-perform evidence-based methods of psychotherapy (Barkham et al., 2021).

The Allure of Brain Imaging

It is tempting to look at a brain scan and assume it offers an understanding of psychopathology. The media have greatly promoted the allure of brain imaging. This is a story of one picture being worth a thousand words.

Brightly colored images have a great impact, even when they tend to tell us things we already know. (One of my colleagues, an expert on borderline personality disorder, told me that he never quite believed that his patients see neutral faces as angry until this misperception was demonstrated in an imaging study (Donegan et al., 2003).

Functional magnetic imaging (fMRI) is a window on brain activity. It has even been suggested as a way of reading the mind (Rose, 2016). But this method, in spite of its power, only tells us whether blood flow is increasing in given regions. And even if regions do "light up" when a task is performed, this hardly account for the billions of interacting neurons behind every observation. Some researchers have questioned the assumption that signals from specific brain regions accurately reflect their neuronal activity (Logothetis, 2008; Turner, 2016). Moreover, we need to keep in mind that we are not seeing real colors, but a computerized image based on the average blood flow to one region compared to others. Also, since neural networks are widely distributed, fMRI is not always informative about neuro-connectivity.

Another issue is that correspondences between fMRI findings and thought processes depend on the context in which they are measured (Sahakian and Gottward, 2017). From the perspective of clinical science, Satel and Lilienfeld (2013) assessed fMRI as a useful but often ambiguous representation of a highly complex system. Since each brain region is involved in a host of experiences and interacts with other regions, seeing one area light up does not necessarily correlate with behavior or emotions, not to speak of higher cognitive functions. A final limitation of imaging is that imaging is very expensive. This is probably why most published studies have samples too small to allow generalization of their findings (Ioannidis, 2015).

None of the comments should be taken to deny that fMRI has been a boon to brain research. But that progress lies at the level of basic science, not clinical science. The question is whether it is, as some have claimed, a "window on the brain". Future methods may be more advanced and not suffer from the same limitations, but we are a long way from having a tool that can explain brain and mind.

The Myth of the Chemical Imbalance

A long-standing trend in biological psychiatry is to look for biomarkers associated with psychopathology. These are usually believed to involve changes in brain biochemistry that reflect abnormalities in neurotransmission. This research agenda goes back over half a century, when it was discovered that monoamines (serotonin, norepinephrine, and dopamine) are crucial to circuity affecting emotions. For decades, it was believed that imbalances in these neurotransmitters could account for depression, as well as for psychoses (France et al., 2007). It was also believed that drugs such as antidepressants and antipsychotics work by restoring this imbalance.

The simplicity of these hypotheses has been difficult to resist. Moreover, the pharmaceutical industry aggressively promoted these ideas, and many articles on neurochemistry have featured well-designed colored pictures of the synapse. There have even been claims that individual differences in temperament and personality could be explained by differences in neurochemistry, with each trait domain corresponding to a specific neurotransmitter (Cloninger, 1987). But while psychiatric drugs do change the activity of neurotransmitters, we still do not really know quite how they work to change the mind.

As more data emerged, we learned just how complex neurochemistry can be. At this point, it is fair to say that the most simplistic theories (such as monoamine theories of depression and psychosis) have been disproven. And it is also clear that psychiatric drugs, even when effective, do not work only by changing the activity of specific neurotransmitters. At a clinical level, pharmacological agents such as antidepressants, although currently prescribed to over 10% of the population, do not predictably help people suffering from depression or other internalizing disorders (Cipriani et al., 2018). Yet the wish for a quick fix for human suffering can still shape attitudes in patients, particularly if they prefer to explain their suffering as coming from external forces rather than from their own personality.

The rise and fall of the chemical imbalance model is a classic case of oversimplification and hubris. But this story has another message for us – we should not underestimate the complexities of mind and brain. We would eventually like to cut the Gordian knot of neuroscience, but doing so will require time and patience.

Reductionism, Complexity, and Emergence

Reductionism is a key research strategy for science. In both psychiatry and psychology, it describes a perspective in which processes at the level of the neuron and neural circuitry are examined to account for the effects of higher-level phenomena, including consciousness, mood, behavior, and relationships (Cobb, 2020). The idea mental disorders should be seen as brain disorders is true in a general sense, since there can be no mind without a brain. But it should not be taken to mean that we can understand all mental phenomena through processes of neurotransmission or neurocircuitry.

Those experts who support reductionism, including former directors of mental health research in the US and Canada (Insel and Quirion, 2005), have encouraged psychiatry to adopt reductionism. They also advocate for psychiatry to rejoin neurology, a split that occurred around the end of the 19th century. These scientists may have a strong belief in biochemistry, but fail to recognize that psychology is as important as a basic science for psychopathology. Knowing how little interest most neurologists have in psychology, the abolition of psychiatry followed by a merger with neurology would be a major disaster for patients. Those who take this position show a lack of interest in the psychosocial factors that increase the risk for psychopathology.

In a hierarchy of possible observations (sometimes cleverly referred to as "from neuron to neighborhood"), neuroscience does not deserve automatic primacy. It can explain mechanisms at a cellular level or in neural networks, leading to findings that have illuminated important brain mechanisms (Gorman, 2019). The question is whether, in an enormously complex system like the human brain, consciousness and mental activity can be reduced to these simpler levels.

The problem with reductionism is its incorrect belief that lower levels of analysis can account for phenomena that occur at higher levels. That is not even true in chemistry or physics. A simple example is that water is not simply an amalgam of the properties of hydrogen and oxygen. That is why chemistry remains a separate discipline from physics. And even in physics, one would not look to quantum theory to account for phenomena such as planetary or galactic orbits. This is not to say that reductionism is always misguided, but that it does not necessarily have priority over other strategies. In psychology this means that we must also study *mind*, i.e. the faculty that makes us aware of the world and our own experiences.

One need not be a philosophical dualist, or deny that brain mechanisms underlie psychological phenomena, to question the idea that the complexity of the human mind can be fully understood at a molecular level. By privileging neuroscience, and creating a hierarchy in which life experiences play a secondary role, reductionism downgrades the role of psychosocial factors in human development. As a witty saying puts it, not everything that can be easily counted counts, and not everything that counts can be easily counted. Reductionism has been a potent strategy in the physical sciences, but it does not provide an explanation of either brain or mind.

For a better approach, we need to invoke the construct of *emergence* (Gold, 2009; Gibb et al., 2019). This term means that characteristics can emerge at higher and more complex levels of analysis that *cannot* be accounted for at lower or simpler levels. In short, the whole is more than the sum of its parts.

All highly complex systems tend to produce emergent phenomena that cannot be explained by their components (Koch, 2014). The human brain has at least 85 billion neurons (linked by trillions of synapses), and an even larger number of glia. Neural networks are widely distributed, a fact that is not always apparent from imaging – even if the bright colors of brain scans that "light up" at specific sites seem to imply localization. The systems that influence thought, emotions, and behavior tend to be directed by the frontal cortex, but are based on activity in a very wide range of brain areas.

The complexity of the brain is almost unimaginable, making it unlikely that it can ever be understood by reductionism. Instead, we are in need of models that embrace this complexity, combining biological and psychosocial influences on thought, emotion, and behavior. In short, the mind needs to be studied at an emergent level (Kagan, 2006).

These issues are not just theoretical. Reductionistic models in molecular psychiatry tend to support a focus on drug treatment (Paris, 2017). This rather crude way of applying neuroscience to practice assumes that psychological problems are determined at a cellular level or the activity of a neural network.

In contrast, everything psychotherapists do with patients is based on a different set of assumptions. When they deal with the mind, they can address consciousness and assume that patients have ability to change. This is because therapists see people as having *free will*, i.e. the power of acting without the constraint of necessity (List, 2019). Even as our understanding of neuroscience grows, it does not follow the thoughts, emotions and behaviors are predetermined by biological mechanisms.

Debates about free will have gone on for millennia, but the arguments in its favor are strong (Dennett, 2003), and psychology is incomprehensible without that assumption. The point is that while physical laws are predictable in principle, mental processes need not be. This distinction, which has been called "compatibilism" (Gold, 2009), allows therapists and their patients to work on the assumption that, in spite of either nature or nurture, people have enough free will to change their lives.

Again, it may be necessary to explain that emergence is not a form of dualism. (I have had to carefully monitor my thoughts on complexity when talking to biological researchers.) Thoughts cannot exist outside the brain. Even so, mind is the highest and most complex level at which brain functions can be studied. Mind is the main subject of cognitive psychology. Without considering mind, one cannot do research on subjectivity (Kagan, 2006). Finally, responses to the environment can produce brain changes, some of which involve *neuroplasticity,* in which circuits can be modified to deal with changing circumstances (LeDoux, 2002). Free will is an essential part of our responses to environmental challenges.

The idea that mental disorders are "nothing but" brain disorders has done serious damage to my discipline. Psychosocial factors play a major role in the most common mental disorders, and are also relevant to understanding the origins of psychoses. I have heard more than once about medical students interested in psychiatry being discouraged by faculty members, who believe it is only a matter of time until mental illness will be entirely explained by changes in the brain. In their view, the sooner psychiatry disappears, the better. I believe that this hostility to my discipline is based on an almost universal fear of mental illness.

A recent issue of the journal *Behavioral and Brain Sciences* was entirely devoted to the relationship of mental disorders to the brain. The target article, by the Dutch psychologist Denny Borsboom et al. (2019) had as its title "Mental disorders are brain disorders – not really". It argued for a different model, using sophisticated mathematics, in which symptoms are linked with each other a *network* structure. In this model, symptoms are features of psychopathology that interact at points called "nodes" that can have variable strength (Boschloo et al., 2015).

A network model, as briefly discussed in Chapter 1, allows for the complexity of psychopathology by focusing on the overlaps between symptoms. It examines psychopathology at a mental level, and as a product of the brain as a whole – not of any particular region, or of the mechanics of neurochemistry or neuroconnectivity. In some ways, the model is consistent with DSM-5 and ICD-11, in that it focuses on symptoms rather than on unproven theories about etiology. The network model is also consistent with dimensional models such as HiToP, and with an interactive and biopsychosocial model of psychopathology. (See discussion of the biopsychosocial model of psychiatry in Chapter 7.)

As Borsboom et al. (2019, p. 137) explain:

> …mental disorders arise from direct interactions between symptoms…. At the heart of the theory lies the notion that symptoms of psychopathology are causally connected through myriads of biological, psychological and societal mechanisms. If these causal relations are sufficiently strong, symptoms can generate a level of feedback that renders them self-sustaining…This idea naturally leads to a comprehensive model of psychopathology, encompassing a common explanatory model for mental disorders, as well as novel definitions of associated concepts such as mental health, resilience, vulnerability and liability.

In line with the format of this journal (*Brain and Behavioral Sciences*), a large number of comments on Borsboom's target article, 27 in all, were published. Some were critical, but most were supportive. Here are some comments by a leader in medical research, John Ioannidis (2019, p. 23):

> There is enormous investment in basic neuroscience research and intensive searches for informative biomarkers of treatment response and toxicity. The yield is close to nil. Even optimists acknowledge that, currently, there is still no clinically useful way to predict which patients will respond best to widely used medications such as antidepressants. If mental health problems are mostly not brain disorders, the dearth of useful neuroscience-derived biomarkers is only to be expected. To overcome this dead end, we should shift emphasis away from the research paradigm that considers mental health problems to be mostly brain disorders and move towards exploring other, potentially more fruitful paths. First, this would mean reducing emphasis on identifying etiological brain pathways, and through them, biological markers and surrogate outcomes. If consistently strong and clinically useful biological markers/surrogates do not exist, perpetually searching for them would be in vain.

Ionnaddiis' view is that the lack of progress in applying neuroscience to mental health practice does not support continuing on the same path, hoping for a major scientific breakthrough, but embarking on a different approach. There is an enormous gap between the level of neurons and higher level functions such as mind, thought, emotion and behavior. Behavior, emotions, and cognitive processes cannot be reduced to cellular mechanisms. Moreover, processes that are deterministic on a cellular level can still be subject to free will and intentionality at the level of behavior (List, 2019). We need to study the brain, but that does not exclude studying the mind at a mental level.

Perhaps the most serious problem with biological reductionism is its failure to develop a theory of psychopathology based on the Darwinian principle of natural selection. As Brune (2016) points out in his textbook of evolutionary psychiatry, most research focuses on *proximal* causes of abnormality, rather than on *ultimate* causes rooted in Darwinian mechanisms. In other words, we need a model that explains why problematic cognitions, emotions and behaviors are so common, in spite of natural selection. In other words, what looks maladaptive may have developed because it was originally adaptive in the environment in which we originally evolved. Thus, one should search for potentially adaptive aspects of psychopathology that have kept them in the gene pool. These questions arise from a evolutionary theory that studies organisms as a whole, and that cannot be reduced to processes at the level of neurons or their connections. For example one can understand anxiety disorders as driven by an alarm system that is needed, but that goes off too readily. One can also understand substance use disorders and many forms of personality disorder as based on emotional dysregulation and an inability to control behavioral impulses. But while these models can ultimately be rooted in neuroscience, they describe mental function as a whole.

At present, all systems of classifying psychopathology, from DSM to HiTOP or network theory, describe symptoms but fail almost entirely to explain *why* they emerge. A useful etiological model of mental disorders would need to provide both distal and ultimate explanations, and would need to move beyond reductionism to take multiple levels of analysis into account. It would also need to be based on Darwinian principles and concern itself with whether variations in thought, behavior, and emotion, have an underlying basis in functioning.

Many clinicians and researchers, used to linear ways of thinking, find interactive models uncomfortably complex. In the same way as neuroscience researchers search (albeit unsuccessfully) for single genes, single neurotransmitters, or single neural pathways to explain mental disorders, they are attracted to simple theories of all kinds. (As Chapter 5 will discuss, a similar problem afflicts clinical psychology, e.g. the way that one of its most prominent current theories claims that trauma accounts, more or less by itself, for many forms of psychopathology.)

Some Tentative Conclusions

Neuroscience has provided us with information on the brain that, for those of us who can remember where the field was 60 years ago, is impressive.

On the level of basic science, progress is undeniable. It is a bet on the future that may or may not pay off. At this point, applying its findings to clinical practice is another story. A more achievable and practically relevant alternative, as recommended years ago by Caspi and Moffit (2006), would be to integrate neuroscience with psychosocial research that takes a longitudinal (not cross-sectional) approach to development. As the next two chapters will show, this requires studying people over time with tools drawn from both of these domains.

In summary, while neuroscience has shed important light on brain function and has the potential to tell us many important things about psychopathology, it focuses on only one level of a vast hierarchy. What we need is a better theory of mind, and a better understanding of how higher-level constructs, such as personality, influence the way people think, feel, and behave.

5 Childhood Adversities and Adult Functioning

Nature, Nurture, and Childhood

Assumptions that personality and psychopathology are shaped primarily by nature or by nurture have a long history. These polarities reflect different views of the world. A focus on nurture is in accord with a modern idea that nothing is inevitable, and that life can always be made better. A focus on nature emphasizes limits on development reflecting genetic factors that can override environmental effects.

The idea that nurture is the most crucial factor in development reached an apex around the middle of the 20th century, but goes back much further. The 17th-century English philosopher John Locke proposed that the mind is a "blank slate" at birth, and this idea has been interpreted to mean that individual differences between people are almost entirely shaped by social learning. The view that families are the main factor shaping the personalities of children has long been held, and it has been particularly influential in the social sciences (Degler, 1991). The anthropologist Margaret Mead (1935, p. 191) spoke for many when she wrote: "Human nature is almost unbelievably malleable, responding accurately and contrastingly to contrasting cultural conditions".

There is (and always has been) a political dimension to this debate. Conservatives tend to adopt what Pinker (2002) calls a "tragic vision", i.e. that individual differences are innate, and that human nature sets a limit on progress that needs to be respected. In contrast, a "Utopian vision" proposes that differences in opportunity and achievement are external to the individual, and that they can and should be redressed. The idea that we are, in a famous phrase, "created equal", has been interpreted, particularly by Marxists, to mean that social reforms can radically change what has long been believed to be human nature.

A tragic vision has sometimes been associated with genetic determinism. This relationship helps to explain why political liberals have often been reluctant to accept scientific findings on the heritability of personality and psychopathology. (One of my teachers refused to believe that schizophrenia is heritable because he believed that thinking in that way would lead to hopelessness.)

DOI: 10.4324/9781003156215-5

An Utopian vision is implicit in many areas of psychology. In spite of strong evidence for heritability, the top journals in child development continue to publish articles showing correlations between early adversity and adult functioning, without considering genetic effects. Under the influence of Freud and his followers, the idea that psychological problems are rooted in childhood experiences became central both to therapy and to modern culture, and only much later came under question (Furedi, 2003). This bias was pointed out by Judith Rich Harris (2009). In a widely discussed book, she used the findings of behavior genetics to support the view that parenting is not the crucial factor driving the risk for psychopathology or personality traits. Instead, Harris proposed that interactions between genes and the wider social environment are more important.

In the last several decades, the triumphs of genetics and neuroscience have encouraged people to attribute psychological problems to heredity or to "chemical imbalances". The mantra that "mental disorders are brain disorders" takes the blame for psychopathology away from both patients and their families. In contrast, blaming parents is one of the hazards of practicing clinical psychology, and you do not have to be a therapist to believe that parents often harm children.

In a well-known poem, Philip Larkin (1988, p. 180) embraced the same idea:

Man hands out misery to man.

It deepens like a coastal shelf.

Get out as early as you can,

And don't have any kids yourself.

Childhood and Psychopathology

Fifty years ago, when I was training to be a psychiatrist, my teachers, as well as many mental health professionals, took it for granted that childhood adversity is the main cause of adult psychopathology. Few questioned this belief, even though it was based on clinical impressions, rather than on data. We were not yet in the era of evidence-based medicine. Even in fields like internal medicine or surgery, theory and practice were mainly guided by expert opinion, not research. In clinical psychology, the idea of evidence-based practice was only beginning. Students apprenticed themselves to teachers, and almost never asked them "where is your data?"

Today, mental health clinicians are much more humble, and expert opinion is much more rooted in empirical evidence. Speculative theories of child development such as psychoanalysis that have not been supported by empirical data have had to be either heavily revised or discarded (Paris, 2019).

Over the decades, psychological treatments became more oriented to current problems, and less to exploration of the past. This is one of the reasons why cognitive behavior therapy (CBT; Beck, 1979) became so popular. Another reason is that this method has earned a strong evidence base. CBT does have a developmental theory ("cognitive schemas"), but that is not its main or only focus. Rather, CBT teaches patients to manage their thoughts, emotions, and behaviors better to deal with current stressors. In my own clinical work and research on personality disorders, I have, like many others working in the field, been greatly influenced by the work of Marsha Linehan (1993). Linehan's theory is that BPD results from an interaction between a genetic factor (emotional dysregulation) and an environmental factor (invalidation of emotions in the family). Thus, the focus of "dialectical behavior therapy" for patients with BPD involves teaching patients to regulating emotions and to find sources of validation for those feelings. This is the most evidence-based method of treatment for these difficult patients, no doubt because it is based on a strong theory, and not on the currently fashionable view that this form of psychopathology is caused by traumatic events early in life (Paris, 2020a).

None of these developments mean that childhood experiences are irrelevant, or that they are not risk factors for psychopathology. Severe adversities do raise the risk – but usually in interaction with many other factors, both genetic and environmental. That is why mental health professionals should base their work on integrative gene–environment models that consider the interplay between nature and nurture.

For mental disorders like psychoses, which have a stronger genetic component, biology should and does take precedence. But neuroscience does not know how to explain them – not to speak of accounting for depression and anxiety, which are the most common symptoms seen in clinical practice. Progress in biological research has illuminated some of the mechanisms behind mental disorders, but has failed to integrate biology with environmental risks, beyond fuzzy constructs such as "stress" or "trauma".

Meanwhile, biological psychiatry, with its narrow emphasis on neuroscience, has seriously overshot the mark. The belief that psychopathology is almost entirely due to genes (and/or aberrant neural circuitry) is a vast oversimplification. Supported by the current *DSM* system, the theory and practice of psychiatry has come to depend on the assessment of symptoms, while downplaying the role of life experiences. The result is a practice based on symptoms treated with interventions that often consist only of drugs. This is a travesty of what psychiatry should be all about.

Clinical psychologists use different models, but some its practitioners are also oriented to symptoms. This leads them to offer all-purpose CBT skills (such as relaxation or mindfulness exercises). On the plus side, some of principles of emotion regulation have become part of the average clinician's tool kit. But, if CBT therapists were more aware of research in developmental psychopathology, they would give greater weight to life histories in understanding their patients.

The Impact of Adversity

There is a vast body of research on the relationship between early life experiences and adult psychopathology. It provides strong evidence that childhood trauma and neglect are risk factors for problems in adulthood (Cicchetti, 2016). But these risks need to be framed by individual differences in temperament that shape the vulnerability to adversity. Genes alone and environment alone tend to have weak effects, while interactions between genes and environment are most likely to lead to psychological problems.

The problem with this line of research is that, with few exceptions, studies of childhood adversity describe correlations that do not necessarily prove causality. (See the detailed discussion of this issue in Chapter 8.) Even as correlations, many of these relationships can be statistically significant, but not strong enough to be predictive of outcomes. For example, one large-scale prospective study found that childhood abuse increases the risk of adult psychopathology, but only accounts for 5% of the outcome (Fergusson et al., 2011). Thus, while adversity is a risk factor, most people who suffer childhood trauma never develop a mental disorder, and many people with adult mental disorders have not had a traumatic childhood (Rutter, 2012. The relationship between adverse experiences in childhood and adult symptoms is largely based on associations that do not allow for accurate prediction. Statistically significant findings usually account for only a small percentage of outcome variance.

The missing elements that help to explain the EW is temperament and personality. Some children are highly vulnerable to life stressors. Others shrug them off and move on. That is what we mean by *resilience* (Rutter, 2012). (See Chapter 7 for a detailed discussion.)

Another way of describing these individual differences is the construct of "differential susceptibility to the environment" (Belsky and Pluess, 2009). In that model, children with high temperamental susceptibility are not only more affected by negative life experiences, but also benefit more than others from positive experiences. The idea of unusual sensitivity to the environment is also similar to the concept of "high reactive" temperament in children (Kagan, 1994).

This relationship has also been subject to empirical research. Using a scale to identify highly sensitive children (Pluess et al., 2018), Assary et al. (2020) conducted a twin study of adolescents, which found that about half of the variance in the trait of sensitivity to the environment is heritable, and that separate pathways process positive and negative experiences. These findings support the overall theory that childhood adversities have a more powerful effect on highly reactive children. This is also the same kind of model developed by Linehan (1993) to account for BPD.

Since temperamental factors are crucial in whether or not adversity in development leads to sequelae, research and practice need to be "genetically informed" (Moffit et al., 2005). That may well be a major project for the future. At this point, genes have complex interactions that are hardly understood, and current measures of temperament are too approximate for accurate prediction. But while waiting for more definitive research findings, we can still train ourselves to think interactively and avoid attributing complex outcomes to simple causes.

Another difficulty with studies of childhood environment and adult outcome derives from broad and imprecise measures of life adversities. I have already described the problematic use of fuzzy concepts such as "stress" or "trauma". Both these terms have been subject over time to what has been called *concept creep*, in which definitions expand to include phenomena that were not part of the original construct (Haslam, 2016).

For example, a recent review article (Lippard and Nemeroff, 2020) measured psychological risks for adult mental disorders as a single variable called "child maltreatment". That term is quite misleading because it conflates a very wide range of life experiences. Do failures to respond consistently to emotional needs or a critical attitude imply maltreatment – or should that term be reserved for sexual or physical abuse? The term "emotional abuse" (Loring, 1994) is a meaningful construct when it refers to constant criticism of children, but it has sometimes been used to describe all kinds of faults in parenting. Emotional neglect, i.e. the failure to validate feelings in children, is generally a more crucial factor in development, but is not strictly a form of maltreatment.

Kagan (2006) advised researchers to avoid using such broad constructs, and to consider the parameters and contexts in which maltreatment is most likely. Doing so could make the study of development even more challenging. But given the complexity of the pathways from childhood to adulthood, we have no other choice.

Adversity in Childhood

Children can suffer from many adverse events, including family dysfunction, traumas such as sexual or physical abuse, family breakdown, emotional neglect, and poverty. Yet the long-term outcome of each of these risk factors is variable. These adversities have few specific relationships with adult psychopathology.

Once again, research on these life events, each of which has been thought to increase the risk for adult symptoms, describes statistical risks that are not strong enough to be usefully predictive. In most cases, when evidence linking risks to outcome is exposed to close critical scrutiny, it shows that only a minority of those exposed will suffer long-term sequelae. Let us now examine some of the research on each type of risk.

The quality of parenting

The basic tasks of parenting are to love children well enough to make them feel secure, and then to provide them with encouragement to leave and live their own lives. The Australian psychiatrist Gordon Parker (1983) termed these two dimensions *affection* and *control* (the latter being the opposite of support for autonomy). Parker developed a self-report measure, the Parental Bonding Index, to measure these constructs. Using this measure, psychopathology has been found to be associated both with low affection and high levels of control.

However, researchers have also found major differences in the perceptions of parenting and family atmosphere between children growing up in the same family. Specifically, behavior genetics finds that retrospective measures of parenting have the same level of heritability as personality traits (Plomin, 2018). Parents can, and do, treat different children differently, but, to a large extent, parental behaviors are a response to variations in the temperament of the child, and the degree of fit with the temperament of parents (Rutter and Rutter, 1993). Some children need more affection than others, and their feelings of emotional neglect have to be seen in the light of that vulnerability.

Retrospective measures of parenting are colored by a recall bias in which people in *current* distress remember the past in a more negative way. One meta-analysis (Baldwin et al., 2019) found poor agreement between prospective and retrospective measures of childhood maltreatment. This is why we need more prospective studies, in which parenting is directly measured during childhood, after which cohorts of affected children are followed into adulthood. There are now several such studies (I will review them in Chapters 6 and 7). Research into resilience suggests that most children have an innate capacity to overcome defects in parenting (Rutter, 2012).

As the British psychoanalyst Donald Winnicott (1958) famously remarked, parenting does not have to be always good – only *good enough*. Or, in the view of Jerome Kagan (2010), children will grow up in their own way unless parents put serious obstacles in their way. And even when parenting is not "good enough", other life experiences can compensate for its deficiencies.

My conclusion is that parents have to be *highly* toxic to their children to produce consistent negative effects, and that the effects of bad parenting are amplified by genetic vulnerability. One example of this pathway occurs when parents themselves suffer from mental disorders. A good deal of evidence shows that children raised by parents who have significant psychopathology are at higher risk (Simpson-Adkins and Daiches, 2018). While these associations also reflect shared heredity, one can readily imagine how parental mental disorders can seriously interfere with the tasks of parenting, leading to neglect and abuse.

Short of overt mental illness, a low quality of family life will usually have a statistical, but not predictable, relationship to psychological outcomes in children. Children respond particularly badly to severe marital conflict and/ or family violence, and they may even feel relieved if a family break-up terminates exposure to such stressors (Rutter and Rutter, 1993). Yet although toxic parenting leads to worse effects than mediocre parenting, children can survive such experiences. They may feel inner emotional scars, but need not become seriously dysfunctional in life. The ultimate outcome of children's experiences with parenting often depends on other, largely innate temperamental characteristics, as well as on factors outside the family environment (Cicchetti, 2016; Rutter, 2012).

Finally, if parenting were as crucial as we often assume, we should expect to see consistent psychopathology in children raised *without* a family. Foster care is known to be a risk factor for psychopathology (Wade et al., 2019), but not all children are affected in the way, and it is difficult to separate the effects of inadequate care from the reasons for children going into care in the first place, or from a shared heredity. In a famous study of Romanian orphans (Rutter et al., 2012), abandoned infants who had been kept in low-quality settings (mostly left uncared for in cribs) were followed for many years. Most of those who moved into adoptive homes improved rapidly, and the majority functioned well by adulthood. But the longer children had been in orphanages, the worse they did later in life.

In summary, the quality of rearing does not, by itself, determine whether or not a child grows up to develop psychological symptoms. Given the inevitable vicissitudes of family life, this discrepancy may be fortunate. Having a capacity for resilience early in development should increase survival, which makes sense in the light of natural selection.

Childhood trauma

Trauma is currently a very fashionable topic in clinical psychology. Since its introduction in *DSM*-III, the construct of post-traumatic stress disorder (PTSD), once a rarity in clinical usage, has become one of the most commonly diagnosed and studied of all forms of psychopathology (Horwitz, 2018).

Yet it does not follow that given a high-enough level of stress, PTSD is inevitable. Evidence from community populations (Breslau et al., 1991, 1998) and from military veterans exposed to combat (Dohrenwend et al., 2006) shows that this assumption is entirely unwarranted. Given very high-risk stressors, 25% of those exposed to life-threatening stressors will develop PTSD, but studies of a broader range of adversities suggest that less than 10% are clinically affected (McNally, 2015; Horwitz, 2018). Moreover, a large body of data shows that this disorder is more determined by characteristics of the individual being stressed than by the nature of adverse events (Yehuda et al., 2015).

Do these principles also apply to children? Many have thought that trauma should affect children, who are cognitively immature and at the mercy of circumstance, more severely than adults. Yet no evidence supports this belief. If anything, as shown in a study of Holocaust survivors (Sigal and Weinfeld, 2001), children can sometimes be *more* resilient than adults.

Childhood sexual abuse (CSA) increases the risk for a number of psychological difficulties in children, leading to both internalizing and externalizing symptoms (Finkelhor, 1990). These findings were originally based on retrospective studies of adults in the community who reported sexual abuse as children (Browne and Finkelhor, 1986). The results showed an increased risk for depression, suicide attempts, substance abuse, and interpersonal problems. On the other hand, those who were severely affected were in the minority, and resilience was common.

These earlier findings, while based on cross-sectional retrospective data, were later confirmed in large-scale prospective studies. A landmark study conducted in New Zealand (Fergusson et al., 1996a, 1996b) followed a cohort of children in the community for 20 years. There was a higher lifetime prevalence of mental disorders in those adults who reported (at age 18) having been exposed to childhood sexual abuse (CSA). Similarly, a project in New York State that followed children for several decades (Cohen et al., 2005) found that sexual abuse, physical abuse, and neglect, particularly when trauma was documented through court records, were associated with symptoms of personality disorders. Widom (1999) conducted a prospective study of children referred to the courts because of sexual abuse or neglect (the choice of this cohort avoided retrospective bias in assessing trauma). The findings were that high rates of PTSD in adults were associated with documented abuse in childhood. A recent review (Nol, 2021) confirmed that CSA is a risk factor for many forms of psychopathology, but it is not necessarily linked with PTSD. Much like the recent pandemic, stress tends to make things worse for those who are already vulnerable.

Even so, none of this research proves that abuse and neglect can cause serious adult psychopathology on their own. In particular, associations between risks and outcomes could be due to latent variables that were not measured. For example. abused children may come from dysfunctional families, where they suffer not from a few incidents of adversity, but from continuous adversity of all kinds. Family dysfunction is a variable that is not always assessed in research, but it accounts for many of the effects of specific events such as sexual abuse (Nash et al., 1993).

These complexities help explain why even the most sophisticated correlational studies have not been able to identify with precision how risk factors affect outcomes. These relationships may also reflect genetic influences, non-shared environment, or a combination of both. Large-scale prospective studies, particularly those using twins, are needed to help sort out these complexities (see Chapter 6 for some examples).

What we see in the data is that pathological outcomes occur only in a minority of those exposed. While the base rate of sexual abuse of any kind in children is high, affecting about 12% of girls and 6% of boys, the impact of childhood sexual abuse (CSA) depends on a number of parameters that define severity. These parameters have been studied for many decades (Browne and Finkelhor, 1986). The most important is the relation to the perpetrator. Abuse by any caretaker, especially a father, is associated with more sequelae than if the abuser is a neighbor or a stranger. More commonly, abuse comes from a stepfather, which has a less severe effect than if the perpetrator is the biological father, but it also tends to be associated with a failure of protection by mothers. Other parameters that influence outcome are the severity of the act (whether intercourse occurred), the frequency and duration of the abuse, and whether the victim was able to inform someone else about what happened. The most common form of sexual abuse in children is a single incident of molestation, not involving penetration, and perpetrated by a non-relative. Such experiences are much less likely, on their own, to lead to long-term sequelae.

Add to this the likelihood that temperamentally vulnerable children have a more intense response to abuse than those who are more resilient. These interactions explain why the majority of those exposed report no significant psychological symptoms in adulthood. That is not to say, of course, that survivors may not experience distress after these experiences, or suffer from painful memories. And needless to say, the ubiquity of resilience cannot be used to condone or minimize such incidents.

Similar conclusions emerge from studies of the long-term effects of physical abuse (Malinovsky-Rummell and Hansen, 1993). About a quarter of children who suffer serious physical abuse (causing injury) from their parents develop psychological symptoms as adults, and there is a relationship between severity and outcome. But physical abuse is also highly inter-correlated with other adversities: family dysfunction or breakdown, and mental illness in parents.

The principle that children who have been beaten are more likely to become violent adults was once a shibboleth, both for therapists and for the media. Yet, there is very slim empirical support for this relationship. It *is* true that those who suffer violence as children are statistically more likely to be violent as adults (Widom, 1989). It is *not* true, however, that most violent adults have been abused during childhood. It is also *not* true that most children who are physically abused will become violent adults.

Once again, the problem derives from the difference between statistically significant effects, based on a minority of cases with a limited capacity for predictability, and large-scale effects in a majority of those exposed to adversity. For example, in a large-scale study of children exposed to family violence, although there was a higher rate of violent behavior by adulthood, the vast majority were never violent at any time (Widom, 1989). Only a sub-group accounted for the reported association, and temperament could at least partially explain these relationships.

Some traumas in childhood have nothing to do with family dysfunction. Few events in this century were as traumatic as the Holocaust. Only a few of those exposed to the genocide lived to see the end of the Second World War. Some children survived to emerge from camps, or from hiding under assumed identities. Yet while holocaust survivors report higher levels of psychological distress than most people (Sigal and Weinfeld, 1989), they do not necessarily develop major psychopathology. Some have even described post-traumatic growth (Frankl, 1959).

The moral of this story is that research on child maltreatment shows that one cannot rely on impressions drawn from clinical cases that may not be borne out in larger community populations.

Family breakdown

The human family, when it remains intact and is well-functioning, is a protective factor against psychopathology. It is usually tragic to lose a parent during childhood. But do such losses necessarily have long-term consequences, leading to serious psychopathology?

One of the most frequently investigated research questions concerns the effects of early bereavement. Parental loss has long been thought to be a risk factor for later depression (Bergman et al., 2017). Yet, using data from the National Longitudinal Survey of Adolescent to Adult Health, Feigelman et al. (2017) found that while adolescence was more difficult for those bereaved earlier in childhood these effects tended to disappear by young adulthood. The problem was that many subjects in this study dropped out of school, leading to other deficits. Thus, the death of a parent need not cause psychopathology by itself, unless accompanied by *other* adversities, such as depression in the surviving parent, or isolation of the nuclear family from social supports. We should also keep in mind that early parental death was a very common experience throughout the history of humanity.

Today, divorce has become as common as parental death used to be. At one time, it was thought that, copared to an unhappy marriag(especially if there is physical violence) divorce might be the lesser evil. Yet only a minority (30%) of divorces are associated with family violence, and it possible that, as shown by a large-scale national survey (Amato and Booth, 1997) quiet divorces can come as a nasty surprise to children and have more long-term sequelae.

Longitudinal studies of birth cohorts (Cherlin et al., 1991) show that, compared to children from intact families, the children of divorce suffer from lower self-esteem and have more psychological symptoms, more interpersonal problems, and are more likely to divorce as adults. But again, these findings reflect outcomes in vulnerable minorities. Risk is not the same as destiny.

Even here, nature plays an important role, as divorce tends to run in families. Behavioral genetic studies of adopted cohorts have documented heritable factors in the risk for divorce, generally related to problematic personality traits (Salvatore et al., 2018). But the inter-generational transmission of marital instability also reflects experiences in the family. Genes have not changed in recent decades, but the divorce rate has.

Moreover, the effects of divorce on children vary depending on factors that go beyond the simple fact of marital breakdown (Amato and Booth, 1997). For example, the parent who raises children may also be affected by loss, while the breakdown of community and extended family ties makes children more dependent on the custodial parent. A bitter divorce and/or parental alienation makes matters much worse for a child. And again, people who have a difficult temperament may be more likely to divorce and to suffer from it more.

Those who divorce early on in a marriage are more likely to remarry. Yet the outcome of remarriage is not always beneficial for children. Remarriage sometimes provides a father-substitute for boys, but girls can feel excluded by the mother's new relationship (Hetherington and Elmore., 2003).

The conclusion of this story is relatively encouraging: most children of divorce grow up normally, and function as adults without developing significant psychopathology. As with other adversities, sequelae are concentrated in a vulnerable minority, and resilience remains the rule.

Social class and poverty

Low socio-economic status or poverty is a major risk factor for psychological problems of all kinds (Kagan, 2006). This is a domain in which child development reflects socio-political factors. By and large, it is better to be rich than poor. Higher socioeconomic status is associated with better physical and mental health, even when other factors are controlled for (Wang and Geng, 2019). Social class is a strong predictor of symptoms, with many mental disorders being more common in lower socioeconomic groups (Robins and Regier, 1991). But that need not always be the case. A Boston inner-city study that followed working class boys into adulthood (Vaillant and Western, 2001) found that most of the cohort achieved upward mobility, particularly if they came from well-functioning families and had access to supportive community networks.

By itself, poverty is a statistical risk factor for psychological sequelae, but most people are resilient. The paradox is that even as Western civilization becomes wealthier, some forms of psychopathology in young people have become *more* common (Twenge, 2017). But like the divorce rate, these outcomes among youth may be shaped by excessively high expectations (Lukianoff and Haidt, 2018). These unrealistic hopes can be shaped by families, but they also derive from society at large, and can be amplified by social media.

Cumulative Adversities

Our immune system helps us to remain healthy even when exposed to pathogens. But when that protection breaks down, we readily fall victim to disease. In the same way, the psychological immune system ensures that many individuals never develop any form of psychopathology, even when exposed to severe stressors. On the other hand, even in relatively normal individuals, defenses can be broken down by *cumulative* levels of adversity.

When enough bad things happen over time, psychological symptoms tend to appear. In children, the total number of adversities during childhood has a stronger relationship to a pathological outcome than the presence of any one risk factor. Rutter and Rutter (1993) reviewed a series of classic studies that demonstrated the cumulative effects of adversity in samples of children at high risk, which were often associated with psychosocial or socioeconomic adversities. The six variables associated with the greatest long-term risk for psychiatric disorder were: (1) severe discord between parents; (2) low social status; (3) large family size; (4) paternal criminality; (5) maternal psychiatric disorder; and (6) child placement. A child with only one of these factors would do as well as those with none. But as additional factors were added on, the risk of disorder increased – in those with four or more, the rate was as high as 20% (even so, there was an 80% rate of resilience.) Moreover, the long-term effects may have represented a "developmental cascade" in which each problematic symptoms leads to another, cementing the cumulative effect of multiple adversities (Rutter, 1991).

There are also childhood adversities that are so severe, and that occur at a crucial point of development, that they are particularly likely to lead to consequences in adulthood. The most impressive data, as already noted, derives from follow-ups of Romanian orphans adopted abroad into healthy families. These issues will be discussed in the next chapter.

It seems reasonable to conclude that the effects of childhood adversity need to be framed within a biopsychosocial model of psychopathology. As Fonagy et al. (2021), noted in a review, and as also argued by Kagan (2010), the strongest predictor of adult psychological symptoms is neither genes nor families, but socioeconomic class. The mechanism for this relationship most likely depends on the availability to social support, which moderates the effects of adverse life events.

Emotion Regulation and Emotional Neglect

My reading of the literature on childhood adversity is that the impact of traumatic events has been greatly over-emphasized, while the effect of emotional neglect has been greatly under-emphasized. Since traumatic experiences are more dramatic, it has been tempting to attribute pathological consequences to them. And as Chapter 9 will discuss, theories that focus on trauma may not need to be the most evidence-based approach to therapy.

In contrast, more subtle adversities can have a stronger effect than single incidents, associated with a cumulative impact. Moreover, assessing the sequelae of childhood adversities is hampered by other problems. One is whether to use a narrow or broad definition of maltreatment. Another derives from the vagaries of memory when adults are questioned about events that happened decades earlier.

A good body of research supports the view that many (if not most) of the risk factors in childhood can be better understood in a different context. Adversities are most pathogenic when multiple and repeated, producing a cumulative impact. Moreover, the impact of trauma depends on support systems. When these fail, one can speak of emotional neglect, which often leads in turn to emotion dysregulation.

Research on emotion regulation has now generated a rather large literature (Gross, 2014). Skills used to manage intense feelings can be modeled and taught in families. While most often studied in personality disorders, emotion dysregulation is implicated in a broad range of psychopathology. While some children have a heritable temperament that makes regulation easier to learn, others have a temperament that makes doing so rather difficult. These interactions can lead to vicious circles in which abnormal temperament creates interpersonal problems, and in which interpersonal conflicts amplify these effects.

Emotional neglect can be viewed as the opposite of affection (Parker, 1983). This is why it may well be the most crucial risk factor for psychopathology. Emotional neglect is the most common form of childhood adversity, and b neglect has both psychological and neurobiological effects that interfere with normal development (Muller et al., 2019). Again, while trauma is more dramatic, it describes an episode, not a pattern. In contrast, neglect is a condition that stays the same for years on end. It bores its way into the psyche and in those who are most vulnerable, can create profound feelings of rejection and unworthiness.

Memory Research and the Myth of Recovered Memories

Over the last few decades, clinical psychology and psychiatry have been influenced by the belief that childhood traumas can produce adult dysfunction. The idea that childhood trauma drives both physical and mental symptoms has been promoted in a number of popular books, such as a bestseller by van der Kolk (2014). It has also been suggested that trauma may be present even in the absence of memories for such events. In a widely quoted book, Herman (1992, p. 5), even claimed that "the ordinary response to atrocities is to banish them from consciousness". (This is an idea that goes back to Sigmund Freud.)

Yet there is no serious evidence that abused children repress memories of adverse events (McNally, 2015). Some may be reluctant to talk about past trauma, but the idea that they entirely forget these events runs counter to a large body of research. PTSD is characterized not by amnesia, but by *hypermnesia* (unwanted and painful recollection). For example, survivors of the Holocaust do not forget what happened to them, even if they do not always want to talk about it.

The idea that memories are stored in the brain as if they were being recorded on tape, is a rather old theory, but is entirely wrong. People do not remember events as they happened. Events are hardly ever recorded in any precise way, are distorted over time, and revised each time they are recalled (Schacter, 1996; McNally, 2003). The further in the past the original event, the more likely it is that memories will be inaccurate.

Research on memory also shows that it is surprisingly easy to create false memories (Loftus and Ketcham1991). That is something that therapists are in a position to do (by aggressively suggesting that trauma must have been present, if symptoms that can be associated with it are). The idea that traumatic memories produce symptoms that can disappear when the memory is "recovered" has no empirical support. Moreover, there is no evidence that trauma has a specific effect on mental mechanisms that leads either to repression or dissociative symptoms (McNally, 2003).

These ideas were the basis of the recovered memory movement, which was more of a cult than a serious scientific project. The idea of recovered memories was based on the assumption that trauma is the key to psychopathology. It is an example of what can ensue when nurture runs rampant, overriding all consideration of nature.

In the past, society has tolerated child abuse, but we do not need to create false memories to counteract this under-reporting. To the surprise of many, the prevalence of child abuse has gone down steeply over the last several decades (Finkelhor, 1990). This change may reflect the current social climate, in which children are watched more carefully and allowed less unsupervised time. This shift in parenting practices may have a downside by interfering with autonomy and exploration (Lukianoff and Haidt, 2018), but children are better protected now than they have been at most times in human history.

Adversity in an Evolutionary Context

If we were as vulnerable to adversity as some clinicians and researchers seem to think, then it would be hard to credit the enormous success of the human species over time. This is why resilience is built into our mental mechanisms. However, an evolutionary perspective might also suggest a role for the family in modulating environmental challenges. Given that the family, with some variations is a human universal, it is unlikely that it plays a minor role in psychological development, even if the behavioral genetic literature has sometimes been interpreted in that way.

To take one example, Belsky (2007) reviewed the evidence for life history analysis, e.g. that a problematic childhood leads to an early puberty, reproductive strategy that does not trust time to offer options better than a pregnancy during adolescence. However, this hypothesis remains controversial.

An association between early puberty and various forms of child abuse was not supported by a recent meta-analysis (Zhang et al., 2019).

Another question of interest for an evolutionary context is whether early adversities are more pathogenic than those that come later in development. If that were so, the survival of humanity would have been put at great risk, given the likelihood of traumatic events in the Paleolithic era. Bowlby (1969) described as our "environment of evolutionary adaptiveness", and that was a time when no parent could expect that all or even most of their children would live long enough to become adults. But children are born with a capacity to bounce back from adversity.

Kagan (1998) described the primacy of early experience as one of "Three Seductive Ideas" that have greatly misled research in child development. Other developmental psychologists (e.g. Lewis, 1997) have also contested this assumption. The problem is that early adversity is often followed by continuous problems over years to come, so that timing is not the crucial factor.

In summary, adversities are hurtful, but severe sequelae are not inevitable. These are the challenges that life presents us with. They raise the risk for psychopathology, but that is not the only possible outcome. But for those who are more sensitive to their environment, the risk is bound to be even higher.

6 Resilience: Surviving a Bad Childhood

The Nature of Resilience

Resilience refers, literally speaking, to the ability to "bounce back" from the impact of adverse life events. We might think of it as a defense system against psychological injury. Just as immunological mechanisms protect us against the physical attack of micro-organisms, resilience mechanisms protect us against the mental effects of adversity. Resilience is therefore not only a matter of luck. It depends on capacities intrinsic to the individual.

Why are children and adults more or less vulnerable to adverse life events? Most people do not develop a mental disorder after a traumatic experience (Breslau et al., 1998). But does the explanation for the ubiquity of resilience lie in nature or in nurture? The answer is, of course, both. Although each of us begins life with unique and heritable temperamental characteristics, personality traits do not emerge *de novo* but are shaped by a multitude of life experiences.

As we have seen, while trauma and maltreatment during childhood are risk factors for psychopathology, most who are exposed to them show resilience. Again, this does not mean they are not affected. If those exposed to adversity are less sensitive to the environment, they will not necessarily develop sequelae.

Mental health clinicians live in an age in which the concept of trauma tends to dominate the practice of psychotherapy. But the impression that many have that trauma necessarily leads to psychopathology is largely due to a biased sample of those who come for treatment. For every patient with a history of childhood adversity, many others with similar experiences have few symptoms and have never come to clinical attention.

Keep in mind that the most severe adversities, especially when they are cumulative, have the capacity to override resilience (Rutter, 2012). Even so, the literature consistently shows that resilience is the rule, not the exception. This conclusion derives from such a large body of data that it is unquestionable (Rutter, 2013).

The ubiquity of resilience also makes good sense in the context of evolutionary psychology (Brune 2016). Natural selection will favor the

DOI: 10.4324/9781003156215-6

development of innate protective mechanisms against stressful events. Adversity is inevitable, and people who cannot bounce back from adversity will be less likely to survive and bear children of their own.

The environment in which our species evolved was, in the famous phrase of the English philosopher Thomas Hobbes, "nasty, brutish, and short". In hunter-gatherer societies, starvation was always a possibility, and predation was far from unheard of, particularly for children. Disease was endemic, and there was no medical treatment to speak of. Parents often died young, and children did not always survive to adulthood. Strangers could be physically dangerous. In short, traumatic events in pre-history would have been much more common than they are now (Pinker, 2018).

Yet our species did not become extinct. Evolution developed mechanisms to deal with exposure to danger and trauma. Humans are characterized by an unusually long childhood and adolescence, providing an opportunity to learn the complex tasks required of an adult. Children are also born with a degree of toughness and an ability to rise above circumstances.

Moreover, traumatic events, especially those involving violence, are much less common than they were a few centuries ago (Pinker, 2018). When such events do occur, we, unlike our ancestors, are more likely to see the world as out of joint. As McNally (2015) has pointed out, even as human life has become better, our expectations have changed, making us more likely to experience and report psychological symptoms after exposure to milder adversities.

Individual Differences in Resilience

Resilience is the antidote to risk. The reason is that any life event, whether negative or positive, can be processed in different ways. Thus, the intensity of reactions to adverse events, whether moderate or severe, shows remarkable variation between individuals. Resilience, a mechanism through which the mind assimilates and processes these experiences, is also linked to personality profiles, most particularly levels of neuroticism (Yehuda, 2002). These traits, rooted in temperament, provide different but generally effective ways of dealing with environmental challenges (Beck and Freeman, 2015). This is why "person–environment interactions" (Plomin, 2018) are much stronger predictors of outcome than exposure to adversity alone.

Children who have predispositions to psychopathology, or who have personality profiles that make them unusually sensitive to stress, are more likely to experience adverse life events as traumatic, and to react badly to them. Moreover, some children are also more likely, because of their temperament, to be *exposed* to adversities (Rutter, 2012). In contrast, children with positive personality traits and lower sensitivity to the environment are more likely to find ways to cope with adversity and to find new pathways of development (Belsky and Pluess, 2009).

Although most children lie on a continuum between these extremes, the average child will have sufficient resourcefulness to weather an average level of adversity. In short, those who rise above adversity have intrinsic temperamental characteristics that open new pathways and attract emotional support (Rutter, 2012). In this way, resilience is a primary example of the interactions between nature and nurture.

Studies using prospective designs have most consistently demonstrated that children are not easily damaged by adverse life experiences. Kagan and Zentner, (1996) remarked on their surprise when they conducted follow-up studies on children at risk, observing that family dysfunction need not necessarily have long-term effects.

The concept of resilience need not imply dismissing or discounting the effects of adversity. Once again, keep in mind that statistical associations are rarely strong enough for useful prediction. The data drawn from most research studies tend to be driven by a sub-sample of people who are already at risk for psychopathology for other reasons, and their findings may not necessarily be applicable to individuals.

Research also does not consistently find that early adversities are more pathogenic than later life events. The reason is that when risks begin early in life, they are likely to continue over time and become cumulative, leading to a "developmental cascade" (Masten and Ciccheti, 2010). For this reason, early trauma can best be seen as a marker for severity of exposure over time. Moreover, most of the important adverse events during childhood, such as family discord, parental psychopathology, and poor socio-economic status, are highly inter-correlated, leading to cumulative effects (Rutter and Rutter, 1993).

Rutter (1989), in his pioneering Isle of Wight Study, found that a combination of multiple adversities (four or more) led to a rate of mental disorder in children in 20% of cases. While that is a large number, 80% of children with the same risk factors did *not* develop psychopathology. This rate supports a general conclusion about the effects of life adversities, a kind of a "20% rule". Or, to paraphrase a cliché, one can see the cup as four-fifths full rather than one-fifth empty.

In summary, single adverse events need not lead to long-term dysfunction, but repeated adversities can. These are the circumstances in which the psychological immune system can be overwhelmed.

Major Research Studies of Resilience in Children

Prospective longitudinal studies, following cohorts of young children into adulthood, are the best way to unravel the mechanisms of resilience. Prospective studies of twins, a method that can control for genetic factors, can provide an even better basis for developing a theory of resilience.

Many longitudinal studies of community populations have documented the effects of chronic adversities on children (Masten and Barnes, 2018). This kind of research, using non-clinical samples avoids focusing on those who end up in treatment. But these samples often lack a large enough number of individuals facing the most serious adversities. For this reason, another method of choice for researchers has been the follow-up of children at risk. Both methods support the general conclusions discussed above, that is, that resilience is ubiquitous, that cumulative adversities are much more pathogenic, and that temperament plays a major role in vulnerability. I will now discuss some of the most important longitudinal studies that have shed light on these relationships.

1 The Hawaii study

A research group in Hawaii led by Emma Werner followed, up to age 30, a cohort of over 500 children born to poverty-stricken plantation workers (Werner and Smith, 1992). This is still one of the best studies of the effects of adversity in childhood. While poverty, particularly when associated with family dysfunction, was a risk for adult mental disorders, most of the children in this study, in spite of being exposed to multiple adversities (such as dysfunctional families and emotional neglect) grew up to be competent adults.

What were the characteristics of the minority in Werner's cohort that *did* develop significant pathology? One was temperament. Positive personality traits proved to be highly protective against the impact of adversity. In particular, children with better social skills and who were more persistent in mastering tasks did better than those who lacked such characteristics. Intelligence was also a protective factor against adversity.

Another important finding of the Hawaii study was that stressful environmental circumstances were associated with consistent sequelae only in a high-risk sub-group, consisting of 10% of the total cohort. Again, these children suffered from multiple adversities, including dysfunction or breakup of the nuclear family, and/or parental mental illness. Moreover, cumulative effects lead to a breakdown of defenses. The larger the total number of risk factors, the greater was the likelihood of a pathological outcome. Two-thirds of children with multiple adversities did develop difficulties of some kind with behavior or mood as adults. While the findings of this study were published decades ago, later research has consistently confirmed them (Masten and Barnes, 2018).

2 The Albany–Saratoga study

Cohen et al (2005) conducted a large-scale longitudinal study of children from 975 families in two counties in upstate New York, in order to determine the predictors of delinquency and substance abuse. A wide range of data was collected on this cohort over several decades.

The results showed that neither parental death and divorce nor child-rearing practices (such as measures of emotional closeness or punishment) were predictive of pathological outcomes. The psychosocial risk factors inside the family associated with the most sequelae were parental mental illness and sociopathy, as well as remarriage after divorce and change of neighborhood. Social class, as well as school and peer influences, were better predictors of delinquency and substance abuse than risk factors inside the family.

3 Birth cohort studies

Researchers can also study the outcome of adversity using large community samples. One of the best-known examples is the British National Longitudinal Study, in which all children born in the UK over a period of several months in 1958 were followed into adulthood (Wadsworth, 2010). Again, research showed that most of those who suffered serious adversities in childhood eventually did well, while a minority developed symptoms, usually when faced with further stressors in adult life. But this study did not measure heritability or personality profiles. Moreover, while the results were statistically significant, the cohort was so large that the findings did not apply to the majority of subjects facing adversity. The results suggested that there is a vulnerable minority who are most affected by life experiences at any stage, and who are most likely to develop pathology under stress.

One of the most influential of all birth cohort follow-ups derives from a longitudinal study of 1000 children born in 1972–3 in Dunedin, New Zealand, followed into their adult years. The research team included some leading researchers in child development: (Terri Moffitt, Avshalom Caspi, and Jay Belsky). Their findings have been nicely summarized in a recent book (Belsky et al., 2020). The study did not measure genetic risks early in life, but it was able to carefully document environmental risks, such as family dysfunction. The results support a strong role for interactions between heritability and childhood adversity that is associated with psychological problems in adulthood. I will further discuss the Dunedin findings in Chapter 7.

Birth cohort studies are not usually designed to take genetic effects fully into account, and most of the published research thus far has told us more about the environment than about gene-environment interplay. Longitudinal follow-up of twins allows for genetically sensitive analyses that separate nature and nurture. Hur and Craig (2013) documented twin registries across the world and located about a hundred of them. Many of these samples are being followed longitudinally. The most clinically relevant findings of this research will be discussed in the next chapter.

The E-Risk study (Fisher et al., 2015) examined similar predictors in a twin birth cohort of 2232 children in the UK, with an over-sampling of families at risk (e.g., teenage mothers). Its use of twin allowed it to control for heredity, and separate that from environmental risk. The participants have up to now been followed to age 18. Some of the findings of this study, with outcomes ranging from risk for victimization during adolescence to self-harm and/or crime, will be discussed in Chapter 7.

In recent years, the availability of genome-wide association studies (GWAS) and polygenic risk scores (PRS) has helped to measure associations between genomic variation and long-term outcomes. For example, a report by Belsky (2018) pooled data from five longitudinal studies in the UK, New Zealand, USA and conducted PRS analyses. The results showed that genes associated with life success partially accounted for upward social mobility, independent of social class origins. While these results would not necessarily be predictive in individual cases, the authors suggest that genetic factors do account for an important portion of individual differences in resilience.

4 Institutionalized children

Children raised in institutions can suffer from severe emotional neglect, adversity well known to increase the risk for psychopathology. But the results of a major study of women who had been reared in institutions early in their childhood (Rutter and Quinton, 1984a) also demonstrated the importance of temperament, the severity of neglect, and the ubiquity of resilience. The data showed that while severe adversity led to a poorer overall outcome, there was enormous variability in outcome within the cohort. Once again, only a minority developed severe psychopathology.

Rutter and Quinton also looked at what mechanisms might explain this variability. One of the most important determinants of long-term outcome concerned the way individuals reacted to life events later on in life. Whether or not they grew up in a reasonable and planned way, as opposed to getting pregnant and marrying impulsively, was a major factor in protecting them against the impact of prior adversities. It is notable that those women whose marriages broke down proved more sensitive to renewed stress, and it was this sub-group that accounted for most of the differences. In contrast, those who married successfully were eventually indistinguishable from those raised in intact and non-dysfunctional families. Although it is not exactly clear what determined these successful choices, it seems likely that those whose marriages worked well-made use of favorable temperamental characteristics, such as higher persistence and lower impulsivity.

Another line of evidence supporting this interpretation is that the women with symptoms during adulthood were much more likely to have had temperamental difficulties during childhood. In contrast, those who did well had a more positive temperament did better in school and in social relationships throughout development and showed a good capacity to plan their lives. As in the Hawaii study, those who were most intelligent were most resilient. These findings nicely demonstrate the mechanisms by which later events can compensate for earlier events.

Yet when environments are consistently and severely adverse, natural mechanisms of resilience can be overwhelmed. Meta-analyses show that the prognosis for children at severe risk is guarded (Lawrence et al., 2006;

Goemans et al., 2015), but it is difficult to determine whether these outcomes are driven by earlier adversities or by unmeasured heritability. Decades ago, Clarke and Clarke (1976) reviewed a series of classical studies on fostered children, a group known to be susceptible to long-term sequelae. When children were placed in a secure and positive environment before age six, the results of early deprivation were *entirely* reversible. Placement at a later age did not have the same salutary effects, since, by that point, many children were too deficient in social skills to take advantage of their new environment.

Studies of orphans adopted after World War II and the Korean War (Winick et al., 1975) support the principle that placement in a good home can reverse the effects of early deprivation. Researchers found that these children, in spite of having been exposed to severe malnutrition and other life-threatening adversities, were indistinguishable from their contemporaries a few years later.

Studies of Romanian orphans adopted into families in America and Britain have provided a unique opportunity, a kind of "natural experiment", to examine these issues (Rutter et al., 2012). As discussed in Chapter 5, this population suffered documented high levels of trauma and neglect. Many of these children were left alone and uncared for in poorly staffed institutions, sometimes over several years. Yet in spite of the massive deprivations they experienced, a majority of these young people were doing reasonably well in early adulthood.

But given the severe nature of the neglect, it is understandable that the longer these children stayed in orphanages, the more damaged they were, often showing subtle social deficits that compromise their ability to overcome adversity . Yet in another large sample (Groze and Ileana, 1996), of 475 Romanian children living in their adoptive homes after approximately 3 years in an orphanage, most had achieved appropriate milestones, while parents tended to report good relationships, few had behavioral problems, and adoptions were stable.

In one of his earlier reports about Romanian orphans in Britain, Rutter (1999) reported that about a third of this group was doing well, and another third was on the way to recovery. The last third was the most disturbed group since they had usually spent more time in the orphanage. This subgroup remained deficient in cognitive functions and in social skills on later follow-up (Rutter et al., 2012). They retained a level of social awkwardness, in which they seemed not to know how to manage meeting new people.

All these studies are hopeful, but also provide examples of how the most severe and cumulative adversities can overcome resilience. Thus far, no one has examined the role of temperament in these populations, or whether some of these children were also exposed to fetal or perinatal risks.

In summary, studies of institutionalized children demonstrate a surprising (but not unlimited) degree of resilience, even in the face of severe neglect.

Cumulative adversities can sometimes overcome this resilience, but a change in environment has the capacity to reverse these sequelae.

The mechanisms of resilience

What mechanisms, either genetic or environmental, account for children's ability to rise above adversity? The factors determining resilience have not yet been fully unraveled by research. While the effects of cumulative adversities are well documented, heritable factors clearly play a role.

Temperament is clearly a major factor in resilience. Both the Werner and Rutter studies suggest that characteristics intrinsic to the child strongly influence competence in the face of adversity. Impulsivity provides a good example. Rutter and Quinton (1984b) observed in institutionalized children that those who respond to stress by internalizing and withdrawing develop less conflict with family and peers than those who externalize their problems and act out impulsively. Although internalization also carries its own long-term risks, it at least avoids the vicious circles so often brought on by externalizing behaviors.

Let us return to the study by Werner and Smith (1992). Here the most prominent traits promoting resilience were an attractive personality, intelligence, persistence, a variety of interests, the capacity to be alone, and an optimistic approach to life. Thus, these children had a number of capacities that helped them to respond flexibly to environmental challenges.

Competent children are not passive recipients of external input, but actively shape their environment to meet their needs (Scarr, 1992). For example, an extraverted child tends to establish a strong social network, but an introverted one can find pleasure in more solitary activities such as reading. Yet if a child does not have extended family and/or a supportive peer group to counter the effects of family dysfunction, the effects of adversity will be greater (Masten et al., 1999).

A well-known prospective study conducted by Vaillant (2012) in a sample of university-educated men confirmed this principle. Somewhat to the surprise of the lead researcher (a psychoanalyst), the quality of childhood experience had little or no predictive value for the extent to which adults achieved psychological maturity. Instead, school performance and defense styles, both of which tend to reflect favorable or unfavorable personality traits, were the best predictors of functioning later in life.

Thus, the most resilient children have positive and effective traits that lead them to do well at school, gain the positive attention of their teachers, find a supportive peer group, and develop attachments to people in their extended family and community. In contrast, a vulnerable child is more likely to experience negative events, and also responds more strongly to them. These temperamental qualities, reflected in personality trait profiles, prevent them from making good use of their environment, leading to negative feedback loops.

For example, impulsive and irritable children respond to adversity by becoming even more difficult, making it more likely that they will be badly treated (Rutter and Quinton, 1984). A long-term follow-up study of children in New Zealand (Caspi et al., 1996) found that observations of impulsivity and anxiety as early as age three allowed the researchers to predict a statistical risk for adult disorders, with children who show early impulsivity being at long-term risk for externalizing disorders.

Children with an anxious temperament can also respond to adversity in a maladaptive way. Becoming more withdrawn interferes with the ability to make use of crucial alternate attachments outside the nuclear family, involving peers, extended family, and community organizations. Caspi et al. (1996) found that anxious children were also at long-term risk for internalizing disorders. We need to keep in mind, once again, that most children in the sample did *not* develop adult psychopathology.

Differences in resilience can also be driven by environmental factors. Clearly, positive experiences are protective against environmental risks. The relative availability or unavailability of these opportunities to develop buffers to the negative impact of adversity Rutter, 1987). To this extent, therefore, resilience reflects not only personal qualities but also good fortune. Yet since not every child can take advantage of favorable circumstances, we must never lose sight of temperament.

The presence of readily accessible social support networks is another important factor in resilience. Social cohesion helps to explain why communities vary in overall levels of psychopathology (Leighton et al., 1963). Social structures are particularly important for children with an abnormal temperament, who may otherwise have difficulty finding a social niche. Traditional societies, which provide guaranteed social roles for almost everyone, protect vulnerable children from developing several forms of psychopathology, most particularly addictions and personality disorders (Paris, 2020b).

In summary, research on resilience shows that even the most troubled children need not develop serious psychopathology later in life. The influence of Freud supported the impression that development is relatively fixed at the end of childhood or adolescence. But many adolescents "straighten out", with two-thirds of children with conduct disorder growing out of delinquency (Robins, 1966). Throughout adult life, people continue to change their ways of coping, sometimes in surprising ways (Vaillant, 1993).

Surviving an unhappy childhood

Research on resilience points to specific strategies that children can use to overcome adversity. On the one hand, constitutional advantages such as intelligence and an attractive personality, are largely a matter of luck. Yet even for those not well endowed with positive temperamental qualities, some behaviors are more useful than others.

First of all, children growing up in a dysfunctional family need to get out of the house and spend time with other people. The more time is spent at home, the worse the outcome. Conversely, positive interactions with uncles, aunts, or grandparents all lead to a better outcome. Similarly, having friends, and spending time at houses with *their* families protects children from parental pathology.

Second of all, connecting with a social community buffers the effects of family dysfunction. Children are attached not only to family and friends, but also to schools, religious groups, and community organizations. A child whose teacher, whose clergyman, or whose youth worker takes a special interest in them is likely to fare better. Rutter (1989) described how these positive experiences can become "turning points" that change the course of development.

Rutter (2012) suggests that, much as we use vaccines to stimulate the immune system, that low doses of potential trauma (such as brief separations from a family) may allow for a "steeling" effect, or what has been called "post-traumatic growth". Moreover, the life course can be marked by turning points, in which a positive factor (such as an important new relationship) comes to cancel out some of the effects of previous adversity. Finally, he notes that resilient children have more positive personality traits.

Research shows that some temperamental qualities are useful for making the best use of environmental opportunities. Werner and Smith (1992) described them as an attractive personality, intelligence, persistence, a variety of interests, the capacity to be alone, and an optimistic approach to life. People are not passive recipients of external inputs but actively shape their environment to meet their needs.

Availability of social support is another important element in resilience. Classical studies of social cohesion have shown how communities that are "socially integrated" have lower levels of psychopathology (Leighton et al., 1963). Support may be particularly important for children with a problematic temperament. In the past, traditional societies, by guaranteeing social roles for almost everyone, protected vulnerable children from psychopathology (Paris, 2020a).

Drawing on qualitative data and self-report questionnaires, Southwick and Charney (2018) wrote a book suggesting what might be key components of temperament affecting resilience. The most important is *optimism* – the ability to recognize that life's challenges, however difficult they are, offer opportunities for psychological growth. While about half the variance in optimism is heritable (Mosing et al., 2009), people who are pessimistic by nature can still be trained to change their view of the world (Cicchetti and Toth, 2018).

Southwick and Charney propose that a positive outlook on life leads to other mechanisms, including a moral compass and a sense that life has both meaning and direction. Moreover, resilient people are able to face fear rather than avoid it. This observation concords with my own experience that avoidant personality traits are particularly difficult to manage, because fear begets more fear, ending in failure.

Resilient children also have the capacity to recognize the reality of adversity. If they grow up in dysfunctional families, they should not see their environment as normal, and spend more time outside the home.

Another key component is *social support*. We are a social species, and even introverts need to have meaningful connections with a community. We also benefit from role models who have themselves overcome adversities in life, and who inspire us.

While some people can readily apply most of these strategies, they can also be learned. For those whose temperament makes doing so more difficult, therapists can teach skills that are better adaptations to adversity.

The ubiquity of resilience carries a hopeful message. The past does not determine the present. No matter how unhappy childhood has been, people usually have the capacity to find something better.

7 Nature–Nurture Interactions

Gene–Environment Interplay

This book has argued that gene–environment interplay is the key to understanding psychological development (Rutter, 2006; Caspi and Moffit, 2006). Nature–nurture interactions do a better job of predicting psychopathology than genes alone, or environment alone. This chapter will provide some useful examples of this principle.

Keep in mind, however, that single genes rarely govern complex behavioral outcomes. Instead, each trait or outcome is influenced by interactions between very large numbers of alleles. It is also important to remember that measures used to measure the environment can be overly broad concepts that do not do justice to the complexity and cumulative effects of environmental factors. A "recipe" for psychopathology is unlikely to be described by interactions between single genes and single stressors. At our present state of knowledge, a search for interactions between single risk factors is therefore unlikely to be fruitful. We can continue this line of research, but we should avoid simplistic models. (Chapter 10 will discuss the need for complex models in more detail.)

Types of Gene–Environment Interplay

We can distinguish between several ways in which genes and environment influence each other (Rutter, 2006). One form of interaction involves *correlations* between G and E (rGE). There are three types of gene–environment correlation.

Passive rGE refers to the fact that the behavior of other people, particularly family members, depends in part on their own genetic makeup, and not just the genes of a child. For example, if one or both parents have antisocial behavior, that can drive family dysfunction, leading to similar outcomes in their children.

Active rGE refers to the fact that genetic effects on children's behavior can shape environments through the choices they make. For example, children who are at risk to develop antisocial behaviors are also more likely to have friends or gangs with those who share these traits.

DOI: 10.4324/9781003156215-7

Evocative rGE refers to the fact that behaviors rooted in heritable traits elicit reactions, both negative and positive, from other people. For example, children with conduct disorder, the precursor of adult antisocial behavior, will often be rejected by peers, or even by their own families.

While all these relationships are correlations, what Rutter calls "true" gene–environment interactions (G×E) occur when children with different genotypes respond to environmental challenges in unique ways that reflect heritable traits. Thus, children with an impulsive temperament are more likely to develop antisocial behaviors when stressed, while those with high neuroticism are more likely to become anxious or depressed.

All these mechanisms can be explored using the methods of behavior genetics (described in Chapters 1 and 2). But this method can only provide a snapshot of effects that can change over time. Thus. the best way to study these interactions is by conducting longitudinal research. Many studies in recent decades have enrolled children at a given age and then followed them regularly into adulthood. Birth cohort studies are even better: the samples are less biased, and measures from earlier periods in development can be included in analyses. Perhaps, the most informative studies have been conducted in large cohorts of monozygotic and dizygotic twins, in which researchers can control for heritability. I will now review some of the most important studies of this kind and show what light they have shed on the problem of separating out risks from many different sources and determining the strength of their relationship to adult outcomes.

Longitudinal Studies of Children

Cohen et al. (2005) conducted the Children in the Community Study (CCS), following over 800 children growing up in the Albany-Saratoga region of New York State into their adult years. One of the main findings of the research was that psychopathology associated with suicidality, violence, or problematic relationships had identifiable markers early in development, related to traits that are also risks for personality disorders. Some of these traits are measurable in childhood, while others are associated with psychopathology that only emerges in adolescence.

Another large-scale project in the US, the Great Smoky Mountains Study, followed 11,000 children into adulthood, and its data have been the basis of many scientific articles (Copeland et al., 2018). One of the main findings was that psychopathology in childhood, as well as the presence of symptoms that did not cross thresholds for diagnosis, was usually associated with the development of further psychopathology in adulthood. While both studies highlight the importance of observing early signs of psychopathology, they do not fully account for trajectories in which measurable symptoms first emerge around puberty. This delayed onset may reflect interactions with hormonal changes as well as the synaptic pruning that occurs during early adolescence (Paus et al., 2008). It also reflects the stressful nature of adolescent development, particularly in modern societies (Romeo, 2013).

Another UK study, the Avon Longitudinal Study of Parents and Children (ALSPAC; Houtepen et al., 2018), was designed to shed light on maternal health, as well as on the prevalence of common childhood adversities. To this end, ALSPAC recruited a cohort of mothers with 14,000 children born in 1991–2. The frequency of adverse events was similar to other samples (4% for sexual abuse, 18% for physical abuse, 25% for bullying, and 32% for parental separation). However, while the study aimed to shed light on gene–environment interactions, it did not examine the effects of genes.

Zanarini et al., 2011) used the ALSPAC cohort to measure early features of BPD at age 11. (While the disorder usually begins in adolescence, some of its features can be observed earlier in development). This study observed that behavior disorders prior to adolescence predicted these features, which usually peak in early to mid-adolescence (Chanen and McCutcheon, 2013). Unfortunately, since funding for further follow-up of this high-risk sub-sample was not renewed, we do not know what happened to these children. This is one of the problems that researchers face in conducting long-term studies. In addition, they need to live long enough to collect and analyze the results.

High-Risk samples

A major problem with studies of normal community populations is that they may miss the important minority of children in which psychopathology is most likely. For this reason, researchers make use of *high-risk samples*. Most of these studies concern children of parents with mental disorders, particularly psychoses. However, research has also been done on environmental risks, such as poverty (as discussed in Chapter 6).

Here I will focus on a follow-up of a cohort considered to be at high risk for behavioral disorders. The Pittsburgh Girls Study (Keenan et al., 2010) has been following a cohort of 2451 girls from the community since middle childhood. The research was planned to over-sample girls raised in urban poverty. It focused on conduct disorder and depression, but its most important results have concerned BPD (Stepp et al., 2016). The findings showed that emotion dysregulation is an early feature of that disorder, and that family conflict interacts with that trait. In some cases, the specific features of BPD can be observed prior to adolescence, but further follow-up showed that girls in the cohort who had related risk factors in childhood were also more likely to develop the disorder and to embark on intimate relationships marked by behavioral impulsivity and poor choices of romantic partners (Lazarus et al., 2019).

Birth cohort studies

If one wants to find out how temperament and environmental risk factors influence development, it might be better to begin longitudinal research on children at infancy rather than at school age. One way to address this obstacle is to use *birth cohorts*, following groups of children born at the same time so that measurements can be made in infancy. Several projects of this kind have been conducted, each with a different focus and different measures of risks and outcomes

Many of these birth cohort studies have been conducted in the UK, e.gthe National Survey of Health and Development (NSHD; Wadsworth, 2014). Each of these research programs recruited between 15 and 20,000 children. However, the focus of these projects was on general health rather than on psychopathology or personality.

An Australian birth cohort of 3778 families (Kiseley et al., 2018) focused on the relationship between documented child abuse and psychopathology. Documentation is important because memories of childhood experiences in adults are colored by recent events. The results showed that childhood maltreatment, particularly emotional abuse and neglect, predicted psychopathology in young adulthood. These relationships were not significant for sexual abuse, but they became statistically significant when more than one form of maltreatment was present.

As discussed in Chapter 5, a large-scale study of child abuse and neglect in New Zealand was reported by Fergusson et al. (1996a, 1996b). It followed a birth cohort of 1265 children for 30 years. The main finding was that abuse and neglect were statistically (albeit not consistently) predictors of substance use and antisocial behavior.

The Dunedin study

The Dunedin Multidisciplinary Health and Development Study is a birth cohort of over 1000 children born between 1972 and 1973 in New Zealand, and results thus far have been summarized in a recent book aimed at the general reader (Belsky et al., 2020).

It was a great advantage to recruit a sample from a small city where people were less likely to move around. That is why Rutter conducted his most famous study in the Isle of Wight, and not in London. In the Dunedin sample, researchers have been able to track these subjects even when they did move far away. The results of this study have had great impact on developmental psychology, and they were the subject of a television series in 2016.

The most widely cited reports from the Dunedin study emerged under the leadership of the husband-and-wife team of Avshalom Caspi and Terri Moffitt, now at Duke University. Caspi and Moffitt collaborated with Rutter, with whom they have authored a review of many of the main findings of this research (Rutter et al., 2006).

Two papers published by this team (Caspi et al., 2002; Caspi et al., 2003) have been among the most quoted in all of psychology. The 2002 paper on antisocial behavior has been cited over five thousand times, while the 2003 paper on depression has been cited more than ten thousand times, and it was one of the top papers of that year ranked by the journal *Science*. These findings have been considered foundational in the study of gene–environment interactions in psychopathology.

Both reports showed that while genetic risks and environmental risks, by themselves, do not necessarily raise the risk, the combination of both is significantly related to either antisocial behavior or depression. In each case, the authors selected a genetic locus known to be associated with a specific outcome. Caspi et al. (2002) examined a polymorphism of the monoamine oxidase (MAO) gene, which, when combined with childhood maltreatment, predicted antisocial behavior. Caspi et al. (2003) found that when stressful life events occurred in individuals with copies of the short allele of the serotonin promoter gene, they developed more depression than individuals who were homozygous for the long allele.

Yet these findings of interactions between genes and environment in depression can now be described as doubtful. First and foremost, they have not been consistently replicated (Munato, 2009; Fergusson et al., 2011; Nilsson et al., 2018). Second, the rate of depression was based on the presence of symptoms, and lacked context, failing to distinguish between normal sadness after a loss and clinical depression. Finally, GWAS methods and PCR scores were not available 20 years ago: measuring a single "candidate gene" is clearly not sufficient.

These observations, now two decades old, continue to stir controversy. In a book and nature and nurture in psychological development, Tabery (2014) devoted an entire chapter to the problems with replicating results linking genetic variants to antisocial behavior. A 30-year longitudinal study of 398 males (in a birth cohort from Christchurch, New Zealand) failed to support a gene–environment interaction between MAO alleles and maltreatment in predicting an antisocial outcome (Fergusson et al., 2011). While a meta-analysis of 27 studies provided qualified support for this association (Byrd and Manuck, 2014), Tabery (2014) noted that there have been several meta-analyses, each with conflicting results. Thus. a final conclusion remains up for grabs.

Once again, the problem is that single variants in alleles are unlikely to have a strong relationship to a complex behavioral outcome. In another study, Cicchetti et al. (2012) found that associations with antisocial behavior were much stronger when multiple genetic loci are examined. This has led researchers to carry out analyses of the whole genome (GWAS) yielding polygenic risk scores. But studies using that method have also failed to resolve the controversy.

In depression, findings of gene–environment interactions involving levels of serotonin activity have proved even more difficult to replicate. Two meta-analyses, one based on GWAS data using polygenic risk scores (Peyrot et al., 2018) failed to support the Caspi et al. finding concerning the serotonin promoter gene. Similar problems prevented another meta-analysis in a very large sample from replicating Caspi et al. (Culverhouse et al., 2018). Howard et al. (2019) conducted a GWAS study that found 102 genes associated with depression, each with a very small effect. A 30-year longitudinal study reported by Fergusson and Horwood (2011) failed to support any interaction between depression, childhood trauma, and the gene that controls serotonergic activity. In another large-scale GWAS study, 18 candidate genes had no relationship to depression, and no gene–environment interactions were found (Border et al. 2019). Still, the debate still goes on: in the most recent meta-analysis (Bleys et al., 2018), only a weak relationship was found between depression and the serotonin promoter allele.

However, the findings of gene–environment links to antisocial behavior have gained more support, and they have been replicated (Fergusson et al., 2011). But this still does not mean we are in a firm position to make predictions from childhood about adult outcomes.

Belsky and Pluess (2013) have called attention to another set of alleles, dopamine receptor genes (DRD) that have been associated with pleasureful feelings and externalizing behaviors. However, variations in these alleles are not consistently predictive of psychopathology.

If you are looking for relationships between single genes and clinical categories that are themselves heterogeneous, is it any wonder that the results remain doubtful? Moreover, since psychopathology of all kinds is associated with hundreds of genes, the use of polygenic risk scores is not in a position to resolve the problem.

Genetic studies in medicine have suffered from what has been called a "replication crisis". The reason is that single genes are the proverbial needle in a haystack, and large samples are needed. As Ioannidis (2015) pointed out in a widely quoted paper, many (if not most) research findings in medicine are wrong, and they should not be considered true until repeatedly replicated. Or, as I tell my students – never believe one paper – it is almost always best to wait for a meta-analysis. And even then, meta-analyses can differ depending on what data you put into them.

One might think it would be easier to find links between G–E interactions and psychosis. That relationship was not measured by the Dunedin researchers, probably due to the relatively lower prevalence of such outcomes in the community. We know from behavior genetic data (and may other sources) that a vulnerability to psychosis is heritable (Plomin, 2019). Yet when Zwicker et al. (2018) reviewed the literature, the only secure finding for specificity was a small relationship between one allele and psychosis following cannabis use.

In contrast, more consistent with the Caspi et al. study, there seems to be evidence for gene–environment interplay in conduct disorder (Salvatore and Dick, 2018), as well as for a link of MAO genes to both substance abuse and suicidality (Polimanti et al., 2020). There is some evidence that variants of the DRD4 (dopamine) gene, long linked to attention-deficit hyperactivity disorder (ADHD), can interact with a family environment to produce problems in adolescents (Schlomer et al., 2015).

In summary, one can observe slow progress in the G–E interaction field (Duncan and Keller, 2011; Salvatore and Dick, 2015). Yet we do have enough data to identify replicable relationships with behavioral outcomes. The main reason why the debate is still open after 20 years of research may be the complexity of the variables under study. Considering what we have learned from GWAS research, it is unlikely that any single gene, or even a small number of genes, even in interaction with life adversities, can explain a large percentage of variance in behavioral outcomes, even if they are sometimes statistically significant in large samples. It is possible that antisocial outcomes are more sensitive to genetic effects than heterogeneous constructs such as depression, which probably describe many different clinical entities (Goldberg, 2011).

We should also keep in mind that all these studies, even those with a longitudinal methodology, are ultimately correlational, and do not necessarily demonstrate causality. Moreover, this kind of data cannot distinguish between the genetic and environmental precursors of psychopathology. However, few longitudinal studies have included genetic measures that would allow for the assessment of gene–environment interactions. To do so requires a different research design.

Longitudinal Studies of Twins

Following MZ and DZ twins longitudinally over time allows researchers to control for genetic effects at the same time as measuring interactions with the environment. This is an expensive but unique way to separate the effects of genes and environment.

One of the best-known of these cohorts is the Minnesota Twin Family Study, which begun in 1983 (Krueger and Johnson, 2002). It described 8000 twin pairs who entered the study between ages 11 and 17. The main cohort of twins has also been used to follow adolescents with traits of BPD, estimating the effects of genes and environment at different points of development (Bornovalova et al., 2013).

A related study from Minnesota made headlines by finding a group of MZ twins who had been separated at birth and placed in different families. As it turned out, they were surprisingly similar in behavior as adults.

A major project in the UK, the Environmental Risk (E-risk) Longitudinal Twin Study, which is still another project co-founded by Caspi and Moffitt, has been following a sample of 2232 twins born in 1994–5 (Moffitt et al., 2013). As in previous longitudinal research, E-risk found that child abuse and neglect are statistically related to psychopathology, particularly to conduct disorder (Stern et al., 2018). Another direction of research in the E-risk program has been victimization during adolescence, which seems to have a causal relationship to later psychopathology, above and beyond heritable traits (Schaefer et al., 2018). Latham et al. (2019) reported that later psychopathology could be predicted in those who had been maltreated as children, using a model that generated a "risk calculator". In another recent report, Wertz et al. (2020) found that BPD symptoms at age 12 were exposed to both genetic and environmental risk factors, a combination that predicted poor functioning later in adolescence.

As the E-Risk cohort is entering young adulthood, we await more findings that could shed light on the roles of genes and environment in other forms of psychopathology. There is data from this group at age 18 showing the effects of adolescent victimization (Schaefer et al., 2018), and of multiple (i.e., "complex") traumatic exposures (Lewis et al., 2021). But at this point, it is safe to conclude that data sets such as these, involving longitudinal studies of twins, have not yet fully borne fruit.

The E-Risk study has also examined epigenetic effects in a cohort of over 2000 twins followed prospectively (Wong et al., 2010). Their main finding was that even between genetically identical individuals, changes in gene activity begin in early childhood in response to environmental influences, but these differences are not necessarily stable over time.

Social Risk Factors for Psychopathology

The idea that psychiatry is nothing but the "clinical application of neuroscience" (Insel and Quirion, 2005) reflects a current bias for considering brain research to be the basis of theory and practice in studying and managing psychopathology. But as this book has tried to show, psychology is just as important a basic science for psychiatry. Moreover, the social sciences that study society as a whole – most particularly, sociology and cultural anthropology, are also highly relevant for understanding the risk for psychological symptoms.

For example, one of the most consistent findings in social science research concerns the impact of social class on all kinds of outcomes. Thus, people in lower socioeconomic groups are usually at higher risk for psychopathology (Kagan, 2010). As shown many decades ago (Leighton et al., 1963), another finding is that living under conditions of what has been called "social disintegration" (i.e., the loss of traditional social support systems) is a risk for psychological symptoms. Another factor that can increase risk is immigration to countries where minorities are marginalized, which has an effect on the prevalence of psychosis (Cantor-Grae and Selten, 2005). One can also see changes in the frequency of suicide over time depending on social integration, which the pioneer sociologist Emile Durkheim (1899) described as related to social alienation or "anomie".

Culture need not always produce symptoms *de novo*, but it can affect the symptomatic expression of psychopathology (Shorter, 1997). A good example of changes in a historical context is the relatively recent increase in the prevalence of anorexia nervosa (Brumberg, 1988). Another is the striking differences in the prevalence of substance abuse around the world (Helzer and Canino, 1992), as well as differences in antisocial behavior

(Rutter and Smith, 1995). Finally, there are also social changes that promote resilience. As discussed in Chapter 5, rates of child abuse have gone down greatly in recent years (Finkelhor, 2007), and society now encourages parents to be more protective of children.

The mechanism by which social risk factors have influence generally lies in their effects on family life and the health of the social community. This kind of mediation has been called a level of "social capital" (Bourdieu, 1990). And needless to say, all these risks more strongly affect those who are already temperamentally vulnerable. This leads us toward a model in which social risk factors are transmitted and mediated by biological and psychological factors, a point of view supporting a broader and highly interactive model of the causes of psychopathology.

The Biopsychosocial Model

The evidence for a reduction of mind to brain is insufficient, nor is it likely that future investigations based on this principle alone will ever fully account for psychopathology. Similarly, the reduction of psychological factors to trauma, maltreatment, or stress fails to consider individual differences in response to the environment. Finally, to blame social factors for psychopathology fails to explain why most people remain unhealthy under all sorts of social systems. But there is a better alternative.

The key point here is that you cannot reduce complex phenomena to simple theories of the pathways to psychopathology. When you study the mind at a mental level, you will observe emergent phenomena that cannot be identified by a reductionistic approach.

That is why psychopathology requires a *biopsychosocial* model (BPS; Engel, 1977, 1980) that integrates *all* sources of risk for disorders and how they interact with each other. The BPS model is consistent with emergence and with an interactive model.

George Engel was a psychiatrist who worked in a hospital-based consultation service. He proposed that a BPS model should be applied to medicine as a whole, as well as to clinical psychiatry. Engel's concern was that a purely biomedical model fails to take into account the psychological and social context of illness, and consider interactions between biological, psychological, and social factors.

Over the next few decades, the BPS model has had its ups and downs. Some, including myself, consider it to be only common sense (ignoring how easy it is for clinicians to focus exclusively on either biological or psychosocial factors). Yet Ghaemi (2010) dismissed the model as vague and unhelpful. He does not see it as integrative because in practice it turned out to be a little better than eclecticism. Gorman (2018) suggested discarding BPS on the grounds that psychosocial factors affect the brain, and that they are therefore equally biological. But this objection can be met by remembering that these factors cannot be understood separately, but through their interactions.

Nature–Nurture Interactions 91

One of the best defenses of the BPS model comes from a book by Bolton and Gillett (2019), which was a collaboration between a philosopher-psychologist and a bioethicist-neurosurgeon. These authors suggest that biological and psychosocial factors create systems of regulatory control that differ from physical and chemical laws because they can break down, providing a basis for the difference between health and disease.

I view the BPS model as central to psychiatry. Since influences from many domains in complex interactions shape personality and psychopathology, clinicians need to adopt model that integrates biological and psychosocial risks the BPS model has the potential to help replace the all-too-frequent reduction of psychology to biology

Over the next few decades, the BPS model has had its ups and downs. Some consider it to be only common sense (ignoring the tendency of clinicians to focus exclusively on biological or psychosocial factors). Others, like Ghaemi (2010) dismiss BPS as simply providing an eclectic list of risk factors. But that view misses the point of nature–nurture interaction. One of the best defenses of the BPS model comes from a book by Bolton and Gillett (2019) a collaboration between a philosopher-psychologist and a bioethicist-neurosurgeon. In their view (p.1), developing a BPS model is a necessity to counter "historical prejudices against psychosocial causation deriving from physicalist reductionism…"

I view the BPS model as essential to psychiatry, both in research and practice. But many people, used to linear theories, find interactive pathways uncomfortably complex and tend to be attracted to simpler models. Yet reductionism is almost always a misleading oversimplification of causal pathways. Some researchers have searched (albeit unsuccessfully) for single genes, single neurotransmitters, or single neural pathways to explain mental disorders, while others seem to think that psychological trauma accounts, more or less by itself, for many forms of psychopathology. But we will not be able to answer the most pressing questions in our field without becoming more comfortable with multicausality.

Psychology and History: Two Multicausal Disciplines

The problems discussed in this book are not unique to the disciplines of psychology, psychiatry, or neuroscience. Any domain which attempts to account for human behavior must face the same problem. Individual humans are complex and unpredictable, and human societies are even less predictable. Thus, historians who attempt to explain why the war began cannot reasonably limit themselves to single causal factors, but they must always consider interactions between multiple causes of different kinds. And as in human development, there are unpredictable and random events, some lucky and some unlucky that drive history. Who can say, for example, what the 20th century have been like if, in August 1914, Archduke Franz Ferdinand's car had not made a wrong turn in Sarajevo, allowing a terrorist to assassinate him? Similarly, unpredictable events can turn human lives in an unanticipated direction.

These issues challenge us to consider what research needs to prove causality. We do not have the option of the hard sciences to conduct experiments. But in contemporary social science research, it is no longer common for published papers to report univariate analyses, in which one attempts to show whether a single independent variable is associated with changes in a dependent variable. The reason is that even if you find a statistically significant relationship, how do you know whether other variables you did not measure are even more important? Today, unless data analysis is multivariate, social science research papers may not be easily publishable.

As this way of thinking sunk in, statistical methods have become more sophisticated. The more complex procedures can examine relationships between multiple independent variables and multiple dependent variables. One of the more sophisticated methods is structural equation modeling. This rather complex procedure allows researchers to separate relationships between predictors from each other and can therefore be shown to have a unique effect on outcomes. The main limitation of these procedures is that you need a much larger sample (whose recruitment has to be supported by more money) to conduct a valid data analysis. And even so, you can never be sure you have included all possible variables that contribute to causality.

In spite of all these problems, we need to think about psychopathology using multivariate models of causality, and to study it using multivariate statistical models. To do so, we need to draw on a broad range of factors not limited to either biology, psychology, or the social sciences. Finally, as the next chapter will show, this perspective can usefully inform clinical practice.

8 Problems with Causality

Causality Reconsidered

This book has emphasized how much we do not know about psychopathology and personality. That is inevitable, given how complicated the pathways are that shape human behavior. Moreover, one cannot predict what people do with their lives in the same way as scientists use physics. To believe that disciplines such as psychology and history that describe human behavior are predictive and deterministic may be comforting for those who seek certainty. But such ideas are based not on facts, but on faith.

Moreover, many errors in understanding psychological outcomes come from misunderstandings about causality. When the American writer HL Mencken stated: "for every complex problem there is an answer that is clear, simple, and wrong", he was talking about the fatal attraction to simplicity. But there is an even larger issue: whether predictive models in the social sciences or history can ever be more than approximate. By and large, outcomes of interest cannot be predicted by one or two variables.

If we really knew how to predict the future, the stock market would look quite different. Even the weather is only partially predictable, given that large effects can result from very small initial conditions. It is kind of hubris to think that psychological development can ever be a fully predictive science.

I am also reminded of some financial columns in Canadian newspapers that purport to tell readers whether their currency will rise or fall in relation to the all-powerful American dollar. Almost all these predictions are wrong, but no one ever checks on them. Yet they just keep coming. It would be nice if the world was more predictable, but it is not. Random or chance events, even when very rare, can have massive effects. Taleb (2010) has described that kind of event as a "black swan". Most of the important events of human history, such as wars and epidemics, fit that description.

How Medical Research Studies Causality

Medical research aims to identify risk factors that are major predictors of disease. But most illnesses have multiple causes, and the few exceptions derive from cases in which, as in Huntington's disease, a single gene is responsible for the condition. Even in infectious diseases, the cause is not only the pathogen but also lies within the strength of the immune system. And in diseases such as heart attacks, strokes, and cancer it takes "multiple hits" to produce diagnosable illness.

Sometimes a single risk factor dominates the picture. Many decades ago, the British epidemiologist Austin Bradford Hill (1965) commented on the fact that smoking is associated with lung cancer. This risk factor is not universal, but it is clearly one of the major sources of causality. When Hill was criticized on the grounds that there were no randomized clinical trials to confirm the relationship, he responded by pointing out that causality is not solely determined by randomized controlled trials, but it needs to be confirmed by multiple observations from multiple points of view. Since Hill lived in an earlier era that focused on single causes of pathology, I will adapt his argument for the multiple interacting networks of causality that characterize the complex pathways to psychopathology.

Hill listed nine criteria, but I will focus on four of them. One should begin with the *strength* (i.e., effect size) of the association, a point that can be missed when researchers are satisfied with statistically significant associations. It is rare in psychopathological research to find a large effect size for *any* risk factor. Instead, factors claimed to be causal, whether derived from genes, neural processes, or environmental stressors, often have relationships that are weak and inconsistent within a sample. That is why many statistically oriented psychologists, such as Jacob Cohen (1994), have recommended that we drop the qualitative criterion for a significance level of $p < .05$. Cohen suggested replacing this arbitrary cut-off point with a quantitative measure called *effect size* (based on overall change, measured in standard deviation units). Since then, while some scientific journals have made this switch, the $p = .05$ criterion lives on, probably because it is much easier to reach, and allows researchers to claim causality even when relationships are weak (Ritchie, 2020). Using effect sizes would help us to acknowledge that almost all the relationships we observe in research are complex, multifactorial, and interactive.

The second criterion proposed by Hill is *consistency* (i.e., reproducibility). This issue mirrors the current concern with a "replication crisis" in psychology and medicine. That is why I tell students not to believe any scientific finding until there is enough data for a meta-analysis. And even then, meta-analyses can yield different results, depending on methodologies and choice of articles to consider (Stegenga, 2018), and we often have to wait for multiple meta-analyses.

A third criterion is *specificity*. As we have seen, risk factors in abnormal psychology tend to be non-specific, and can be found in many different forms of psychopathology. This need not deny an etiological role, but specificity for any risk factor is more likely to appear when research takes interactions with other risks into account. This is why multivariate analyses have become standard in psychology.

A fourth criterion is the presence of a dose-response relationship. We have seen how the trauma literature conflates minor or isolated adverse life events with major and repeated events, as well as how genetic studies in which single genes, and even multiple genes, explain only a small percentage of the variance.

I should also note that psychopathology is a discipline whose methods are almost entirely observational and naturalistic. Thus, although biomarkers might be discovered in the future, we have very few laboratory findings on which to ground clinical observations. It is interesting that in spite of their lack of understanding of etiology, that mental health clinicians do as well as other physicians in helping most of the patients they see (Leucht et al., 2012).

Caseness and the Base Rate Fallacy

If a risk factor is sufficiently ubiquitous, then even when it is frequently associated with an outcome, the relationship may not be truly causal. This has been called the *base rate fallacy*. When the incidence of an outcome is high, you can expect to find more false positives than false negatives. A good example is death by suicide. Fatalities are usually preceded by suicidal ideation and/or attempts. But they cannot be predicted either by attempts or ideation. The reason is that while fatal behaviors are rather rare, attempts are common, and ideation is almost ubiquitous. One result of this discrepancy is that most predictions of whether people will die by suicide, even if based on complex algorithms using known risk factors, are almost always wrong (Paris, in press).

To establish whether a biomarker or an adverse life event is a valid cause of clinically significant symptoms, we need to decide what cut-off point to use. In other words: *what is a case?* This well-known problem in clinical epidemiology arises from the fact that most forms of disorder lie on a continuum with normality, with pathology emerging only on the extremes (Goldberg and Huxley, 1992). Therefore, to the extent that adverse experiences are frequent in the general population, many patients are bound to report them. Yet non-patients who have had the same experiences may not develop the same sequelae.

To know what a case is, we must also address the difference between *distress* and *disorder*. This is best demonstrated by the lack of boundaries between sadness, in which episodes are universal, and clinically significant depression, which affects only a proportion of those exposed to adversity (Horwitz and Wakefield, 2007). Thus, while distress is ubiquitous, disorder is not. This issue has become relevant recently in assessing claims that environmental stressors (such as the COVID pandemic) are associated with mental disorders—as opposed to self-reported symptoms.

This problem with determining "caseness" also has implications for measuring resilience. When we are conservative about defining psychopathology, most people appear highly resilient. When we are overly liberal in defining normal variations as pathological, resilience is less obvious.

Some might argue that we miss important effects of adversity by counting only those who have clinical levels of psychopathology. In this view, we should give equal weight to those affected in any perceptible way, even if they have no diagnosable disorder. But that point of view leads to misleading conclusions, largely because it runs directly into the base rate problem.

These problems explain why current definitions of psychopathology are too broad, especially when they are based on DSM definitions (Frances, 2013). An earlier version of the DSM manual was used in the large-scale National Comorbidity Survey conducted in a sample of the US population (Kessler et al., 1994). The results, which were later replicated (Kessler et al., 2005), seemed to show that at least a third of the population have a measurable mental disorder over a lifetime. This very high estimate has often been quoted as a way to encourage people to take mental illness seriously. But DSM manuals describe many syndromes that do not actually have a major effect on functioning. If we only considered those that *are* severe (schizophrenia, major mood disorders, heavy substance abuse, highly dysfunctional personality disorders), a much smaller percentage of the population would be considered as affected. Once we open the door to diagnosing distress, being mildly troubled can become universal.

In summary, we need to avoid defining caseness in a way that makes the distinction between normality and pathology meaningless. Models that pathologize all forms of psychological suffering run the risk of applying a standard of mental health that turns almost everyone into a patient. We should not make diagnoses without a clear-cut impairment in functioning. Moreover, this problem would not disappear (and might even be made worse) if we replaced categories with dimensions. A bell-curve of quantitative data measuring symptoms or dysfunctions would still need some kind of cut-off point to determine caseness.

Why Risk Factors Do Not Prove Causality

We can browse the web almost any day and read about results of the latest research on risk factors for physical and mental illnesses. Over morning coffee, we learn that researchers are considering whether how much alcohol intake is safe, whether it is dangerous to be too fat or too thin, and how much people should exercise. Even so, we need not become unnecessarily concerned. All of these purported dangers are *risks*, but they may not be *causes*. Risk factors consist of anything that makes disease statistically more likely. But we need to know more precisely how likely a negative outcome is before claiming causality. If the base rate in the population as a whole is 1%, and a risk factor doubles it to 2%, such data would provide little reason to intervene or change one's lifestyle.

Nonetheless one can find many good examples in medicine of risk factors that meet most criteria for being truly causal. As we have seen, some of the best examples concern the relationship of cigarette smoking to lung cancer and to cardiovascular disease. We know that smoking frequently leads to these kinds of pathology, and we also have a good idea of the mechanism by which exposure to tobacco leads to pathology. Even if these relationships are only statistical, there is can be little doubt that they are etiological. Ironically, Roland Fisher, one of the pioneers of statistics in research, was a heavy smoker and tried to debunk this link, which was one reason why Bradford Hill wrote his classic article.

In contrast, the association between negative life events (or genetic markers) and psychopathology is neither strong nor specific. It also lacks a well-established pathogenic mechanism. Most people exposed to any of these risk factors never become ill, and if they do, they rarely suffer from symptoms that are specific to the risk. When relationships are purely statistical, they need not, and usually do not, apply to any particular individual. Thus, while from a retrospective point of view we seem to be seeing causality, from a prospective point of view, we cannot predict which individuals exposed to any risk factor will developmental disorders.

In general, while many risk factors *contribute* to a pathological outcome, they should not be thought of individually as either necessary or sufficient conditions. The causes of psychological symptoms are almost never single risks, but the result of complex interactions between many factors. These pathways can involve what Ciccheti (2016) calls *equifinality* (the same result emerging from different causes) and *multifinality* (different results emerging from the same cause).

Reminder: Correlation is Not Causation

Correlation does not prove causation. This saying is so well known that it has become a cliché. Yet the principle behind it is often ignored. For example, the difference between correlation and causation is crucial to understanding the relationships between childhood experiences and adult disorders. When researchers find such associations, they need not be etiological in any way.

Moreover, associations between risk and outcome may result from *latent variables* not measured in the study. To consider an example, people who drink too much are more likely to develop lung cancer. But alcohol does not cause lung cancer. The explanation is that people who drink more also smoke more and that tobacco is the latent variable leading to disease.

To consider an example close to the experience of psychotherapists, children who are sexually abused are more likely to develop a wide range of psychological problems as adults. Yet we have seen that this kind of abuse, by itself, need not be the primary or only cause of these outcomes. Children who are traumatized by abuse tend to come from dysfunctional families, in which emotional neglect is prominent if not universal (Paris, 2000a). Thus neglect and failure of validation may be the latent variable driving this association.

In summary, adversities are multiple and inter-correlated. As a result, researchers are likely to draw faulty conclusions from research in which one or two risks are examined for their effects on the outcome. They need to carry out *multivariate* studies that can measure many risks. These methods provide a way of assessing a wide range of potential factors, rather than being confined to one or two. The main obstacle is that the more variables are studied, the larger the sample needs to be (larger samples in research require more funding). And underpowered studies are one of the main causes of non-replication in medical research (Ionaniddis, 2015). Finally, no matter how many additional variables are added, important ones can still be missed. That is why scientific papers often end with a call for further research.

Differences Between Clinical and Community Populations

Clinicians do not see a random sample of the population. Their patients belong to a sub-group who have a more than average sensitivity to the environment. Therefore, observations in clinical settings cannot be generalized to non-clinical groups. Moreover, clinical impressions often lead to incorrect conclusions about cause and effect. Practitioners may find associations between adversities and disorders in patients that may not apply to community populations, since clinical populations are, almost by definition, more vulnerable.

A project conducted at my own university department provides an example of this principle. Since the end of the Second World War, a number of clinicians have been interested in understanding the effects of the Holocaust, both on the survivors themselves, and on their children. Clinical observations had given the impression that most survivors suffered from post-traumatic symptoms, and that their children suffered difficulties associated with guilty feelings about their damaged parents. However, when a research group examined a large community sample of survivors (Eaton et al., 1982), they found that while nearly half of those who had been in camps reported at least some form of distress, the majority did not meet the criteria for any diagnosable mental disorder, and many were actually asymptomatic. Similarly, in community samples of the children of Holocaust survivors, who had previously been believed to be at particular risk, they are no more likely to develop significant psychopathology (Sigal and Weinfeld, 2001).

These results should not be interpreted as implying that there were *no* psychological consequences to surviving the Holocaust. Life events can cause distress, even if they do not necessarily lead to disorder. The point is that clinical populations, in which disorders are more frequently observed, are unrepresentative of community populations. Holocaust survivors who develop disabling disorders may have had other vulnerability factors. Even so, resilience remained the rule-- however horrific their experiences, survivors do not necessarily have clinical pathology. Their children also tend to have more symptoms related to stress, possibly on the basis of epigenetic mechanisms (Yehuda and Lerner, 2018), but these problems are usually sub-clinical.

The Problem of Recall Bias

Seventy years ago, Akira Kurosawa directed the classical Japanese film "Rashomon". The plot concerned a murder, and how several different observers (the victim, the perpetrator, and witnesses) all had contradictory perceptions of what happened. In addition to the reconstructive quality of long-term memory, even memories of recent events can depend on one's point of view. This is why when a classical study of psychotherapy (Mintz et al., 1973) found no relationship between ratings of patients, therapists, and outside observers as to whether a particular session had been productive, the researchers called it a "Rashomon effect".

Similar findings apply to the recall of highly memorable events such as the Kennedy assassination and 9–11 (Hirst et al., 2009), as well as to eyewitness testimony in a courtroom (Loftus and Ketcham, 1991). Moreover, much the same problem affects the reliability of memory in children, adults, or outside observers when they describe the positive or negative features of a family. This is one of the main reasons for conducting prospective studies to determine the true likelihood of causality.

Vagaries of recollection are even more severe for long-term memories. Most studies of childhood experience are conducted in adult patients who are asked to recall events many years in the past. Yet, as has often been shown (Maughan and Rutter, 1997), the way we remember childhood is strongly influenced by our present state of mind. In a classic study, Yarrow et al. (1970) compared mothers' and children's memories of the quality of early childhood experiences to direct observations of family life (that had been made years earlier for another purpose). The results showed little or no relationship between the way parents and children recalled the past. The nature of these memories was much more strongly associated with the quality of *current* relationships between mothers and children.

The concept of *recall bias* describes how the way we remember the past is determined by the present, and it is a problem for all surveys that depend on recollection (Coughlin, 1990; Schacter, 1996). People who are happy in the present are more likely to forget bad events and to remember good ones, while people who are unhappy in the present are more likely to focus on bad memories and to discount good ones. Problems with the validity of past information are even more complex in patients who externalize their current difficulties, preferring to hold others responsible. It is impossible to tell whether such reports represent objective reality or perceptions. Again, only prospective studies can answer such questions.

Another problem with relying on retrospective reports in clinical samples is that many are often conducted on populations of patients in treatment with therapists who believe that adult problems are due to an unhappy childhood, and who tend to shape perceptions of the past to conform to these beliefs. It is not just false memories, but *selective* memories that produce difficulties in knowing the truth about the past. There are many variables that can affect child development, but it is easier to remember the most dramatic incidents. As discussed in Chapter 7, this is a problem both for psychologists and for historians.

Statistical Significance vs. Clinical Significance

When perusing scientific journals, most readers, to rapidly assess the results, scan the abstract first. When a hypothesis is confirmed by data, the words *significant*, or even *highly significant* will appear in the text. The "take-home message" becomes a claim for demonstration of a cause-effect relationship. Yet a deeper understanding of statistics shows that this need not be the case (Ritchie, 2020). A risk factor can be statistically significant even when it does not apply to *most* cases.

To illustrate the problem, let us return to an important prospective study of the impact of marital conflict and divorce on children (Amato and Booth, 1997). Marital discord and divorce did predict a number of psychological problems among children when they reached adulthood. The authors, who were research sociologists, used sophisticated statistical analyses, making use of regression equations that can sort out which variables, above and beyond any of the others, predicted outcome. In this case, standardized regression coefficients for an overall model were *highly* significant, accounting for about 20–25% of the outcome variance. In the context of psychosocial research, in which there is always a high "signal to noise" ratio, that is a remarkable finding.

Nevertheless, one cannot conclude from such results that children or divorce are *necessarily* damaged by divorce. The risk is high enough to suggest that couples with children may want to think twice about ending a marriage (as discussed in Chapter 5, high levels of family conflict can sometimes make family dissolution a positive experience, but marriages that have ended in spite of low levels of conflict tend to cause more long-term damage to children). Moreover, none of the analyses accounted for the *other* 75% of the variance. In other words, even though having parents who are unhappily married makes it more likely that children will have problems with intimacy as adults, more often than not, there will be no such association. Thus, most people who come from unhappy families can achieve normal levels of self-esteem and intimacy. Conversely, while coming from a happy family makes it more likely that children will grow up to be happy and successful, there is no assurance that this will be the case.

This example shows why clinicians who follow the research literature need to understand the difference between *statistical significance* and *clinical significance*. As everyone who has taken an introductory statistics course knows, a finding is significant when one can say, at least ninety-five times out of a hundred, that the results in this particular sample is not a false positive, but represents what would be found if one had conducted the same study on an entire population.

But differences that are statistically significant may not be large enough to be "significant" in the real world. Statistical significance only proves that there is *some* association between the variables under study. It does not mean that the relationship applies to most people in the sample. By and large, few studies do well in accounting for a large percentage of outcome variance. Group differences tend to mask enormous heterogeneity, with some subjects affected positively, others negatively, and some not at all.

Let us consider some examples. It is quite possible for a finding to be highly significant, even if it applies very strongly *only* to a sub-group. This is an important issue in clinical trials of drugs: a result can be significant if a few patients do extraordinarily well, even if most obtain no benefit. Alternatively, a finding that is statistically significant, and that applies to most subjects in the sample, may still be too weak to attain clinical significance. In antidepressant trials, for example, it is possible for a drug to reduce some symptoms but not others, leaving most patients clinically depressed.

Finally, the statistical "power" of any study depends on sample size. But sometimes a research study can have too much power for its own good. More findings become reportable if the sample is so large that even small differences attain statistical significance. Although this is not often an issue in clinical research (where the problem usually consists of finding enough subjects), it arises frequently in large-scale community surveys.

Again, this is why Cohen (1994) argued that statistical significance is not a sufficient criterion, by itself, to determine the reliability of a research finding. Instead of a simple "yes–no" question, researchers need to know "how much". Cohen proposed that one way this can be accomplished is by determining *effect size*, a statistic that describes a quantitative, and not just a qualitative difference between groups.

The best way to determine the quantitative effects of a research finding is through multivariate statistical techniques, which can measure how much of the variance in outcome is accounted for by each of several independent variables. Finding factors that explain a large percentage of the variance is relatively rare. In the real world, there are just too many factors, measured or unmeasured, that can influence outcomes. And most studies that do yield such results turn out to be less impressive when they are replicated.

When an adverse life experience or a genetic marker is statistically associated with symptoms, and when that relationship is clinically significant, we tend to conclude that it constitutes a risk factor, i.e., that it is at least one among many factors that can lead to a pathological outcome. Yet we will be still a long way from being able to say that the adversity *causes* an outcome, or that when we see a specific outcome in a clinical setting, we should expect to find a history of particular adversity.

These methodological and statistical problems are by no means abstruse and theoretical. On the contrary, these issues are crucial for understanding the nature of the relationship between psychological risk factors and psychopathology. *Some* people are badly affected by their childhood. It is this vulnerable sub-group that accounts for most of the statistically significant relationships between exposure and outcome reported in the literature, even when the majority of those exposed are doing reasonably well. For this reason, conclusions about relationships between childhood and adult functioning are, in any individual case, just as likely to be wrong as right.

We should not depend on claims by therapists that they have unlocked the keys to psychopathology. No matter how much experience clinicians have, the formulations they use to account for causation are often wrong. That is because clinical methods are incapable of determining cause and effect relationships. At the same time, research methods can also produce misleading results that fail to establish causation. Once again, long-term prospective research in community samples (preferably using twins to control for common genes) is the most unquestionable way to determine the effects of childhood experience.

Therapists should never forget the principle that no one can make general conclusions about the human condition from clinical experience. Instead of relying on the opinions of prestigious "experts", clinicians would do well to familiarize themselves with the research literature on child development and developmental psychopathology (Cicchetti, 2016).

Fatal Attractions to Explanations and Attributions

False beliefs in psychology do not easily die out. Many survive and continue to influence the next generation. Why do new facts not lead to the correction of old errors? Why does illogic so often defeat logic?

Social psychologists have long been interested in understanding why people come to idiosyncratic conclusions about the world. This area of research is termed *attribution theory* (Sutherland, 1992; Weiner and Graham, 1999), and consists of formal studies about how people explain sequences of events in their lives. These attributions tell us a lot about the role of personality in understanding one's own life history. In particular, they tell us the importance of narrative—the process by which complex pathways are turned into an intelligible story.

By and large, people prefer any explanation to no explanation. We prefer to prove something true than something that is untrue. When confronted with a complex sequence of events, most of us will be uncomfortable with not having at least some adequate theory. For this reason, we have trouble withholding judgment about cause and effect.

These problems have been well studied in cognitive science, and they are best described in a classic book by Daniel Kahnemann (2011). Biases affect all decision-making. But they may have a particular effect on the judgments of clinical psychologists (Dawes, 1994).

This leads to an *availability bias*, the tendency to explain events on the basis of what lies closest at hand. These explanations provide an illusion that we can control our environment. What most readily comes to mind often derives from beliefs that are commonly held in one's culture. Attributions based on an availability bias also color observations in both clinical and research settings, leading to misleading associations between risks and outcomes.

Second, people overvalue previous harm when experiencing present adversity. This tendency to rewrite one's personal history in the light of present suffering is another example of recall bias (Weiner and Graham, 1999). People may not prefer to explain life failures in terms of *personal* inadequacy. Blaming others provides a readily available explanation.

Third, the *fundamental attribution error* describes the fact that we typically attribute our *own* behavior as a reaction to a situation, while we tend to attribute the behavior of *other* people to internal dispositions such as personality. In other words, when people tell their stories, they prefer to present themselves as victims of circumstance, rather than as the authors of their own distress. It is the task of therapy to correct these perceptions. But too often, out of a need to be empathic and be "on the patient's side", clinicians are inclined to accept and validate biased attributions. The concept of *locus of control* is another way to divide people into those who typically attribute problems to external factors and those who attribute problems to their own failings. These differences, which reflect externalizing or internalizing personality traits. are associated with specific problems in psychotherapy (see Chapter 9).

Unfortunately, psychotherapy, by its very nature, tends to pathologize human problems and many forms of therapy seek causes in the past. This encourages patients to see themselves as victims of traumatic events. Such conclusions are neither fair to the facts, nor necessarily therapeutic. These applications of research to clinical practice will be discussed in the last two chapters.

9 Implications for Psychotherapy

The most important clinical implications of an integrative nature–nurture model of psychopathology affect the practice of psychotherapy. Mental health care remains split between psychotherapists who believe that nurture is the main cause of mental disorders and biological psychiatrists who attribute psychopathology to defects derived from nature. These differences have led to a serious divide in practice. Many psychiatrists today spend little time with patients, offering a "15-minute hour" every few weeks, which focuses on renewing or revising prescriptions. Psychotherapists are more interested in the person and their life course, but some work within a paradigm that focuses on symptoms, and that fails to take temperament and personality into account.

Nature, Nurture, and Psychotherapy

Psychological treatments have traditionally emphasized nurture and downplayed nature. This bias is most obvious in psycho-dynamically oriented therapies. Their methods are based on developmental theories that emphasize the impact of childhood adversity, which drive many of their interventions. Like many others of my generation who trained in the 1960s, I was taught by psycho-dynamically oriented teachers who compensated for a lack of evidence with charisma and rhetoric. Later in my career, I came to value the approach of cognitive behavior therapy. Yet CBT also lacks a well-developed model of individual differences, leading it to offer many of the same interventions to patients with very different problems.

There are hundreds of psychotherapies on the market, but some general principles apply to all of them. The evidence for the overall efficacy of psychotherapy for a wide range of patients over a wide range of methods is very strong. Research shows that talking therapies are superior to no treatment or to "treatment as usual" (i.e., whatever is done usually) in most clinical settings. Smith et al. (1980) reached that conclusion in a large-scale metanalysis forty years ago. Specifically, psychological treatments are as efficacious as medicine or education (which is to say they do not always work, but often do, and are usually worth trying). Research over the next few decades has consistently supported this conclusion (Barkham et al., 2021).

DOI: 10.4324/9781003156215-9

Yet psychotherapy, in spite of its strong evidence base, is under-utilized in mental health care. In the current age of neuroscience and high-tech interventions, its value is not appreciated. In part, the problem reflects disappointment with overblown claims in the past. Over many decades, psychoanalysis claimed, without support from research data, to be a cure for almost every psychological problem (Paris, 2019). Disillusionment was inevitable, leading to suspicion about all forms of the "talking cure". Cognitive behavioral therapy (CBT) is now the method that most clinical psychologists offer, and its efficacy has been supported by thousands of studies (Hoffman et al., 2012).

Since CBT occupies the niche of a default therapy, it has sometimes been called a "gold standard" (David et al., 2018). For many patients, that method does offer the best option. Yet large-scale studies do not consistently demonstrate its superiority to support, (e.g., from counseling). Moreover, like many other forms of treatment, CBT is only effective in 50% of patients (Pybis et al., 2017).

Another reason why the "default" form of psychotherapy today tends to be CBT (Cook et al., 2010) is that this method has stimulated more research. Moreover, CBT is oriented to the present and not the past. It also has a very large bag of tricks, from which every therapist has something to learn. Yet CBT, while it can be considered a gold standard, has sometimes been hyped as a cure-all for psychological problems of all kinds. But this kind of treatment is not a "cure-all", nor are any of the hundreds of variants of therapies on the market.

The main reasons why psychotherapy is not prescribed as often as it should be done not lie in its evidence base, but in time and money. While most interventions in practice are brief, psychological treatment has a tendency to drag on for months to years, making it too expensive for most patients. There is actually little evidence that doing so makes a difference. For one thing, almost all research has been on brief courses of therapy lasting for 10–20 weeks (Barkham et al., 2021). Moreover, research on the length of therapy fails to show that longer is necessarily better.

A classical study in a large and representative clinical sample by Howard et al. (1986) found that most improvement in therapy occurs within 20 sessions or less and that longer durations do not usually yield better results, even when applied to more dysfunctional patients. This finding was later replicated by Barkham et al. (2006) in a UK sample of 1868 patients receiving time-limited therapy: the data showed no relationship between number of sessions and outcome.

Moreover, research does not support interminable therapies in which patients discuss their childhood for years without changing the way they function in the present (Paris, 2019). In current practice, long-term treatment is no longer that common, and most therapies today tend to be brief. CBT was originally designed to be time-limited, and its evidence base depends on seeing patients for months, not years. Other time-limited approaches, such as brief psychodynamic psychotherapy, also have a good track record in clinical trials (Abbass et al., 2014).

Finally, CBT suffers from some of the same problems as other therapies, in that it also can go on for too long. If standard interventions fail to produce a symptomatic remission, therapists are tempted to continue as long as the insurance lasts. This is most likely to happen in patients with personality disorders, who are less likely than those with depression or anxiety without a PD to benefit from psychotherapy (Newton-Howes et al., 2006). The underlying reason is that personality traits are resistant to modification. And that is why attempting to do the impossible is a danger for any method, especially when it fails to take nature into account.

Yet some currently popular forms of psychotherapy are still based on past events rather than current problems, and patients can spend years exploring their past. The assumption that adult problems can be traced to early traumatic experiences can be used to explain many things, which is why it continues to have currency. This even applies to methods of CBT designed for patients with trauma histories. For example, trauma-focused CBT (TFCBT) has been successfully tested in children and adolescents (Cohen, 2006), as well as in adults (Bisson, 2013). Yet clinical trials have not shown that TFCBT is superior to standard CBT (Kar, 2011). This may be because therapists are using the wrong theory, one that privileges trauma over other environmental risk factors.

Unfortunately, market forces have led to a proliferation of acronym-based therapies that all claim to be unique. This development presents a major problem for the overall credibility of the field. Competition for market share does not lend itself to scientific scrutiny. We do not need brand names, which should be replaced by an integrated model corresponding to what research tells us about the non-specific and specific factors in outcomes (Wampold and Imel, 2015).

The practice of psychotherapy depends in part on our views about nature and nurture. The problem is that not everyone agrees as to what human nature is. Some see it as largely fixed, while others see it as infinitely malleable. Pinker (2002) addressed these issues at book-length some years ago. He challenged what he called the "standard social science model" in which the environment determines almost everything, offering a better framework for understanding how evolution has (and has not) programmed thoughts, behaviors, and emotions. Pinker pointed out that people are influenced by a mixture of heritable personality traits, some of which can be aggressive and destructive, while others are more cooperative and constructive.

Human nature, with all its imperfections, is what we all have to deal with, both in daily life and in psychotherapy. There is no "blank slate" at birth, no childhood innocence, and no such thing as noble savages living in harmony with the world. We are all flawed in specific says, and we cannot blame society for spoiling the perfection of an imagined state of nature.

Rather, reason has to be harnessed to control our demons and to encourage the "better angels of our nature" (Pinker, 2011, 2019).

In the past, many therapists ignored temperament and thought that children are blank slates on which families write behavioral programs. If you think that is true, you may be tempted to encourage patients to blame parents for problems in children. And, if you believe that human nature is infinitely malleable, you may set unreachable goals in therapy that make it go on for too long.

Since we are all born different, we have temperamental biases that reflect unique ways of processing life events. This principle does not contradict the fact that family dysfunction can be a risk factor for almost every kind of psychopathology. The point is that adversity does not affect every child in the same way. That is why the relationship between childhood and adulthood is extremely complex and multi-determined.

Another issue concerns whether all forms of psychotherapy are designed to reach well-defined goals. The task of treatment is not to get patients to reach an ideal level of mental health. Instead, it should help to build a life that fits the patient's temperament, making use of positive traits while controlling negative ones. When patients stop looking for someone to blame, they are in a better position to change their life narrative from one of victimhood to one of the agency.

Therapies that are "trauma-focused" run the risk of supporting a sense of victimhood patients. The narrative that emerges is like a detective story: once the misdeeds of perpetrators are identified, life can return to normal. A different view is that once patients learn to function better, they can process their past more usefully, even if some events have been traumatic. As Linehan (1993) put it, people need to "radically accept" most difficulties in their past life to move on and deal with current problems.

Nature and Biological Psychiatry

A different and rather opposite problem emerges in the contemporary practice of psychiatry. Its orientation has become almost exclusively based on biological theories about human nature, and practice tends to be almost exclusively psychopharmacological. Most physicians are either relatively untrained or uninterested in psychotherapy, and while that tended not to be the case in the past for psychiatrists, that is the case today. I see, with dismay, students being trained to evaluate patients based on a series of checklists designed to make categorical diagnoses and identify potential targets for drug treatment. Clinicians then follow algorithms that lead them to try many drugs to see which, if any, are effective. Some psychiatrists have become practitioners who do not know what is going on in the lives of their patients. They may see people for just enough time to decide whether to adjust a prescription.

Forty years ago, I applauded the third edition of the Diagnostic and statistical manual of mental disorders (American Psychiatric Association, 1980), when it changed the focus of previous editions from unproven theories to observable symptoms. I did not anticipate that its diagnoses would come to replace an understanding of the life course and personality of patients. The result is that mental health services have come to resemble internal medicine, with a focus on biology and a failure to understand psychology. Moreover, treatment methods in psychiatry are based on categorical diagnoses that psychiatrists hope can be targeted by prescriptions. In reality, psychiatric diagnoses are inexact and slippery. It remains to be seen whether dimensional models could make practice more evidence-based or lead to better treatment outcomes.

It is undeniable that drugs are indispensable for the management of severe mental disorders such as psychoses. But the results of pharmacological interventions in the most common forms of disorder, most particularly depression and anxiety, are not superior to well-planned courses of psychotherapy (Abbass et al., 2014). For some problems, such as substance use (McHugh et al., 2010), eating disorders (Halmi et al., 2005), and personality disorders (Paris, 2015a), psychotherapy is the main treatment, and pharmacotherapy only plays an adjunctive role.

The problem is not that nature is not important, but that our understanding of it is too primitive. While no single theory can account for the complexity of human psychology, treatments should be at least consistent with what is known from research. Making this happen requires adopting an integrative biopsychosocial model. Integrating nature and nurture would do more justice to the complex roots of psychopathology, and it is a point of view that can be incorporated into mental health practice.

How Psychotherapy Works

Research has shed a great deal of light on how psychotherapy works. This literature is so vast that I will mainly rely on reviews and meta-analyses describing consistent findings in a large number of studies. But here are some general principles, supported by the latest edition of a standard textbook (Barkham et al., 2021).

1 Psychotherapy is effective for a wide variety of psychological problems.
2 Therapy usually works rapidly, with results apparent after a few months, and most patients do not require years of treatment.
3 When psychotherapy works, patients usually continue on an upward trajectory, even after formal treatment ends.
4 The outcome of psychotherapy does not necessarily depend on specific techniques; the best predictors of success are "common factors", such as a positive therapeutic relationship in which patients feel understood.

Psychotherapy has suffered from the existence of multiple schools of thought, each identified by a catchy acronym (usually consisting of 3 or 4 letters). Some wags have remarked that therapy has become more acronym-based than evidence-based. There is little need for so many competing methods, most of which are based on the prestige of a founder, and that are not very different from existing approaches. Instead of research support, new therapies are put on the market through books that lack a base in research but are illustrated by a few case histories. That is not evidence-based therapy, but eminence-based therapy.

I support the principle of *psychotherapy integration* (Norcross and Goldfried, 2005). This movement aims to meld together the best ideas from all sources, either by creating a single basic method for practice or by encouraging therapists to be open to other types of interventions. The movement publishes the Journal of Psychotherapy Integration, sponsored by the Society for the Exploration of Psychotherapy Integration (SEPI), which also organizes a yearly research congress. Its concept of integration aims to be consistent with empirical evidence, most particularly the *absence* of differences between various methods (Barth et al., 2013).

While research studies have rarely compared integrative therapy to more specific methods, data from comparative trials between therapies has shown that theoretical models are much less important than many clinicians think (Wampold and Imel, 2015). Also, therapies based on integrative models (e.g., interpersonal psychotherapy, schema-focused therapy, cognitive analytic therapy) have as good evidential support as CBT (Zarbo et al., 2015).

A single form of psychotherapy would apply the best ideas from all sources. It could draw on the psychodynamic tradition of understanding life histories but rely on cognitive methods to initiate and promote change. An integrated psychotherapy would make good use of the *common factors* that make psychotherapy work. In one research report, Laska et al. (2014) described the relative contribution of the most important common factors: consensus about goals 11.5%, empathy 9%, therapeutic alliance 7.5%, affirmation 7.3%, genuineness 5.7%, other therapist qualities 5%. Specific treatment interventions accounted for less than 1% of the variance.

Since all these factors add up to only about half of the total variance in outcome, we still have much more to learn about how therapy works. Given our limited knowledge of what actually leads to change in treatment, we need to keep an open mind about which interventions work best for which patients. Integrative therapy has the potential to take individual differences into account. For example, research suggests that patients with internalizing symptoms are more responsive to self-examination, while those with externalizing symptoms may require more emphasis on behavioral change (Zarbo et al., 2015). This observation points to the importance of factoring in personality trait profiles when planning therapeutic interventions.

Working with Personality in Psychotherapy

One of the duties of mental health clinicians is to offer patients an explanation of why they are suffering. But this requirement may not always be met in a useful way. Today every patient expects a diagnosis, and many go online to look their illness category up on the web. Doing so may be reasonable when patients have severe mental illnesses that have about the same level of validity as most medical illnesses (think of schizophrenia and bipolar-I disorder). But it is not as reasonable for the more common disorders, or for disorders that are not widely known or understood. Some of these categories are rather heterogeneous and have fuzzy boundaries (think of major depression).

Understandably, but unfortunately, patients *believe* in these diagnoses and talk about the diagnostic process as if it were entirely scientific (it is not). By and large, people feel comforted by giving their suffering a name, associated with trust that they are receiving appropriate treatment. As a consulting psychiatrist, I see many patients who have been unsuccessfully treated for extended periods with polypharmacy regimes are reluctant to give up any of these medications. Even though many of them have received diagnoses that might be challenged, the clinic to them for support.

Is there an alternative? I think so. Patients need to understand that since diagnosis is an inexact science, offering labels can only be an approximation. They also need to know that since everybody is different, these categories are by no means set in stone, but are a way of describing commonalities in symptoms that allow for more specific ways of treatment (Paris, 2020d).

Problems can also emerge when patients are treated by psychotherapists who do not see any value in diagnosis. For these clinicians, every case is unique. While they are right up to a point, that stance interferes with the appraisal of research findings that shed light on the likelihood that specific treatments will be helpful.

If we were to adopt a dimensional approach to mental disorders, our task might be even more complicated. The rather arcane terminology used in current models may not guide us in how we explain psychopathology to patients. Most (if not all) of these ideas can be explained using simple words. Since DSM diagnoses are still what people believe, I use them and encourage patients to look them up online and come to their own conclusions, but warn patients not to consider these categories as based on hard science.

For example, I am often asked by patients suffering from BPD to explain what caused their illness. My answer is something like this: "you were born with strong emotions and were unusually sensitive to your environment so that when no one in your life knew how to deal with the problem, you became desperate and developed symptoms that reflected that desperation". That is gene–environment (or nature–nurture) talk, and you do not need a higher degree to understand it.

This kind of explanation avoids the twin perils of telling people that their genes and neural networks are at fault, which might make them feel helpless, or that their families are at fault, which can trap them in a cage of resentment.

Similar concepts based on nature–nurture interactions can be applied to the interventions clinicians provide. If patients are overly sensitive and emotional, we can teach them ways of regulating their feelings (this is the central idea behind dialectical behavior therapy). If patients have had neglectful or traumatic rearing environments, we can teach them to accept what cannot now be changed, to learn new life skills, and to move on. In a fine turn of phrase, Linehan's (1993) term "radical acceptance" nicely captures that concept.

This point of view on what is possible in psychotherapy is essentially the same as a "serenity prayer" suggested by the American philosopher Reinhold Neibuhr, later adopted by Alcoholics Anonymous: "…grant me the serenity to accept the things I cannot change, courage to change the things I can, and wisdom to know the difference".

One of the most important contributions of these principles to practice involves taking individual differences in temperament and personality into account. Depression is a symptom, but it may need different treatment in patients with different trait profiles. A patient with high neuroticism may require careful handling to get past their tendency to avoid situations due to fear. A patient with high levels of externalizing psychopathology may need to control impulses (e.g., to drown their sorrows in substance use) before having the courage to come to grips with disappointments in life.

A person-centered approach to the treatment of psychopathology needs to be personality-sensitive and requires an assessment of the life course. I consider this to be a major conceptual basis for conducting psychotherapy.

10 Implications for Prevention and Management

Implications of Research for Early Intervention and Prevention

In recent years, there has been a movement to prevent the development of mental disorders through early intervention. This approach to at-risk populations is based on the concept of clinical staging (Cross et al., 2014). The idea is to manage psychopathology prior to vicious cycles that can set symptoms in stone.

Developing interventions that are preventive would make the most sense if we knew for sure who was most likely to develop psychopathology. But we do not know how to make such predictions with clinically relevant accuracy. In fact, as Cuijpers et al. (2021) usefully point out, most people with risk factors for psychopathology will never develop a mental disorder.

Psychological development is marked by both continuities and discontinuities. While early childhood temperament and early adversities can be statistically predictive of adult symptoms, people change a good deal over time, sometimes in rather unpredictable ways.

The problem of unpredictability arises from the complexity of the pathways to psychopathology. The effects of genes are reflected in inborn temperamental patterns. Yet heritable risks are only half the story. By and large, gene–environment interplay is the most crucial factor in outcome. Even if parents are less crucial for development than previously assumed, they play an important role reflecting what Chess and Thomas (1984) called "goodness of fit". Thus, families may have few problems raising a child with one kind of temperament, but much more difficulty with another.

Finally, psychopathology reflects changes in society as a whole. In past eras, most parents were struggling just to survive and could not consistently attend to the emotional needs of their children. Today, as parents have a more secure life, they can be overprotective (Lukianoff and Haidt, 2018). They may also, for better or for worse, be highly supportive of the value of very child. (Twenge, 2017). But self-esteem is not sufficient to develop life skills and can lead to over-confidence and self-absorption when unjustified by concrete accomplishments. Another difference between the past and the present is that young people are expected to find their own occupations, their own intimate attachments, and their own supports outside the family, tasks that create great difficulty for many young people (Paris, 2020c).

In 1963, the British Broadcasting Corporation televised a program, called "Seven Up!", about 14 seven-year-old children drawn from different socioeconomic backgrounds. The cohort was then re-interviewed every seven years, and the last installment of the series in 2019 was called "63 Up". This cohort was, of course, small and unrepresentative, and the assessments were unsystematic. Yet the prominent continuities and discontinuities in their lives provided the series with a sense of drama that gave the program a cult following. While the advantaged children tended to lead advantaged lives, some disadvantaged children did surprisingly well. Some advantaged children had to get past a difficult adolescence, while one disadvantaged child only developed significant psychopathology in his 20's (later making a partial recovery).

Research in developmental psychopathology leads to similar conclusions about the limited value of prediction. We cannot assume that the future is absolutely predictable, either by temperament or by previous life events. This is one reason why a broader paradigm can help us move beyond an illusory determinism.

Like historical events, psychological outcomes are multi-determined but ultimately unpredictable—on anything more than a statistical basis. We can view the relationships between risk factors to outcome in much the same way as weather reports. They will be correct more times than not, but will not be precise, and can sometimes be surprisingly wrong. This uncertainty is not just because we do not know enough. It relates to "chaotic" processes in which small changes can produce large effects. In complex systems, it is impossible to predict the future when so many variables are involved.

Consider the following example. A boy of mixed race is abandoned by his alcoholic father with whom he has minimal contact for years, after which the father dies in a car accident. He is raised by his mother and grandparents. He lives for a time with his mother and a stepfather in a developing country half the world away. The mother is an unstable woman who marries and divorces once again, makes little use of her higher education, and is not consistently available.

One might think that this story describes a child with a high risk for psychopathology. But the man I am writing about is Barack Obama, who served as President of the United States for 8 years and who is widely admired around the world.

The only possible conclusion is that we are not victims of circumstance. More than previously believed, character shapes destiny. Given reasonable opportunity, some succeed, while others fall by the wayside. Part of the explanation lies in heritable traits that promote resilience. Another piece of the puzzle is whether the effects of dysfunctional families are compensated by extended family and community. Another piece lies in society, depending on how easily it offers opportunities for those who are disadvantaged.

This having been said, still, another part of the explanation of unpredictable outcomes in development lies in luck. There is room in the world for many kinds of temperament. People who do not easily fit in have to find a niche that suits them (Tyrer and Tyrer, 2018). To avoid psychopathology, they need to have many pieces of the puzzle in place, but a good temperament can go far to overcome serious risk factors.

This brings us back to the question of whether psychopathology can be prevented. In the course of the last century, some held the view that happier families can be fostered by a combination of therapy and education. Others have believed that social change and a better distribution of wealth will do the trick.

Other things being equal, it is better to have a good family than a bad one. But these effects, even when statistically significant, are not as strong as one might think. This book has raised questions about the consistency of the relationship between childhood experience and adult functioning. There was a time when mental health professionals thought they could prevent mental illness by educating families. They have since learned to be humble about the practicality of prevention. There is little or no evidence that psychosocial interventions can accomplish such a task.

It is also better to be rich than poor, but the link between wealth and adult functioning is equally weak. A recent study using measures of happiness (Jebb et al., 2018) found that while happiness generally goes up with higher income, that is only true up to a point (the curve flattens out at $75K to $100K a year). We are fortunate today to live in a society where no one needs to starve to death, but the relationship of income level to psychological functioning is not straight but curvilinear.

Moreover, the evidence that early clinical interventions in children and adolescents prevent later development of psychopathology is also weak. For example, while depression and conduct disorder in childhood predict psychiatric symptoms in adulthood (Fombonne et al., 2001), we do not know which children will be affected and which will be resilient, or whether early intervention can prevent negative sequelae.

Until we understand more about the origins of psychopathology, we would be wise to use our limited resources to treat the people we are in the best position to help. We can put aside dreams of prevention until such interventions earn a solid level of support from research.

Implications for Models of Developmental Psychopathology

The point of view that emerges from the research described in this book may come as a surprise to clinicians who were trained in older models. The evidence is not in accord with once standard theories that attribute adult psychopathology primarily to childhood experiences or to family dysfunction. A shift to models based on gene–environment interplay has been in the works for a long time but now seems to have reached a turning point. These models are even beginning to be accepted by experts who have been committed to psychoanalysis (Fonagy et al., 2021).

But when we use the term "psychodynamics", we need to redefine such ideas to be consistent with recent versions of psychoanalytic theory. The most important developments have come from *attachment theory*, a thorough revision of psychoanalysis developed by the British psychiatrist John Bowlby, which has been the subject of a very large body of systematic research (Cassidy and Shaver, 2018). But the original attachment model, like other derivatives of psychoanalysis, assumed that early life experiences, by themselves, can shape personality in ways that determine the nature of adult psychopathology. It described four "attachment styles" (secure, insecure, avoidant, and disorganized) which were assumed to be stable over time.

Recently, a group of research psychoanalysts who have written a great deal about attachment, critically examined the evidence for this hypothesis, and found it wanting (Luytens et al., 2021). They pointed out six problems. The first is the lack of a strong relationship between attachment in infancy or early childhood with measures later in childhood. That finding is consistent with the temperament literature. The second is the relatively weak relationship between attachment styles in childhood and in adulthood. The third is that attachment is not the same in various sociocultural or historical contexts. The fourth is that the intergenerational transmission of attachment styles is weak. The fifth is that attachment styles show a strong genetic influence. The sixth is that attachment styles do not strongly predict responses to treatments such as psychotherapy. For all these reasons, the authors suggest that attachment is not only located in individuals but also reflects the effects of social interactions.

These problems affect almost all theories of developmental psychology. Risk factors once thought to be crucial, largely based on correlational data, are not predictive of outcomes when other risks are considered. This is why Harris (2009) argued that research on psychological development that does not acknowledge the effects of heritable traits might be generally considered to be invalid.

But to be fair to both sides of the nature–nurture divide, it should be pointed out that there are also no consistent biological predictors of psychopathology. Neither genes nor neural connections have the capacity to show anything but relatively weak correlations with developmental outcomes.

The lesson is clear. We need better models and better research, most particularly large-scale longitudinal studies that can assess many risk factors in the same individuals. And these studies benefit greatly when samples consist of twin pairs. It may also follow that as long as our measures of outcomes are limited to roughly defined diagnostic categories, our ability to determine the causes of psychopathology must be hamstrung. This raises the question of whether dimensional models could do a better job.

Implications of Dimensional Models for Treatment

1 The p factor

As discussed in Chapter 1, one can measure a general risk for psychopathology that affects all categories and all dimensions of mental disorder. It is called the "p factor" because of an analogy with the "g factor" that measures general intelligence. Caspi et al. (2014, p.119) explain the concepts behind a p factor as follows:

> "Psychiatric disorders were initially explained by three higher-order factors (Internalizing, Externalizing, and Thought Disorder) but explained even better with one General Psychopathology dimension. We have called this dimension the p factor because it conceptually parallels a familiar dimension in psychological science: the g factor of general intelligence. Higher p scores are associated with more life impairment, greater familiality, worse developmental histories, and more compromised early-life brain function. The p factor explains why it is challenging to find causes, consequences, biomarkers, and treatments with specificity to individual mental disorders."

Factor analysis of genetic data shows that the p factor accounts for nearly half the heritable variance in most mental disorders (Selzam et al., 2018). Thus, the higher the p factor, the more likely one is to develop *some* form of mental disorder. Also, a high p helps account for comorbidity between categories, as well as the tendency of psychopathology to move from one category to another over time. Finally, the p factor describes a trait-like vulnerability that lies on the interface of personality and psychopathology.

Clinicians can benefit from knowing that patients are broadly vulnerable to psychopathology, not just to a specific category of disorder. With this in mind, they could spend less time worrying about making a "correct" diagnosis when patients present with a confusingly wide range of symptoms. They would also be in a better position to avoid basing treatment on symptomatic checklists that fail to consider personality and psychopathology as a whole. This is not to say we should not make diagnoses, both for clinical communication and research. We just have to avoid believing in them as "real" entities, as opposed to provisional constructs that function as a way of describing psychopathology.

One caveat: there are situations in mental health care where making the right diagnosis can make a large difference. These scenarios arise mainly in the psychoses. Here we use different types of medication for bipolar disorder than we do for schizophrenia. Yet in many other clinical presentations, the label one uses may not make a meaningful difference, since treatment choices will not vary that much. That applies to many internalizing and externalizing disorders.

It makes a difference which of these domains of psychopathology best describe a patient. It is not really that useful to diagnose internalizing patients as having a mixture of anxiety, depression, and somatization, as all derive from the same higher-order dimension. For the same reason, it is not always helpful to think about externalizing patients as having specific patterns such as antisocial behavior, substance use, or other impulse control disorders—if all derive from the same higher-order dimension of psychopathology.

Broader domains patterns (such as the p factor) may be of particular value for clinicians who work with children and adolescents (Roland, 2019). The large-scale comorbidity that is so confusing in adult patients is even more massive earlier in development. If one is wedded to making multiple diagnoses, comorbidity will emerge in *most* patients who have externalizing or internalizing symptoms. That is why the Child Behavior Check List (CBCL, Achenbach and McConaughy, 1997), which provides a scoring system for these dimensions, has been so popular in clinical settings for children.

By and large, the more common the clinical picture, the more the DSM system is sorely wanting. One of the consequences of the system is that patients may be treated separately for each of their symptoms. Thus, multiple diagnoses become the basis for multiple interventions, each supposedly specific for one clinical feature. Polypharmacy based on DSM checklists is a frequent result. The same problem can affect psychotherapy, particularly in CBT, where specific symptoms may be targeted. However, a dimensional model of psychopathology can be useful if it views complex interacting problems as reflecting larger domains.

Research on the p factor is in concordance with the fact that general methods of treatment can be effective for a wide range of psychological problems. This is consistent with many observations, including the fact that psychological treatments of all kinds yield similar results (Wampold and Imel, 2015). These findings are also consistent with evidence that therapy directed at personality traits and the quality of interpersonal relationships is effective for symptoms (Lipsitz and Markowitz, 2016). Another example is *Dialectical Behavior Therapy* (DBT; Linehan, 1993), which offers a wide range of specific interventions, but retains a theoretically based focus on emotion regulation that has trans-diagnostic benefits for patients in many categories of disorder (Sloan et al., 2017;).

The p factor is also consistent with the view that personality traits are a key to understanding psychopathology. In personality disorders, in which maladaptive traits are the main focus of intervention, symptoms remit when patients develop a better sense of self and adopt better ways of handling relationships. This is why PD patients tend to get better with time but recover faster with psychotherapy (Paris, 2000a). Since the non-specific effects of psychological therapy run parallel to the common factors that predict outcome, adopting an integrative approach to psychotherapy may maximize these effects.

2 Internalizing disorders

This dimension of psychopathology includes disorders in which suffering is internal rather than manifested in behavior with others. This domain accounts for many clinical presentations, such as major depression, generalized anxiety disorder, panic disorder, post-traumatic stress disorder (PTSD), and obsessive-compulsive disorder (OCD). These patients tend to have personality traits profiles characterized by Neuroticism, as well as a tendency toward strategies of avoidance, that can sometimes be a barrier to effective therapy.

As we have seen in studies of temperament, internalizing traits can be observed early in childhood, and reflect both genes and environment. Goldberg and Huxley (1992) observed that depression and anxiety tend to co-occur and that most people who seek psychological help have features of both. Somatic symptom disorders can also be understood as socially acceptable ways of expressing inward psychological distress (Dimsdale, 2017). For that reason, these clinical presentations can change over time. Similarly, anorexia nervosa expresses inner distress in a manner that social forces have made more prevalent (Treasure et al., 2020).

The pharmacological agents we call "antidepressants" might be better called "antineurotics". That is because they have the same capacity to reduce anxiety as they do for depression (Pigott et a;, 2010). Even so, specific serotonin reuptake inhibitors (SSRIs), are only about 50% effective for depression, with a relatively small advantage over placebos (Fournier et al., 2010). They seem to work best when depression is an episode, as opposed to chronic depression associated with dysfunction in careers and/or interpersonal relationships. This helps explain why SSRIs tend to be unhelpful when patients also meet the criteria for a personality disorder (Newton-Howes et al., 2006). These drugs reduce symptomatic distress, but they do not have much effect on the maladaptive personality traits that drive so much of psychopathology.

The psychological treatment of internalizing disorders also tends to show broad (rather than diagnosis-specific) effects. CBT is a generic therapy that can be prescribed for most of the categories in this spectrum. Even in depression, the condition for which CBT was originally developed, its efficacy is not consistent, generally falling in a 50% range (Cuijpers et al., 2013).

Again, we need to look at personality to understand why this is the case. Even when neuroticism is reduced with treatment, it never quite goes away. Moreover, many people who are high on neuroticism rely on a strategy of avoidance to reduce mental distress. This pattern stands in the way of progress in therapy. Also, given that humans are a social species, avoidance can lead to a vicious circle in which isolation interferes with the ability to connect successfully with others, with symptoms becoming worse over time. Combatting this scenario, mainly through behavioral activation, can be a major challenge for clinicians.

3 Externalizing disorders

Due to their effects on other people, externalizing disorders have been the subject of a larger body of research than those marked by internalizing disorders. This spectrum includes substance use, antisocial behavior, and disruptive behavior in children: conduct disorder, oppositional defiant disorder, and attention-deficit hyperactivity disorder (ADHD). Again, personality traits related to these behaviors appear early in life and are influenced by heritable factors (Belsky et al., 2020).

Antisocial personality and psychopathy are among the more frequent outcomes of conduct disorder in childhood, which is, in turn, based on a temperamental profile that promotes externalization (Black, 2008). Many patients with substance use or the hyperactive type of ADHD also have these traits. At the extreme, antisocial PD is an example of a "pure" personality disorder, in the sense that inner suffering is almost entirely absent, and problems derive from making other people suffer. The partially related category of BPD shows a mixture of externalization and internalization: these patients, above and beyond emotion dysregulation, suffer from impulsivity and chronic suicidality (Paris, 2020a). This overlap between domains makes it difficult to fit the clinical picture of BPD into HiToP; research has actually shown that BPD is correlated most strongly with the p factor (Gluschkoff et al., 2021).

Externalizing disorders tend to be more difficult to treat. By externalizing problems (or denying them entirely), these patients have difficulty committing to psychotherapy. There is also data showing that patients with a mix of problems that include both externalizing internalizing symptoms, can benefit from therapies that target their personality traits (Paris, 2020a). This would include patients with substance use and BPD. This is probably why dialectical behavior therapy (DBT) has been widely used for cases that are "transdiagnostic" and cross over many domains (Ritschel et al., 2015).

4 Psychoses

The most important categories in this domain are schizophrenia and bipolarity. Since the time of the early 20th-century psychiatrist Emil Kraepelin (1923), psychiatrists have believed that these are two separate conditions that can be separated by their course and symptomatology. As noted above, this distinction has been supported by the effects of lithium therapy, which works for bipolarity, but not for schizophrenia.

However, the Kraepelinian dichotomy has been greatly weakened by recent research. In particular, one finds genetic associations for psychosis as a whole, not for separate disorders (Craddock and Owen, 2005). One explanation could be that while genetic risk is shared, there could be many other genes that interact with the ones that are associated with psychotic symptoms. It is also likely that both conditions are heterogeneous. It has long been argued that schizophrenia is not a distinct disorder, but a syndrome (Kahn et al., 2015). Recent research has also found that some patients with bipolarity are lithium-responsive, while others are not, suggesting that they have a different biological pattern and may not have the same form of pathology (Grof et al, 1994).

With rare exceptions, one cannot treat psychoses without antipsychotic medication. But these drugs, although highly efficacious for symptoms, do not address the personality changes associated with a psychotic illness. For this reason, adaptations of CBT have been used to help partially recovered patients, either to mitigate chronic delusions (Lincoln and Pedersen, 2019) or simply to help troubled people manage their lives.

In summary, the broad dimensions of quantitative models show us how temperament and personality are linked and shape the development of psychopathology. Failure to understand this relationship can lead to an over-reliance on methods used to control specific symptoms, and personality disorders are associated with more limited benefits from psychopharmacology, as well with some standard forms of psychotherapy (Paris, 2020b).

Integrating Theoretical Models into Clinical Practice

Current models of psychiatric and psychological treatment can be impersonal. Sensitivity to personality traits can help put the person back into the clinical encounter. In line with this point of view, the HiToP consortium (Ruggero et al., 2019) suggests that their model addresses the broader dimensions of psychopathology, with greater potential value for the conduct of psychotherapy (Hopwood et al., in press).

Some of the clinical presentations associated with major domains of psychopathology can be managed with symptom-based interventions, and in many cases that may be all that is required. But a personality-based perspective encourages clinicians to go beyond symptoms and to explore what patients are doing right and wrong in their lives. It is these maladaptive patterns that drive most of the symptoms that we see. A focus on maladaptive personality traits is also highly consistent with strong evidence for the effectiveness of psychotherapy, for a range of patients from the least to the most severely ill (Barkham et al., 2021).

Fragmentation in the mental health system has worked against biopsychosocial treatment. Many contemporary psychiatrists do little but prescribe drugs and do not practice psychotherapy in any structured or evidence-based way. This bias often leads to polypharmacy and ineffective changes of medication that (at best) capitalize on placebo effects. Moreover, split treatments put clinical psychologists, who carry out most psychological interventions, in a difficult position. They are left to wonder if they are missing something if their patients have not been seen by a physician. What they do not always realize is that referring most patients to a psychiatrist guarantees that they will receive drugs.

If psychologists had the right to prescribe, the situation could even get worse. Currently, the majority of patients are receiving prescriptions, most often from primary care providers. The result is that 13% of the population (18% of women and 7% of men) are currently taking antidepressants, often for extended periods of time (Brody and Gu, 2020). The reason is that once you are on these agents, both patients and physicians are reluctant to stop them. What we see is not an epidemic of depression, but of prescriptions.

The problems with psychological and psychosocial treatment are of a different nature. The demand for psychotherapy greatly exceeds the supply of providers: due to lack of insurance coverage, access is spotty at best. Add to that the fact that the standard of care for psychological interventions is less well established, with a choice of an alphabet soup of acronyms for methods which may not actually be that different from each other.

Nonetheless, the biopsychosocial model supports nature-nurture integration, offering a useful perspective for therapists. First of all, it promotes a holistic point of view that considers individual differences in personality. Second, it is important to recognize the biological factors in psychopathology, which should guide clinicians to set limited but realistic goals for treatment. Finally, taking personality traits into account encourages therapists to help patients find a niche that is consistent with their personality profile (Tyrer, 2008).

In all these ways, a broader model of psychopathology could encourage clinicians to go beyond symptom control and offer much-needed psychological therapies and rehabilitation services for the chronically ill. That may be the greatest failure of the current health system. Allen Frances (2020) points out that the National Institute of Mental Health has bet the farm on neuroscience, and that is where most of its grant money goes. At the same time research on developmental psychopathology, psychotherapy, or access to treatment is more rarely supported.

By and large, research on psychosocial interventions suffers most severely from current priorities. This occurs in spite of the fact that the research literature on these topics is just as extensive as that in neuroscience. Perhaps, the people in charge of funding never read psychology journals. But the belief that neuroscience will solve the mysteries of mental illness on its own invests us in a future that may never arrive, while it denies people in distress the right to better treatment in the present.

Biological treatments for mental disorders are seen, correctly, as making psychiatry look more like internal medicine. But this may not be a compliment! I wonder if most patients are satisfied with the quality of their relationship to the physicians who see them.

Moreover, research shows that psychotherapy is just as effective, if not more effective in the treatment of depression and anxiety as medications (Cuijpers et al., 2008). Somehow governments, and the population at large, have failed to move past the stigma attached to receiving talking therapy, and are more comfortable with a strictly medical model. This problem can only be remediated by changing our views about the mental illness itself. That would allow us to address the massive underfunding of resources that accompanies the stigma.

Meanwhile, the latest data (GBD, 2019*Diseases and Injuries Collaborators*, 2020) shows that depression ranks 13th in a list of global burden for diseases, and its burden has increased by 60% in the last three decades. It also remains difficult to reduce the stigma for all forms of psychopathology, probably because we are all afraid of becoming mentally ill. Denial of the reality can be based either on the idea that illness reflects little except biological variation or on the idea that people who seek treatment just need to get their act together. Often, it requires a member of one's own family to suffer from a mental disorder to change people's minds.

Implications for Parenting

Parents today often believe that whatever goes wrong with their children could be their fault, and many worry about being blamed for psychopathology. But every child is born with a unique set of traits. That is why we cannot determine the effectiveness of parenting without considering the nature of the child. Different approaches will be appropriate for different children, and the same parental behavior can be successful or unsuccessful, depending on how well it fits individual differences in temperament.

The quality of parenting is generally more important in raising children with temperamental vulnerabilities than it is in raising children with easier temperaments. In children with heritable vulnerabilities, rearing practices can be more problematic (Kagan, 2010). Thus, inconsistent discipline can amplify impulsivity, but this parenting style may not have dramatically negative effects on an anxious child. Similarly, overprotective parenting can amplify anxiety, even though this parenting style may not have major effects on an impulsive child. Again, the issue is "goodness of fit".

A child with an easy temperament is more likely to compensate for minor degrees of neglect and to be resilient to adverse experiences. But a child with a difficult temperament, particularly an impulsive one, needs to be handled with sufficient discipline to avoid vicious circles, in which conflict and rejection feed on each other. Similarly, an inhibited child with a slow to warm up temperament needs to be exposed to social interactions to avoid a vicious circle, in which anxiety and overprotection feed on each other.

Thinking interactively can also help counter some long-held beliefs among mental health clinicians. One, mainly held by contemporary psychiatrists, is that psychopathology is almost entirely biological and is treatable with drugs. The other view, mainly held by psychotherapists, is that parents are to blame for psychopathology and that every patient should be offered talking therapy to address these problems. Since neither of these views are evidence-based or rooted in an understanding of complex causality, they are not helpful to patients or their families (Paris, 2000b).

Complexity Reconsidered

We can be misled by the tendency of our minds to prefer simplicity. Multivariate thinking and complexity require much more mental effort. In psychopathology, from the idea of a "gene for" every illness or trait to theories about the effects of childhood abuse, univariate theories often attract a following. But eventually, it becomes clear that they fail to predict or account for psychological outcomes.

The problem of predicting any outcome when multiple interacting variables are involved can also be seen in the hard sciences. For example, in astronomy, it is not possible to compute planetary orbits with complete accuracy when three bodies are involved. We imagine that the universe functions in all aspects like a machine, but such scientific views are out of date. Philosophers may disagree as to whether quantum uncertainty applies to the macroscopic world. But it is well-established that linear models with single causes and single effects do not do justice to causality in the real world. Complex and interactive causal pathways that lack strong predictability are particularly the province of disciplines such as psychology or history.

Complexity theory is a fairly new field of scientific research (Rickels et al., 2007; Gibb et al., 2019). It studies nonlinear systems with very large numbers of interacting variables that are too complex to be accurately predicted. The study of multivariate causal systems also shows that complexity leads to new and different properties, i.e., emergence. This theoretical model has been used to explain phenomena as diverse as economics, traffic jams, and the flight of birds.

Complexity theory has also been applied to psychology, including pathways of development (Guastello et al., 2009) as well as change in psychotherapy (Hayes and Andrews, 2020). Clearly, psychological development is not as strictly determined as many domains of physics. For this reason, even if we could fully understand and measure every interaction involved in complexity, the model that emerges would still not tell the whole story.

As discussed in Chapter 3, *emergence is* one of the most important implications of complexity (Gold, 2019). This term refers to the development of new properties in a system that parts of a system could not produce alone. Or to put it more simply, the whole is greater than the sum of its parts. I do not deny that in the history of science, much progress has often come from strategies based on reduction. Atoms explain a good deal about molecules, as do quarks about atomic nuclei. And reductionism in medicine has also led to great discoveries, such as treating diabetes with insulin. But no one would attempt to explain human behavior in terms of molecules, atoms, or quarks, not to speak of neurotransmitters. This is why, while paying due respect to what reductionistic science can achieve, we need to study the mind at an emergent mental level.

Complexity can also lead to *self-organization*, which is a key property of living things. In this way, matter undergoing evolutionary change counters the effects of increasing entropy. and may also allow organisms to have both consciousness and free will (Dennett, 2003).

Developmental psychopathology is a discipline that has adopted a strong emphasis on complexity. That is why the relationship between risks and outcomes shows both *multifinality* and *equifinality* (Ciccheti and Rogosch 1996). Multifinality means that the same risk factors can lead to entirely diverse outcomes. Equifinality means that the same form of psychopathology can arise from entirely different pathways involving temperament and experience. Thus, similar risk factors lead to all kinds of symptoms in patients, and too few or no symptoms in non-patients. These principles help explain why we cannot assume that patients who have any given symptom must have been exposed to the same risk factor, or that any risk factor leads to a similar outcome. There is no single recipe for the cake of psychopathology, even if one needs to know the ingredients.

The message of this book is that it is not useful to look for simple explanations of the highly complex phenomena associated with psychopathology. A point of view that acknowledges complexity could be the best way to look at how development shapes outcomes.

Complexity is also relevant to how research on psychopathology is conducted. When I was a student, most studies were univariate and used statistical tests such as t-tests and chi-squares. Today, it is difficult to get published unless your statistics are multivariate. But there are still problems. First of all, you need a much larger sample to conduct that kind of analysis. And since larger samples are more costly, researchers may fall into the all-too-common trap of a convenience sample, such as using students in a psychology course. Needless to say, undergraduate students in a psychology class are not representative of the population as a whole, not to speak of people in other parts of them world (Henrich, 2020). The other relatively simple option is to choose people who answer queries on the internet, but that group can also be quite unrepresentative.

Second, you have to choose which variables to include in your research. But it is rare to see a study in which both biological and psychosocial factors are analyzed in the same population. Finally, traditional tests of statistical significance should be replaced by effect sizes. Most of the time, as we have seen in GWAS research, doing so will show that only a small percentage of the variance has been accounted for. And that is just as it should be.

One of the take-home messages of this book concerns clinical practice. The mental health professions need to stop competing and support a united front to get out the word about what we know and what we do not know about psychopathology. I spent the early years of my career resisting the psychological determinism associated with psychoanalysis, and I was considered something of a rebel for saying so. Now, in my later years, as I have taken a stand against biological reductionism and determinism, I find myself seen as old-fashioned. I often wonder how difficult it is for people to hold multiple points of view in their minds at the same time. Based on the positive evolution of research on psychopathology, I believe it to be possible.

The task of embracing complexity does not, however, necessarily mean we will ever be in a position to make accurate predictions about development, i.e., what kind of adult a child will become. In psychology, we are dealing with a different kind of science than physics. We not only have to give up on reduction, but we also have to accept a much more limited kind of determinism. There will never be iron laws that determine and predict a life course.

In this way, development is much like the weather, which we can only understand using model of chaotic interactions in which complexity yields a large level of unpredictability (Rickels et al., 2007). The development of psychopathology is only predictable on a statistical basis, so one can never be sure of the outcome. For one thing, people also have free will to change the course of their lives. As a clinician who uses psychotherapy to help people develop greater agency, I find the denial of free will to be incomprehensible (not to speak of it being seriously unhelpful).

The research findings described in this book can be understood to provide a stronger underpinning for psychotherapy as a major element in clinical practice. Its decline and unavailability for patients have been a real tragedy. But clinicians who do therapy are also at fault for the problem. By adopting simplistic models, by offering putatively unique procedures that are only variations on a theme, and by claiming to do more than is practicably possible for their patients, they have failed to earn the trust of patients and families. This situation is not getting better, and we are in bad need of a unified model of psychological treatment.

Finally, we need to consider the enormous power of *luck* in psychological development. Even when it comes to the origin of life and the evolution of species, if one could rerun the tape of change, things could easily have turned out very differently. In the same way, human life is full of random and unexpected events that can be turning points, either for better or for worse. So let us not dream of prediction, but be satisfied with probability. Given the complexity of the human mind and the complex and often unpredictable nature of the environment we live in, this is a task that could take centuries—and may still never be complete.

References

Abbass AA, Kisely SR, Town JM, Leichsenring F, Driessen E, De Maat S, Gerber A, Dekker J, Rabung S, Rusalovska S, Crowe E (2014). Short-term psychodynamic psychotherapies for common mental disorders. *Coch. Data. Syst. R.*, Issue 7. Art. No.: CD004687.

Achenbach, TM (1966). The classification of children's psychiatric symptoms: a factor-analytic study. *Psychol. Mono*, 80, 1–37.

Achenbach, TM (2020). Bottom-up and top-down paradigms for psychopathology: a half-century odyssey. *Annu. Rev. Clin. Psychol.*, 16, 1–24.

Achenbach, TM, McConaughy, SH (1997). *Empirically based assessment of child and adolescent psychopathology: practical applications* (2nd ed.). Thousand Oaks.

Akingbuwa, WA, Hammerschlag, AR, Jami, ES, Allegrini, AG et al. (2020). Genetic associations between childhood psychopathology and adult depression and associated traits in 42, 998 individuals: a meta-analysis. *JAMA Psychiat.*, 77, 715–728.

Allegrini, A, Cheessman, R, Rimfeld, K, Plomin R et al (2020). The p factor: genetic analyses support a general dimension of psychopathology in childhood and adolescence. *J. Child Psychol. Psychiat.*, 61, 30–39.

Amato, PR, Booth, A (1997). *A generation at risk*. Cambridge, MA: Harvard University Press.

American Psychiatric Association. (2013). *Diagnostic and statistical manual of mental disorders* (5th ed.). Arlington, VA: Author.

Arribas-Avilon, M, Bartlett, A, Avilon, A (2019). *Psychiatric genetics: from hereditary madness to big biology*. London UK: Routledge.

Assary, E, Zavos, H, Krapohl, E, Keers, R, Luess, M (2020). Genetic architecture of environmental sensitivity reflects multiple heritable components: a twin study with adolescents. *Molec. Psychiat.*, 10.1038/s41380-020-0783-8.

Bak RO, Gomez-Ospina N, Porteus MH (2018). Gene editing on center stage. *Trend. Genet.*, 34, 600–611.

Baldwin JR, Reuben A, Newbury JB, Danese A (2019). Agreement between prospective and retrospective measures of childhood maltreatment: a systematic review and meta-analysis. *JAMA Psychiat.*, 76, 584–593.

Barkham, M, Lutz W, Castonguay, LG, eds (2021). *Bergin and Garfield's handbook of psychotherapy and behavior change* (7th ed.). New York: Wiley.

Bass, E, Davis, L (1988). *The courage to heal*. New York: Harper and Row.

Barkham, M, Connell, J, Stiles WB, Evans, C (2006). Dose–effect relations and responsive regulation of treatment duration: the good enough level. *J. Clin. Consult. Psychol.*, 74, 160–167.

Barth J, Munder T, Gerger H, Nüesch E, Trelle S, Znoj H, Jüni P, Cuijpers P (2013). Comparative efficacy of seven psychotherapeutic interventions for patients with depression: a network meta-analysis. *PLoS Med.*, 10(5). e1001454. doi: 10.1371/journal.pmed.1001454.

Beck, AT (1979). *Cognitive therapy and the emotional disorders.* New York: Penguin.

Beck, AT, Freeman, A (2015). *Cognitive therapy of personality disorders* (3rd ed.). New York: Guilford.

Belsky, D (2018). Genetic analysis of social-class mobility in five longitudinal studies. *PNAS*, 115(31), E7275–E7284.

Belsky DW, Caspi A, Arseneault L, Bleidorn W, Fonagy P, Goodman M, Houts R, Moffitt TE (2012). Etiological features of borderline personality related characteristics in a birth cohort of 12-year-old children. *Dev. Psychopathol.*, 24, 251–265.

Belsky, J (2007). *Childhood experiences and reproductive strategies.* In L Barrett & R Dunbar (Eds.), *Oxford handbook of evolutionary psychology* (pp. 242–250). New York: Oxford University Press.

Belsky, J, Pluess, M (2009). The nature (and nurture?) of plasticity in early human development. *Perspect. Psychol. Sci.*, 4, 345–351.

Belsky J, Caspi, A, Moffitt, T, Poulton, R (2020). *The origins of you: how childhood shapes later life.* Cambridge: Harvard Univ Press.

Belsky, J, Pluess, M (2013). Genetic moderation of early child-care effects on social functioning across childhood. *Child Devel.*, 84, 1209–1225.

Bergman, A, Axberg, U, Hanson, E (2017). When a parent dies – a systematic review of the effects of support programs for parentally bereaved children and their caregivers. *BMC Palliat. Care.*, 16, 39.

Bisson J, AM (2013). Psychological treatment of post-traumatic stress disorder (PTSD). *Coc. Data. Syst. Rev.* Update in Cochrane Database Syst Rev. 12:CD003388. PMID: 17636720Top of Form.

Black, DW (2008). *Bad boys, bad men: confronting antisocial personality disorder (sociopathy)* (2nd ed.). New York: Oxford University Press.

Bleys, D, Luyten, P, Soenens, B, Claes, B (2018). Gene-environment interactions between stress and 5-HTTLPR in depression: a meta-analytic update. *J. Affect Dis.*, 226, 339–345.

Bolton D, Gillett G (2019). *The biopsychosocial model of health and disease: new philosophical and scientific developments.* Houndmills, UK: Palgrave.

Border R, Johnson EC, Evans LM, Smolen A, Berley N, Sullivan PF, Keller MC (2019). No support for historical candidate gene or candidate gene-by-interaction hypotheses for major depression across multiple large samples. *Am. J. Psychiat.*, 176, 376–387.

Bogdan, R, Baranger, A, Agrawal, A (2018). Polygenic risk scores in clinical psychology: bridging genomic risk to individual differences. *Ann. Rev. Clin. Psychol.*, 14, 119–157.

Bornovalova MA, Hicks BM, Iacono WG, McGue M (2013). Longitudinal twin study of borderline personality disorder traits and substance use in adolescence: developmental change, reciprocal effects, and genetic and environmental influences. *Pers. Disord.*, 4, 23–32.

Borsboom, D, Cramer, AOJ, Kalis, A (2019). Brain disorders? Not really: why network structures block reductionism in psychopathology research. *Behav. Brain Sci.*, 42(e2), 1–63. doi: 10.1017/S0140525X17002266.

Boschloo, J, van Borkulou, CD, Keyes, KM, Borsboom D (2015). The network structure of symptoms in the *Diagnostic and Statistical Manual of Mental Disorders*. PLOS One. 10.1371/journal.pone.0137621.
Bourdieu, P (1990). *In other words: essays toward a reflective sociology*. Stanford, CA: Stanford University Press.
Boyce, WT (2019). *The orchid and the dandelion*. New York, Penguin.
Breslau, N, Davis, GC, Andreski, P (1991). Traumatic events and posttraumatic stress disorder in an urban population of young adults. *Arch. Gen. Psychiat.*, 48, 216–222.
Breslau, N, Kessler, R, Chilcoat, HD, Schultz, LR, Davis, GC, Andreski, P (1998). Trauma and posttraumatic stress disorder in the community: the 1996 Detroit area survey of trauma. *Arch. Gen. Psychiat.*, 55, 626–632.
Brody, D, Gu, Q (2020). Antidepressant use among adults: United States, 2015–2018. *NCHS Data Brief No. 377*, https://www.cdc.gov/nchs/products/databriefs/db377.htm.
Browne, A, Finkelhor, D (1986). Impact of child sexual abuse: a review of the literature. *Psychol. Bull.*, 99, 66–77.
Brune, M (2016). *Textbook of evolutionary psychiatry and psychosomatic medicine: the origins of psychopathology*. New York: Oxford University Press.
Burt, SA (2011). Rethinking environmental contributions to child and adolescent psychopathology: a meta-analysis of shared environmental influences. *Psychol. Bull.*, 135, 608–637.
Buss, D (2019). *Evolutionary psychology: the new science of the mind* (6th ed.). London: Routledge.
Brumberg, JJ (1988). *Fasting girls: the emergence of anorexia nervosa as a modern disease*. Cambridge MA: Harvard University Press.
Byrd AL, Manuck SB (2014). MAOA, childhood maltreatment, and antisocial behavior: meta-analysis of a gene-environment interaction. *Biol. Psychiat.*, 75, 9–17.
Cahalan, S (2019). *The great pretender: the undercover mission that changed our understanding of madness*. New York: Grand Central Publishing.
Campbell WK, Miller JD (2011). *Handbook of narcissism and narcissistic personality disorder*. New York: Wiley.
Cantor-Graee, E, Selten JP (2005). Schizophrenia and migration: a meta-analysis and review. *Am. J. Psychiat.*, 162, 12–24.
Caspi, A, Elder, GH, Bem, DJ (1987). Moving against the world: life-course patterns of explosive children. *Develop. Psychol.*, 23, 308–313.
Caspi, A, Moffitt, T (2006). Gene–environment interactions in psychiatry: joining forces with neuroscience. *Nat. Rev. Neurosci.*, 7(7), 583–590. doi: 10.1038/nrn1925. PMID: 16791147.
Caspi, A, Moffitt, TE, Newman, DL, Silva, PA (1996). Behavioral observations at age three predict adult psychiatric disorders: longitudinal evidence from a birth cohort. *Arch. Gen. Psychiat.*, 53, 1033–1039.
Caspi, A, McClay, J, Moffitt, TE, Mill, J, Martin, J, Craig, IW (2002). Role of genotype in the cycle of violence in maltreated children. *Science*, 297, 851–854.
Caspi, A, Sugden, K, Moffitt, TE, Taylor, A, Craig IW, Harrington, H (2003). Influence of life stress on depression: moderation by a polymorphism in the 5-HTT gene. *Science*, 301, 386–389.
Caspi A, Roberts BW, Shiner RL (2005). Personality development: stability and change. *Ann. Rev. Psychol.*, 56, 453–484.

Caspi A, Houts RM, Belsky DW (2014). The p Factor: one general psychopathology factor in the structure of psychiatric disorders?. *Clin. Psychol. Sci.*, 2, 119–137.
Cassidy, J, Shaver PR (2018). *Handbook of attachment. Third edition theory, research, and clinical applications.* Guilford.
Cattell, RB (1946). *Description and measurement of personality.* Cambridge, MA: Harvard University Press.
Cherlin, AJ, Fustenberg, F, Chase-Lansdale, L, Kiernan, K et al. (1991). Longitudinal studies of effects of divorce on children in Great Britain and the United States. *Science*, 252, 1386–1389.
Chanen, AM, McCutcheon, L (2013). Prevention and early intervention for borderline personality disorder: current status and recent evidence. *Brit. J. Psychiat.*, 202, S24–S29.
Chess, S, Thomas, A (1984). *Origins and evolution of behavior disorders: from infancy to adult life.* New York: Brunner/Mazel.
Chess S, Thomas A (1990). The New York longitudinal study: the young adult periods. *Can. J. Psychiat.*, 35, 557–561.
Chess, S, Thomas, A (1999). *Goodness of fit.* New York: Brunner-Maze.
Cicchetti, D, ed. (2016). *Developmental psychopathology* (3rd ed.) New York: Wiley.
Cicchetti, D, Toth, SL (2018). Using the science of developmental psychopathology to inform child and adolescent psychotherapy. In JR Weisz & AE Kazdin (Eds.), *Evidence-based psychotherapies for children and adolescents* (pp. 484–500). The Guilford Press.
Cicchetti D, Rogosch FA, Thibodeau EL (2012). The effects of child maltreatment on early signs of antisocial behavior: genetic moderation by tryptophan hydroxylase, serotonin transporter, and monoamine oxidase A genes. *Dev. Psychopathol.*, 24, 907–928.
Cipriani A, Leucht, S, Ionaddidis, JPA, Geddes, J (2018). Comparative efficacy and acceptability of 21 antidepressant drugs for the acute treatment of adults with major depressive disorder: a systematic review and network meta-analysis. *Lancet*, 391, 1357–1366.
Clark, LS (2005). Temperament as a unifying basis for personality and psychopathology. *J. Abn. Psychol.*, 114, 505–521.
Clarke, AM, Clarke, ADP (1976). *Early experience: myth and evidence.* London: Open Books.
Cloninger, CR (1987). A systematic method for clinical description and classification of personality variants: a proposal. *Arch. Gen. Psychiat.*, 44, 573–588.
Cloninger, CR (1994). *The Temperament and Character Inventory (TCI). A guide to its development and use.* St. Louis, MO: Center for Psychobiology of Personality, Washington University.
Cobb, M (2020). *The idea of the brain.* New York: Basic Books.
Cohen, J (1994). The earth is round (p < .05). *Am. Psychol.*, 49, 997–1003.
Cohen, JA (2006). *Treating trauma and traumatic grief in children and adolescents.* New York: Guilford Press.
Cohen, P, Crawford, TN, Johnson, JG, Kasen, S (2005). The children in the community study of developmental course of personality disorder. *J. Personal. Disord.*, 19, 466–486.
Connely, R, Platt, L (2014). Cohort profile: UK Millennium Cohort Study (MCS). *Inter. J. Epidemiol.*, 43, 1719–1725.

Conway, CC, Forbes MK, Forbush KT, Eaton NR et al. (2019). A hierarchical taxonomy of psychopathology can transform Mental Health Research. *Perspect. Psychol. Sci.*, 14, 419–436.

Conway, CC, Latzman, RD, Krueger, RF (2020). A meta-structural model of common clinical disorder and personality disorder symptoms. *J. Pers. Dis.* 34, 88–106.

Cook, JM, Biyanova, T, Elhai, J, Schnurr, PP, Coyne, JC (2010). What do psychotherapists really do in practice? An Internet study of over 2,000 practitioners. *Psychotherapy,* 47, 260–267.

Copeland, WE, Shanahan, L, Hinseley, C, Costello, J, et al. (2018). Association of childhood trauma exposure with adult psychiatric disorders and functional outcomes. *JAMA Network Open*, 1, e184493.

Costa, PT, Widiger, TA (Eds.). (2013). *Personality disorders and the five-factor model of personality* (3rd ed.). Washington, DC: American Psychological Association.

Coughlin, SS (1990). Recall bias in epidemiologic studies. *J. Clin. Epidem.*, 43, 87–91.

Cross, PM, Hermens, DF, Scott, EM, McGorry, PD (2014). A clinical staging model for early intervention youth mental health services. *Psychiat. Serv.*, 65, 139–143.

Craddock, N, & Owen, MJ (2005). The beginning of the end for the Kraepelinian dichotomy. *Br. J. Psychiat.*, 186, 364–366.

Cross-Disorder Group of the Psychiatric Genomics Consortium (2019). Genomic relationships, novel loci, and pleiotropic mechanisms across eight psychiatric disorders. *Cell.* 12, 179, 1469–1482.

Crowell, SE, Beauchaine, TP, Linehan, MM (2009). A biosocial developmental model of borderline personality: Elaborating and extending Linehan's theory. *Psychol. Bull.*, 135, 495–510.

Cuijpers, P, Sijbrandij, M, Koole, SL, Andersson, F et al. (2013). The efficacy of psychotherapy and pharmacotherapy in treating depressive and anxiety disorders: a meta-analysis of direct comparisons. *World Psychiat.*, 12, 137–148.

Cuijpers, P, Smit, P, Furukawa A (2021). Most at-risk individuals will not develop a mental disorder: the limited predictive strength of risk factors. *World Psychiat.*, 20, 224–225.

Culverhouse RC, Saccone NL, Horton AC, Ma Y, Anstey KJ, Banaschewski T, et al. (2018). Collaborative meta-analysis finds no evidence of a strong interaction between stress and 5-HTTLPR genotype contributing to the development of depression. *Mol Psychiatry*, 23, 133–142.

Cuthbert, BN, Insel, TR (2013). Toward the future of psychiatric diagnosis: the seven pillars of RDoC. *BMC Med.*, 11, 126.

Cutting, GR (2015). Cystic fibrosis genetics: from molecular understanding to clinical application. *Nat. Rev. Genet.*, 16, 45–56.

David, D, Cristea, I, Hofmann, SG (2018). Why cognitive behavioral therapy is the current gold standard of psychotherapy. *Front. Psychiat.*, 9, 4–5.

Dawes, RM (1994). *House of cards: psychology and psychotherapy built on myth.* New York: Free Press.

Degler, CN (1991). *In search of human nature: the decline and revival of Darwinism in American social thought.* New York: Oxford University Press.

Dennett, D (2003). *Freedom evolves.* New York: Penguin.

De Young, C, Chmieleski, M, Clark, LA, Condon, DM (2020). The distinction between symptoms and traits in the Hierarchical Taxonomy of Psychopathology (HiTOP). *J Personal.*, in press.

Dimsdale JE (2017). Research on somatization and somatic symptom disorders: ars longa, vita brevis. *Psychosom. Med.*, 79, 971–973.

Dohrenwend BP, Turner JB, Turse NA, Adams BG, Koenen KC, Marshall R (2006). The psychological risks of Vietnam for U.S. veterans: a revisit with new data and methods. *Science*, 313, 979–982.

Donegan, N.H., Sanislow, C.A., Blumberg, H.P., Fulbright, R.K., Lacadie., C., & Skudlarski, P. (2003). Amygdala hyperreactivity in borderline personality disorder: implications for emotional dysregulation. *Biological Psychiat.*, 54, 1284–1293.

Duckworth, AL, Quirk, A, Gallop, R, Hoyle R et al (2019). Cognitive and non-cognitive predictors of success. *Proc. Nat. Acad.Sci.*, 116(47), 23499–23504.

Dudbridge F (2013). Power and predictive accuracy of polygenic risk scores. *PLoS Genet.*, 9, e1003348.

Duncan L, Keller MC (2011). A critical review of the first ten years of measured gene-by-environment interaction research in psychiatry. *Am. J. Psychiat.*, 168, 1041–1049.

Dunn, J, Plomin, R (1990). *Separate lives: why siblings are so different*. New York: Basic.

Dupre, J (2012). *Processes of life: essays in the philosophy of Biology*. New York: Oxford University Press, 2012.

Durkheim, E (1897/1997). *Suicide*. New York: Free Press.

Eaton, NR, Krueger, RF, South, SC, Gruenewald, TL, Seeman, TE, Roberts, BW (2012). Genes, environments, personality, and successful aging: toward a comprehensive developmental model in later life. *J. Geront*, 67, 480–488.

Eaton, WW, Sigal, JJ, Weinfeld, M (1982). Impairment of holocaust survivors after 33 years. *Am. J. Psychiat.*, 139, 773–777.

Eagelman, D (2020). *Livewired: the inside story of the ever-changing brain*. New York: Pantheon.

Engel, GL (1977). The need for a new medical model: a challenge for biomedicine. *Science,* 196(4286), 129–136.

Engel, GL (1980). The clinical application of the biopsychosocial model. *Am. J. Psychiat.*, 137, 535–544.

Eysenck, H, ed. (1982). *A model for personality*. New York: Springer.

Feigelman W, Rosen Z, Joiner T, Silva C, Mueller AS (2017). Examining longer-term effects of parental death in adolescents and young adults: Evidence from the national longitudinal survey of adolescent to adult health. *Death Stud.*, 41, 133–143.

Fergusson, DM, Lynskey, MT, Horwood, J (1996a). Childhood sexual abuse and psychiatric disorder in young adulthood: I: prevalence of sexual abuse and factors associated with sexual abuse. *J. Am. Acad. Child Adoles. Psychiat.*, 34, 1355–1364.

Fergusson, DM, Lynskey, MT, Horwood, J (1996b). Childhood sexual abuse and psychiatric disorder in young adulthood: II: psychiatric outcomes of childhood sexual abuse. *J. Am. Acad. Child Adolesc. Psychiat.*, 34, 1365–1374.

Fergusson DM, Boden JM, Horwood LJ, Miller AL, Kennedy MA (2011). MAOA, abuse exposure and antisocial behaviour: 30-year longitudinal study. *Brit. J. Psychiat.*, 198, 457–463.

Fergusson DM, Horwood LJ, Miller AL, Kennedy MA (2011). Life stress, 5-HTTLPR and mental disorder: findings from a 30-year longitudinal study. *Brit. J. Psychiat.*, 198(2), 129–135.

Finkelhor, D (1990). Early and long-term effects of child sexual abuse: an update. *Profession. Psychol.*, 21, 325–330.

Finkelhor, D (2007). Developmental victimology. In RC Davis, AJ Lurigio, & Herman, S (Eds.), *Victims of crime* (3rd ed., pp. 9–34). Thousand Oaks, CA: Sage Publications.

Fisher HL, Caspi A, Moffitt TE, et al. (2015). Measuring adolescents' exposure to victimization: the Environmental Risk (E-Risk) Longitudinal Twin Study. *Dev. Psychopathol.*, 27, 1399–1416.

Fombonne, E, Wistear, G, Cooper, V, Futter, M (2001). The Maudsley follow-up of child and adolescent depression. *Brit. J. Psychiat.*, 179, 210–217.

Fonagy, P, Campbell C, Constantinou M, Luyten, P et al. (2021). Culture and psychopathology: an attempt at reconsidering the role of social learning. *Devel. Psychopath.*, 1–16. doi:10.1017/S0954579421000092.

Forbes MK, Kotov R, Ruggero CJ, Watson D, Zimmerman M, Krueger RJ (2017). Delineating the joint hierarchical structure of clinical and personality disorders in an outpatient psychiatric sample. *Compr. Psychiatry.*, 79, 19–30.

France, CM, Lysaker, PH, Robinson, RP (2007). The "chemical imbalance" explanation for depression: origins, lay endorsement, and clinical implications. *Profess. Psychol.*, 38, 411–420.

Frances, A (2013). *Saving normal: an insider's revolt against out-of-control psychiatric diagnosis, DSM-5, big pharma, and the medicalization of ordinary life.* New York: William Morrow.

Frances A (2014). RDoC is necessary, but very oversold. *World Psychiat.*, 13, 47–49.

Frances, A (2020). The lure of cool brain research is stifling psychotherapy. https://aeon.co/ideas/.

Frank, JD, Frank, JB (1991). *Persuasion and healing* (3rd ed.). Baltimore: Johns Hopkins University Press.

Frankl, V (1959). *Man's search for meaning.* Boston: Beacon Press.

Furedi, F (2003). *Therapy culture: cultivating vulnerability in an uncertain age.* London: Routledge.

GBD (2019). Diseases and Injuries Collaborators (2020). Global burden of 369 diseases and injuries in 204 countries and territories, 1990–2019: a systematic analysis for the Global Burden of Disease Study 2019. *Lancet*, 396, 1204–1222. 10.1016/S0140-6736(20)30925-9.

Ghaemi, SN (2010). *The rise and fall of the biopsychosocial model: reconciling art and science in psychiatry.* Baltimore: Johns Hopkins University Press.

Gibb, S, Hendry, R, Lancaster, T (2019). *The Routledge handbook of philosophy of emergence.* London: Routledge.

Gluschkoff, K, Jokela, M, Rosenström, T (2021). General psychopathology factor and borderline personality disorder: evidence for substantial overlap from two nationally representative surveys of U.S. adults. *Personal. Disord.*, 12, 86–92.

Goemans, A, Van Geel, M, Vedder, P (2015). Over three decades of longitudinal research on the development of foster children: a meta-analysis. *Child Abuse Negl.*, 42, 121–134.

Gold, I (2009). Reduction in psychiatry. *Can. J. Psychiat.*, 54, 506–512.

Goldberg, D (2011). The heterogeneity of "major depression". *World Psychiat.* 10, 226–228.

Goldberg, D, Huxley, P (1992). *Common mental disorders: a bio-social model.* London, UK: Tavistock/Routledge.

Goldberg, LR (1990). An alternative "Description of personality": the Big-Five factor structure. *J. Personal. Soc. Psychol.*, 59, 1216–1229.

Gorman, J (2019). *Neuroscience at the intersection of mind and brain.* New York: Oxford University Press.

Gottesman II, Gould TD (2003). The endophenotype concept in psychiatry: etymology and strategic intentions. *Am. J. Psychiat.*, 160, 636–645.

Graziano, WG, Tobin, RM (2009). Agreeableness. In MR Leary & RH Hoyle (Eds.), *Handbook of Individual Differences in Social Behavior* (pp. 46–61). New York: Guilford Press.

Gross, JJ (2014). Emotion regulation: conceptual and empirical foundations. In JJ Gross (Ed.), *Handbook of Emotion Regulation* (pp. 3–20). New York, NY, US: Guilford Press.

Gross, JJ (2015). *Handbook of Emotion Regulation*, 2nd edition. New York: Guilford Press.

Guastello, SJ, Koopmans, M, Pincus, D (Eds.). (2009). *Chaos and complexity in psychology: the theory of nonlinear dynamical systems.* Cambridge University Press.

Haig, D (2021). *From Darwin to Derrida: selfish genes, social selves, and the meanings of life.* Cambridge MA: MIT Press.

Hailes, HP, Yu, R, Danese, A, Fazel, S. (2019). Long-term outcomes of childhood sexual abuse: an umbrella review. *Lancet Psychiat.*, 6, 830–839.

Halmi KA (2005). The multimodal treatment of eating disorders. *World Psychiat.*, 4, 69–73.

Harden, KP (2021). "Reports of My Death Were Greatly Exaggerated": behavior genetics in the postgenomic era. *Ann. Rev. Psychol.* (in press).

Hare, RD (1993). *Without conscience: the disturbing world of the psychopaths among us.* New York: Guilford Press.

Harrington A (2019). *Mind fixers: psychiatry's troubled search for the biology of mental illness.* New York: WW Norton.

Harris, JR (2009). *The nurture assumption: why children turn out the way they do*, revised edition, New York: Free Press.

Haslam, N (2016). Concept creep: psychology's expanding concepts of harm and pathology. *Psychol. Inq.*, 27, 1–17.

Hayes, AM, Andrews, LA (2020). A complex systems approach to the study of change in psychotherapy. *BMC Med.*, 18, 197. 10.1186/s12916-020-01662-2.

Hejmans, BT, Tobi EW, Lumey, LH (2008). Persistent epigenetic differences associated with prenatal exposure to famine in humans. *Proc. Natl. Acad. Sci. USA.*, 105, 17046–17049.

Helzer, JE, Canino, GJ eds, (1992). *Alcoholism in North America, Europe, and Asia.* New York: Oxford University Press.

Herman, J (1992). *Trauma and recovery.* New York: Basic Books.

Henrich, J (2020). *The WEIRDest people in the world: how the west became psychologically peculiar and particularly prosperous.* New York: MacMillan.

Herman, J (1992). *Trauma and recovery.* New York: Basic.

Hetherington, E. M., Elmore, A. M. (2003). Risk and resilience in children coping with their parents' divorce and remarriage. In S. S. Luthar (Eds.), *Resilience and vulnerability: Adaptation in the context of childhood adversities* (pp. 182–212). Cambridge University Press.

Hetherington, EM, Kelly, J (2002). *For better or for worse: divorce reconsidered.* New York: Norton.

Hill AB (1965). The environment and disease: association or causation? *Proc. R. Soc. Med.*, 58, 295–300.

Hirst, W, Phelps, EA, Buckner, RL, Schacter, DL, et al. (2009). Long-term memory for the terrorist attack of September 11: flashbulb memories, event memories, and the factors that influence their retention. *J. Experiment. Psychol.*, 138, 161–176.

Hofmann, SG, Asnaani, A, Vonk, IJ, Sawyer, AT, Fang, A (2012). The efficacy of Cognitive Behavioral Therapy: a review of meta-analyses. *Cog. Ther. Res.*, 36, 427–440.

Hopwood, CJ, Mulay, AL, Waught, MH, eds, (2019). *The DSM-5 alternative model for personality disorders*. New York: Routledge.

Hopwood, CJ, Bagby, RM, Gralnick, I, Roe E et al (in press). Integrating psychotherapy with the hierarchical taxonomy of psychopathology (HiTOP). *J. Psychother. Integr.* 10.31234/osf.io/jb8z4.

Horwitz, AV (2018). *PTSD: a short history*. Baltimore: Johns Hopkins Press.

Horwitz, AV, Wakefield, JC (2007). *The loss of sadness: how psychiatry transformed normal sorrow into depressive disorder*. New York: Oxford University Press.

Houtepen LC, Heron J, Suderman MJ, Tilling K, Howe LD (2018). Adverse childhood experiences in the children of the Avon Longitudinal Study of Parents and Children (ALSPAC). *Wellcome Open Res.*, 30, 106.

Howard DM, Adams MJ, Clarke TK, Hafferty JD et al. (2019). Genome-wide meta-analysis of depression identifies 102 independent variants and highlights the importance of the prefrontal brain regions. *Nat. Neurosci.*, 22, 343–352.

Howard, KI, Kopta, SM, Krause, MS, Orlinsky, DE (1986). The dose–effect relationship in psychotherapy. *Am. Psychol.*, 41, 159–164.

Hur, YM, Craig, J.M. (2013). Twin registries worldwide: an important resource for scientific research. *Twin Res. Hum. Genet.*, 16(1), 1–12.

Hyman, S (2010). The diagnosis of mental disorders: the problem of reification. *Ann. Rev. Clin. Psychol.*, 6, 155–179.

Insel, TR, Quirion, R (2005). Psychiatry as a clinical neuroscience discipline. *JAMA*, 294, 2221–2224.

Ioannidis, J (2015). Why most published research findings are false. *PLOS Med.* 2(8), e124g. doi:10.1371/journal.pmed.0020124.

Ioannidis, J (2019). Therapy and prevention for mental health: what if mental diseases are mostly not brain disorders? *Behav. Brain Sci.*, 42. doi:10.1017/S0140525X1800105X.

Jang, KL (2013). UBC twin project: still figuring out what personality is and does. *Twin Res. Hum. Gen.*, 16, 70–72.

Jang, KL (2020). Behavior genetics. In CW Lejeuz, Gratz, KL (Eds.), *The Cambridge handbook of personality disorders*. Cambridge: Cambridge Univ Press.

Jebb AT, Tay L, Diener E, Oishi S (2018). Happiness, income satiation and turning points around the world. *Nat. Hum. Behav.*, 2, 33–38. doi:10.1038/s41562-017-0277-0.

Jung, C (1921). *Psychological types*, translated by HG Barnes, Zurich: Rascher Verlag.

Kagan, J (1994). *Galen's prophecy*. New York: Basic.

Kagan, J (1998). *Three seductive ideas*. Cambridge, MA: Harvard University Press.

Kagan, J (2006). *An argument for mind*. New Haven: Yale University Press.

Kagan, J (2010). *The temperamental thread: how genes, culture, time, and luck make us who we are*. New York: Dana Press.

Kagan, J, Snidman, N (2004). *The long shadow of temperament*. Belknap Press/Harvard University Press.

Kagan, J, Zentner, M (1996). Early childhood predictors of adult psychopathology. *Harvard Rev. Psychiat.*, 3, 341–350.

Kahneman D (2011). *Thinking fast and slow*. New York: Farrar, Strauss & Giroux.

Kandel, ER (2018). *The disordered mind: what unusual brains tell us about ourselves*. New York: Farrar, Strauss & Giroux.

Kar N (2011). Cognitive behavioral therapy for the treatment of post-traumatic stress disorder: a review. *Neuropsychiatr. Dis. Treat*, 7, 167–181.

Kaufman, SB (2019). There is no nature-nurture war. *Scient. Amer.* January.

Keenan, K, Hipwell, A, Chung, T, Stepp, S, Stouthamer-Loeber, M, Loeber, R, McTigue, K (2010). The Pittsburgh Girls Study: overview and initial findings. *J. Clin. Child. Adolesc. Psychol.*, 39, 506–521. 10.1080/15374416.2010.486320.

Kendler, KS (1995). Genetic epidemiology in psychiatry: taking both genes and environment seriously. *Arch. Gen. Psychiat.*, 52, 895–899.

Kendler, KS (1996). Parenting: a genetic epidemiological perspective. *Am. J. Psychiat.*, 153, 11–20.

Kendler, KS (1997). Social support: a genetic epidemiological analysis. *Am. J. Psychiat.*, 154, 1398–1404.

Kendler KS (2019). From many to one to many—the search for causes of psychiatric illness. *JAMA Psychiat.*, 6, 1085–1091.

Kendler KS, Kuhn JW, Prescott CA (2004). Childhood sexual abuse, stressful life events, and risk for major depression in women. *Psychologic. Med.*, 34, 1475–1482.

Kendler, KS, Prescott, CA (2007). *Genes, environment, and psychopathology: understanding the causes of psychiatric and substance use disorders.* New York: Guilford.

Kendler, KS, Aggen HS, Gillespie, N, Krueger, RF (2019). The structure of genetic and environmental influences on normative personality, abnormal personality traits, and personality disorder symptoms. *Psychol. Med.*, 49, 1392–1399.

Kendler, KS, Ohlsson, H, Sundquist, J Edwards, AC (2020). The sources of parent-child transmission of risk for suicide attempt and deaths by suicide in Swedish national samples. *Am. J. Psychiat.*, 177, 938–945.

Kennair, LEO (2003). Evolutionary psychology and psychopathology. *Curr. Opin. Psychiat.*, 16, 691–699.

Kern, M, Friedman, H, Martin, L, Reynolds, C, et al (2009). Conscientiousness, career success, and longevity: a lifespan analysis. *Ann. Behav. Med.*, 37, 154–163.

Kessler, RC, McGonagle, KA, Nelson, CB, Hughes, M, Eshelman, S, Wittchen, HU, Kendler, KS (1994). Lifetime and 12-month prevalence of DSM-III-R psychiatric disorders in the United States. *Arch. Gen. Psychiat.*, 51, 8–19.

Kessler, RC, Berglund, P, Merikangas KR (2005); Lifetime prevalence and age-of-onset distributions of DSM-IV disorders in the National Comorbidity Survey Replication. *Arch. Gen. Psychiat.*, 62, 593–602.

Kimonis, ER, Frick, PJ (2016). Externalizing disorders of childhood and adolescence. In JE Maddux & BA Winstead (Eds.), *Psychopathology: foundations for a contemporary understanding* (pp. 365–389). London: Routledge.

Kisely, S, Abajobir, A, Mills, R, Strathearn, L, Clavarino, A, Najman, J (2018). Child maltreatment and mental health problems in adulthood: birth cohort study. *Brit. J. Psychiat.*, 213(6), 698–703.

Knopik, V, Neiderhiser, JM, Defries, JC, Plomin, R (2017). *Behavioral genetics* (7th ed.). New York: WH Freeman.

Koch, C (2014). *Consciousness: confessions of a Romantic Reductionist*. Cambridge MA: MIT Press.

Koenigsberg, HW (2010). Affective instability: toward an integration of neuroscience and psychological perspectives. *J. Personal. Disord.*, 24, 60–82.

Kotov, R, Gamez, W, Schmidt, F, Watson, D et al. (2010). Linking "big" personality traits to anxiety, depressive, and substance use disorders: a Meta-Analysis. *Psychol. Bull.*, 136, 768–821.

Kotov R, Krueger RF, Watson D, Achenbach TM, Althoff RR, Bagby RM, ... Zimmerman M (2017). The Hierarchical Taxonomy of Psychopathology (HiTOP). A dimensional alternative to traditional nosologies. *J. Abnorm. Psychol.*, 126, 454–477.

Kotov, R, Jonas KG, Carpenter WT, Dretsch, MN et al (2020). Validity and utility of Hierarchical Taxonomy of Psychopathology (HiTOP). I. Psychosis superspectrum. *World Psychiat.*, 19, 151–172.

Kotov, R, Krueger, RF, Watson, D, Cicero D et al. (2021, in press). The Hierarchical Taxonomy of Psychopathology (HiTOP). A quantitative nosology based on consensus of evidence. *Ann. Rev. Clin. Psychol.*, 17, 83–100.

Krueger RF (1999). The structure of common mental disorders. *Arch. Gen. Psychiat.*, 56, 921–926.

Krueger, RF, Johnson, W (2002). The Minnesota Twin Registry: current status and future directions. *Twin Res.*, 5, 488–492.

Krueger, R, Tackett, J (2003). Personality and psychopathology: working toward the bigger picture. *J. Pers. Dis.*, 17, 101–129.

Krueger RF, Markon KE (2006). Reinterpreting comorbidity: a model-based approach to understanding and classifying psychopathology. *Annu. Rev. Clin. Psychol.*, 2006, 2, 111–133.

Krueger, RF, Kotov, R, Watson, D, Forbes, MK, Eaton, NR, Ruggero, CJ, et al. (2018). Progress in achieving quantitative classification of psychopathology. *World Psychiat.*, 17, 282–293.

Krueger, RF, Markon, C (2014). The role of the DSM-5 personality trait model in moving toward a quantitative and empirically based approach to classifying personality and psychopathology. *Ann. Rev. Clin. Psychol.*, 10, 477–501.

Krueger RF, Watson D, Widiger TA (2020). The vibrant intersection of personality and psychopathology research. *J. Res. Personal.*, 84, 103890 .

Larkin, P (1988). *Collected poems.* London: Faber and Faber.

Laska, KM, Gurman, AS, Wampold, BE (2014). Expanding the lens of evidence-based practice in psychotherapy: a common factors perspective. *Psychotherapy,* 5, 467–481.

Latham, RM, Meehan, AJ, Fisher, HL, et al. (2019). Development of an individualized risk calculator for poor functioning in young people victimized during childhood: A longitudinal cohort study. *Child Abuse Neglect*, 98, 10410188.

Lawrence CR, Carlson EA, Egeland B (2006). The impact of foster care on development. *Dev. Psychopathol.*, 18, 57–76.

Lazarus, SA, Choukas-Bradley S, Beeney, JE, Stepp, SD (2019). Too much too soon? Borderline personality disorder symptoms and romantic relationships in adolescent girls. *J. Abnorm. Child Psychol.*, 47, 1995–2005.

Leahy, BL, Moore, TM, Kaczkurkin, AN, Said, D (2021). Hierarchical models of psychopathology: empirical support, implications, and remaining issues. *World Psychiat.*, 20, 57–63.

LeDoux JE (2002). *Synaptic self: how our brains become who we are.* New York: Viking.

Leichsenring F, Steinert C, Hoyer J (2016). Psychotherapy versus pharmacotherapy of depression: what's the evidence? *Psychosom. Med. Psychother.*, 62, 190–195.

Leighton DC, Harding JS, Macklin DB (1963). *The character of danger: psychiatric symptoms in selected communities.* New York: Basic.

Leucht, S, Hierl S, Klslling, JM (2012). Putting the efficacy of psychiatric and general medicine medication into perspective: review of meta- analyses. *Brit. J. Psychiat.* 200, 97–106.

Lewis, M (1997). *Altering fate.* New York: Guilford.
Lewis, SJ, Koenen, KC, Ambler, A, Danese, A (2021). Unravelling the contribution of complex trauma to psychopathology and cognitive deficits: a cohort study *Brit. J. Psychiat.* doi: 10.1192/bjp.2021.57.
Lincoln, TM, Pedersen, A (2019). An overview of the evidence for psychological interventions for psychosis: results from meta-analyses. *Clin. Psychol. Europe*, 1, 1–23.
Linden, D (2020). *Unique: the new science of human individuality.* New York: Basic Books.
Linehan, MM (1993). *Cognitive-behavioral treatment of borderline personality disorder.* New York: Guilford Press.
Lippard ETC, Nemeroff CB (2020). The devastating clinical consequences of child abuse and neglect: increased disease vulnerability and poor treatment response in mood disorders. *Am. J. Psychiat.*, 177, 20–36.
Lipsitz, JD, Markowitz, JC (2016). Interpersonal theory. In JC Norcross, GR VandenBos, DK Freedheim, & BO Olatunji (Eds.), *APA handbook of clinical psychology: theory and research* (pp. 183–212). Washington DC: American Psychological Association.
List, C (2019). *Why free will is real.* Cambridge MA: Harvard University Press.
Littlefield, AK, Lane, SP, Gette, JA, Watts, AL, Sher, KJ (2021). The "Big Everything": integrating and investigating dimensional models of psychopathology, personality, personality pathology, and cognitive functioning. *Personal. Disord.*, 12, 103–114.
Logothetis NK (2008). What we can do and what we cannot do with fMRI. *Nature*, 12, 453(7197), 869–878. doi: 10.1038/nature06976. PMID: 18548064.
Loftus, EF, Ketcham, K (1991). *Witness for the defense; the accused, the eyewitness, and the expert who puts memory on trial.* NY: St. Martin's Press.
Loring, MT (1994). *Emotional abuse: the trauma and the treatment.* New York: Lexington.
Lukianoff G, Haidt J (2018). *The coddling of the American mind.* New York: Penguin.
Luytens, P, Campbell, C, Fonagy, P (2021). Rethinking the relationship between attachment and personality disorder. *Curr. Opin. Psychol.*, 37, 109–113.
Malinovsky-Rummell, R, Hansen, DJ (1993). Long-term consequences of physical abuse. *Psychol. Bull.*, 114(1), 68–79.
Manolio TA, Collins FS, Cox NJ, Goldstein DB, Hindorff LA, et al. (2009). Finding the missing heritability of complex diseases. *Nature.* 461, 747–753.
Masten, A, Burt, K, Tellegen, A (2004). Resources and resilience in the transition to adulthood: continuity and change. *Develop. Psychopathol.*, 16, 1071–1094.
Masten, A, Cichetti, D (2010). Developmental cascades. *Devel. Psychopathol.*, 22, 491–495.
Masten, AS, Barnes, AJ (2018). Resilience in children: developmental perspectives. *Children (Basel, Switzerland)*, 5, 98–108. 10.3390/children5070098.
Maughan, B, Rutter, M (1997). Retrospective reporting of childhood adversity. *J. Personal. Disor.*, 11, 4–18.
McHugh, PR (2008). *Try to remember: Psychiatry as clash over meaning, memory, and mind.* New York: Dana Press.
McNally, R (2003). *Remembering trauma.* Cambridge MA: Harvard University Press.
McNally, RJ (2015). Is PTSD a transhistorical phenomenon? In Hinton, DE, Good, BJ (Eds.), *Culture and PTSD. trauma in global and historical perspective* (pp. 117–133). Philadelphia: U Pennsylvania Press.
McNally, RJ (2016). Can network analysis transform psychopathology? *Behav. Res. Ther.*, 86, 95–104.

McNally, RJ (2021). Network analysis of psychopathology: controversies and challenges. *Ann. Rev. Clin. Psychol.,* 17 (in press).

Mead, M (1935). *Sex and temperament in three primitive societies.* New York: Morrow.

Millon, T, Davis, R (1995). *Personality disorders: DSM-IV and beyond.* New York: Wiley.

Millon, T, Davis, R (1996). *Disorders of personality.* New York: Wiley.

Minda, JP (2020). *The psychology of thinking.* Thousand Oaks, CA: Sage.

Mintz, J, Auerbach, A, Ljuorsky, L, Johnson, M (1973). Patient's, therapist's and observers' views of psychotherapy: a 'Rashomon' experience or a reasonable consensus? *Brit. J. Med. Psychol.,* 46, 83–89.

Mitchell, K (2018). *Innate: how the wiring of our brains shapes who we are.* Princeton, NJ: Princeton University Press.

Moffitt, TE, Caspi, A, Rutter, MM, Silva, P (2001). *Sex differences in antisocial behaviour: conduct disorder, delinquency, and violence in the dunedin longitudinal study.* Cambridge: Cambridge University Press.

Moffitt, TE, Caspi, A, Rutter, M (2005). Strategy for investigating interactions between measured genes and measured environments. *Arch. Gen. Psychiat.,* 62, 473–481.

Moffitt TE, Houts R, Asherson P (2015). Is Adult ADHD a childhood-onset neurodevelopmental disorder? Evidence from a Four-Decade Longitudinal Cohort Study. *Am. J. Psychiat.,* 172, 967–977.

Moffitt, TEthe Klaus Grawe ThinkTank. (2013). Childhood exposure to violence and lifelong health: clinical intervention science and stress-biology research join forces. *Develop. Psychopathol.,* 25, 1619–1634.

Monroe, SM, Simons, AD (1991). Diathesis-stress theories in the context of life stress research. *Psychol. Bull.,* 110, 406–425.

Mosing, MA, Zietsch, BP, Shekar, SN, et al. (2009). Genetic and environmental influences on optimism and its relationship to mental and self-rated health: A study of aging twins. *Behav. Genet.,* 39, 597.

Müller, LE, Bertsch, K, Bülau, K Herpertz, SC et al. (2019). Emotional neglect in childhood shapes social dysfunctioning in adults by influencing the oxytocin and the attachment system: results from a population-based study. *Int. J. Psychophysiol.,* 136, 73–80.

Nash, MR, Hulsely, TL, Sexton, MC, Harralson, TL, Lambert, W (1993). Long-term effects of childhood sexual abuse: perceived family environment, psychopathology, and dissociation. *J. Consult. Clin. Psychol.,* 61, 276–283.

Nesse, R (2019). *Good reasons for bad feelings: insights from the frontier of evolutionary psychiatry.* New York: Penguin.

Newton-Howes, G, Tyrer, P, Johnson, T (2006). Personality disorder and the outcome of depression: meta-analysis of published studies. *Brit. J. Psychiat.,* 188, 13–20.

Nilsson, KW, Åslund, C, Comasco, E et al. (2018). Gene–environment interaction of monoamine oxidase A in relation to antisocial behaviour: current and future directions. *J. Neural. Transm.,* 125, 1601–1626.

Noll, JG (2021). Child sexual abuse as a unique risk factor for the development of psychopathology: the compounded convergence of mechanisms. *Ann. Rev. Clin. Psychol.,* 17, 439–464.

Norcross, JC, Goldfried, MR (2005). *Handbook of psychotherapy integration.* New York: Oxford University Press.

O'Donnell, K, Meaney, MJ (2020). Epigenetics, development, and psychopathology. *Ann. Rev. Clini. Psychol.,* 16, 327–350.

Olfson, M, Marcus, SC (2010). National trends in outpatient psychotherapy. *Am. J. Psychiat.*, 167, 1456–1463.
Paris, J (2000). *Myths of childhood*. New York: Brunner/Mazel.
Paris, J (2005). The developmental psychopathology of impulsivity and suicidality in borderline personality disorder. *Develop. Psychopathol.*, 17, 1095–1004.
Paris, J (2010). *The use and misuse of psychiatric drugs: an evidence-based guide*. London: John Wiley.
Paris, J (2013). *An intelligent clinician's guide to DSM-5*. New York: Oxford University Press.
Paris, J (2015a). *A concise guide to personality disorders*. American Psychological Association Publishing.
Paris, J (2017). *Psychotherapy in an age of neuroscience*. New York: Oxford University Press.
Paris, J (2019). *An evidence-based critique of contemporary psychoanalysis*. London: Routledge.
Paris, J (2020a). *Nature and nurture in psychiatry*, Washington DC: American Psychiatric Press.
Paris, J (2020b). *The treatment of borderline personality disorder* (2nd ed.). New York: Guilford.
Paris, J (2020c). *Social factors in the personality disorders: finding a niche* (2nd ed.). Cambridge, UK: Cambridge University Press.
Paris, J (2020d). *Overdiagnosis in psychiatry* (2nd ed.) New York: Oxford University Press.
Paris, J (2021). *Myths of trauma*. New York: Oxford University Press.
Paris, J (in press). Do we know how to predict or prevent suicide?: An update. *Prev. Med.*.
Paris, J, Kirmayer, L (2016). The NIMH Research Domain Criteria: A Bridge Too Far. *J Nervous and Mental Diseases*, 204, 26–32.
Parker G (1983). *Parental overprotection: a risk factor in psychosocial development*. New York: Grune and Stratton.
Parker, G (2007). Is depression over-diagnosed? *BMJ*, 225, 328–230.
Patrick, CJ (2018). *Handbook of Psychopathy*. New York: Guilford.
Paus, T, Keshavan, M, Giedd, JN (2008). Why do many psychiatric disorders emerge during adolescence?. *Nature reviews. Neuroscience*, 9, 947–957.
Peyrot WJ, Van der Auwera S, Milaneschi Y, Dolan CV et al. (2018). Does childhood trauma moderate polygenic risk for depression? a meta-analysis of 5765 subjects from the Psychiatric Genomics Consortium. *Biol Psychiatry*, 84, 138–147.
Pigott, HE, Leventhal, AM, Alter, GS, Boren, JJ (2010). Efficacy and effectiveness of antidepressants: Current status of research. *Psychother. Psychosom.*, 79, 267–279. doi:10.1159/000318293.
Pinker S (2002). *The Blank Slate: The Modern Denial of Human Nature*. New York: Viking.
Pinker, S (2011). *The Better Angels of Our Nature*. New York: Penguin.
Pinker, S (2018). *Enlightenment Now*. New York: Penguin.
Plomin, R (2011). Commentary: Why are children in the same family so different? Non-shared environment three decades later. *Int J Epidem* 40, 582–592.
Plomin, R, DeFries, JC, Knopik, VS, Neiderhiser, JM (2016). Top 10 Replicated Findings from Behavioral Genetics. *Perspect Psychol Sci* 11, 3–23.

Plomin, R (2018). *Blueprint: How DNA Makes Us Who We Are*. Cambridge, MA: MIT Press.

Pluess, M, Assary, F, Lioneeti, F, Lester, KJ et al. (2018). Environmental Sensitivity in Children: Development of the Highly Sensitive Child Scale and Identification of Sensitivity Groups. *Devel Psychol* 54, 51–70.

Polderman, T, Benyamin, B, de Leeuw, C et al. (2015). Meta-analysis of the heritability of human traits based on fifty years of twin studies. *Nat Genet* 47, 702–709.

Polimanti, R, Levey, D, Pathak, D, Wendt, F et al. (2020). Complex multi-environment gene interactions linked to the interplay between polysubstance dependence and suicidal behaviors (preprint) medRxiv 2020.01.14.20017509; doi: 10.1101/2020.01.14.20017509.

Power, C, Elliott, J (2006). Cohort profile: 1958 British birth cohort (National Child Development Study). *Int J Epidemiology*, 35, 34–41.

Pybis, J, Saxon, D, Hill, A et al. (2017). The comparative effectiveness and efficiency of cognitive behaviour therapy and generic counselling in the treatment of depression: evidence from the 2nd UK National Audit of psychological therapies. *BMC Psychiatry* 17, 215–220.

Regier DA, Narrow WE, Clarke DE, Kraemer HC, Kuramoto SJ, Kuhl EA, Kupfer DJ (2013). DSM-5 field trials in the United States and Canada, Part II: test-retest reliability of selected categorical diagnoses. *Am J Psychiatry*, 170, 59–70.

Rind, B, Tromovitch, P (1997). A meta-analytic review of findings from national samples on psychological correlates of child sexual abuse. *J Sexual Research*, 34, 237–255.

Rickles, D, Hawe, P, Shiell, A (2007). A simple guide to chaos and complexity. *J Epidemiol Community Health*, 61, 933–937.

Ritchie, S (2020). *Science Fictions How Fraud, Bias, Negligence, and Hype Undermine the Search for Truth*. New York: Metropolitan Books.

Ritschel LA, Lim NE, Stewart LM (2015). Transdiagnostic Applications of DBT for Adolescents and Adults. *Am J Psychother*, 69, 111–128.

Robins, L (1966). *Deviant children grown up*. Baltimore: Williams and Wilkins.

Robins, LN, Regier, DA (1991). *Psychiatric Disorders in America*, New York: Free Press.

Roland, A (2019). The psychopathology p factor: will it revolutionise the science and practice of child and adolescent psychiatry? *J Child Psychol Psychiat* 60, 497–499.

Romeo RD (2013). The Teenage Brain: The stress response and the adolescent brain. *Current Directions in Psychological Science*, 22, 140–145.

Romer, AL, Elliott, ML, Knodt, AR, et al (2021). Pervasively thinner neocortex as a transdiagnostic feature of general psychopathology. *Am J Psychiatry*, 178(2), 174–182.

Rose, N (2016). Reading the Human Brain: How the Mind Became Legible. *Body and Society*. 10.1177/1357034X15623363.

Rosenhan, D (1973). On being sane in insane places. *Science* 179, 250–259.

Rothbart, MK, Bates, JE (1998). Temperament. In W Damon (Series Ed.), & N Eisenberg (Vol. Ed.), *Handbook of child psychology: Vol. 3. Social, emotional and personality development*, (5th Ed, pp. 105–176). New York: Wiley.

Rothbart, M (2011). *Becoming Who We Are: Temperament and Personality in Development*. New York: Guilford.

Ruggero, CJ, Kotov, R, Hopwood, CJ, First, M, Clark, LA et al (2019). Integrating the Hierarchical Taxonomy of Psychopathology (HiTOP) into clinical practice. *J Consulting and Clinical Psychology*, 87, 1069–1108.

Rutter, M (1987). Temperament, personality, and personality disorders. *British Journal of Psychiatry*, 150, 443–448.

Rutter, M (1989). Isle of Wight revisited: Twenty-five years of child psychiatric epidemiology. *J Amer Acad Child Adol Psychiat*, 28, 633–653.

Rutter, M (1991). Nature, nurture, and psychopathology: a new look at an old topic. *Development and Psychopathology* 3, 125–136.

Rutter, M (2006). *Genes and Behavior: Nature–nurture interplay explained.* Oxford: Blackwell.

Rutter, M (2013). Annual Research Review: Resilience--clinical implications. *J Child Psychol Psychiat* 54, 474–487.

Rutter M (2012). Resilience as a dynamic concept. *Development and Psychopathology* 24, 335–344.

Rutter, M, Quinton, D (1984a). Long-term follow-up of women institutionalized in childhood. *Brit J Developmental Psychol* 18, 225–234.

Rutter, M, Quinton, D (1984b). Parental psychiatric disorder: Effects on children. *Psychological Medicine*, 14, 853–880.

Rutter, M, Caspi, A, Moffitt, T (2003). Using sex differences in psychopathology to study causal mechanisms: unifying issues and research strategies. *J Child Psychol Psychiat* 44, 1092–1115.

Rutter, M, Moffitt, T, Caspi, A (2006). Gene–environment interplay and psychopathology: Multiple varieties but real effects. *J Child Psychology Psychiatry*, 47, 226–261.

Rutter, M, Kumsta, R, Schlotz, W, Sonuga-Barle, E (2012). Longitudinal studies using a "natural experiment" design: the case of adoptees from Romanian institutions. *J Am Acad Child Adoles Psychiat* 51, 762–770.

Rutter, M, Rutter, M (1993). *Developing minds: Challenge and continuity across the life span.* New York: Basic Books.

Rutter M, Smith, D (1995). *Psychosocial Disorders in Young People: Time Trends and Their Causes*, New York: Wiley.

Sahakian BJ, Gottward, J (2017). *Sex Lies, and Brain Scans.* New York: Oxford University Press.

Salvatore, JE, Dick, DM (2015). Gene-environment interplay: where we are, where we are going. *Journal of Marriage and the Family*, 77, 344–350. 10.1111/jomf.12164.

Salvatore JE, Dick DD (2018). The genetics of conduct disorder. *Neuroscience and Biobehavioral Reviews* 91, 91–10191.

Salvatore JE, Larsson Lönn S, Sundquist J, Sundquist K, Kendler KS (2018). Genetics, the Rearing Environment, and the Intergenerational Transmission of Divorce: A Swedish National Adoption Study. *Psychol Sci.*, 29, 370–378.

Satel, S, Lilienfeld, SO (2013). *Brainwashed: The seductive appeal of mindless neuroscience.* New York: Basic Books.

Saudino KJ (2005). Behavioral genetics and child temperament. *J Dev Behav Pediatr*, 26, 214–223.

Scarr, S (1992). Developmental theories for the 1990s: Development and individual differences. *Child Dev.*, 63, 1–19.

Schacter, DL (1996). *Searching for Memory: The brain, the mind, and the past.* New York: Basic Books.

Schaefer JD, Moffitt TE, Arseneault L, Danese A, Fisher HL, Caspi A et al (2018). Adolescent victimization and early adult psychopathology: approaching causal inference using a longitudinal twin study to rule out noncausal explanations. *Clin Psychol Sci.*, 6, 352–371.

Schlomer GL, Fosco GM, Cleveland HH, Vandenbergh DJ, Feinberg ME (2015). Interparental Relationship Sensitivity Leads to Adolescent Internalizing Problems: Different Genotypes, Different Pathways. *J Marriage Fam.*, 77, 329–343.

Selzam, S, Coleman, J, Caspi, A, Moffitt, T, Plomin, R (2018). A polygenic p factor for major psychiatric disorders. *Transl Psychiat* 8, 205.

Shackelford, T.K., ed. (2013). *The Sage Handbook of Evolutionary Psychology.* Thousand Oaks, CA: Sage.

Shorter, E (1997). *A history of psychiatry.* New York, NY: Wiley.

Sigal, J. J., Weinfeld, M. (1989). *Trauma and rebirth: Intergenerational effects of the Holocaust.* New York: Praeger.

Sigal, JJ, Weinfeld, M, (2001). Do children cope better than adults with potentially traumatic stress? A 40-year follow-up of holocaust survivors. *Psychiat.: Interpers. Biolog. Proc.*, 64, 69–78.

Simpson-Adkins, GJ, Daiches, A (2018). How do children make sense of their parent's mental health difficulties: a meta-synthesis. *J. Child .Fam. Stud.*, 27(9), 2705–2716.

Sloan, E, Hall, K, Moulding, R, Bryce, S, Mildred, H, Staiger, PK (2017). Emotion regulation as a transdiagnostic treatment construct across anxiety, depression, substance, eating and borderline personality disorders: A systematic review. *Clin. Psychol. Rev.*, 57, 141–163. doi:10.1016/j.cpr.2017.09.002. Epub 2017 Sep 11. PMID: 28941927.

Smith, GT, Atkinson, EA, Davis, HA, Oltmanns, JR (2020). The general factor of psychopathology. *Annu. Rev. Clin. Psychol.*, 16, 75–98.

Smith, ML, Glass, GV, Miller, T (1980). *The benefits of psychotherapy.* Baltimore: Johns Hopkins Press.

Sonuga-Barle, EJ, Kennedy, MK, Umstad R, Rutter, M, Maughan, B (2017). Child-to-adult neurodevelopmental and mental health trajectories after early life deprivation: the young adult follow-up of the longitudinal English and Romanian adoptees study. *Lancet*, 389, 15–21.

Southwick, SM, Charney, DS (2018). *Resilience: the science of mastering life's greatest challenges.* Cambridge: Cambridge Univ Press.

Stepp SD, Scott LN, Jones NP, Whalen DJ, Hipwell AE (2016). Negative emotional reactivity as a marker of vulnerability in the development of borderline personality disorder symptoms. *Dev. Psychopathol.*, 28, 213–224.

Stern, A, Agnew-Blais, J, Arsenault, L (2018). Associations between abuse/neglect and ADHD from childhood to young adulthood: a prospective nationally representative twin study. *Child Abuse Neglect*, 81, 274–285.

Stegenga, J (2011). Is meta-analysis the platinum standard of evidence? *Stud. Hist. Philos. Biol. Biomed. Sci.*, 42(4), 497–507. doi:10.1016/j.shpsc.2011.07.003. PMID: 22035723.

Stetenga J (2018). *Medical nihilism.* New York: Oxford University Press.

Stoltenborgh, M, Marian Bakermans-Kranenburg, MJ, van IJzendoorn. MJ (2013). The neglect of child neglect: a meta-analytic review of the prevalence of neglect. *Soc. Psychiat. Psychiat. Epidemiol.*, 48, 345–355.

Tabery, J (2015). *Beyond versus: the struggle to understand the interaction of nature and nurture.* Cambridge, MA: MIT Press.

Taleb, N (2010). *The Black Swan* 2nd edition. New York: Random House.

Tam, V, Patel, N, Turcotte, M et al. (2019). Benefits and limitations of genome-wide association studies. *Nat. Rev. Genet.*, 20, 467–484.

Tellegen, A, Waller, NG (2008). Exploring personality through test construction: development of the multidimensional personality questionnaire. In GJ Boyle, G Matthews & DH Saklofske (Eds.), *The SAGE handbook of personality theory and assessment*, vol 2: Personality measurement and testing; (pp. 261–292). Thousand Oaks, CA: Sage.

Terracciano, A, McCrae, RR (2006). Cross-cultural studies of personality traits and their relevance to psychiatry. *Epidemiol. psichiatria sociale*, 15(3), 176–184.

Terracciano, A, McCrae, R, Costa, P (2008). Personality traits: stability and change with age. *Geriatri. Ag.*, 11, 474–478.

Torgersen S (2011). Personality may be psychopathology, and vice versa. *World Psychiat.*, 10, 112–113.

Treasure, J, Duarte TA, Schmidt, U (2020). Eating disorders. *Lancet*, 395, 899–911.

True, WR, Rice, J, Eisen, SA, Heath, AC, Goldberg, J, Lyons, MJ, Nowak, J (1993). A twin study of genetic and environmental contributions to liability for post-traumatic stress symptoms. *Arch. Gen. Psychiat.*, 50, 257–264.

Trull, TJ, Widiger, TA (2013). Dimensional models of personality: the five-factor model and the DSM-5. *Dial. Clin. Neurosci.*, 15, 135–146.

Turkheimer, E (2000). Three laws of behavior genetics and what they mean. *Curr. Direct. Psychol. Sci.*, 9, 160–164.

Turkheimer, E, Waldron, MC (2000). Nonshared environment: a theoretical, methodological, and quantitative review. *Psychol. Bull.*, 126, 78–108.

Turner R (2016). Uses, misuses, new uses and fundamental limitations of magnetic resonance imaging in cognitive science. *Philos. Trans. R. Soc. Lond.: Biol. Sci.*, 5, 371(1705), 20150349. doi: 10.1098/rstb.2015.0349.

Twenge, J (2017). *iGen: why today's super-connected kids are growing up less rebellious, more tolerant, less happy and completely unprepared for adulthood*. New York: Atria.

Tyrer, P, Tyrer, H (2018). *Nidotherapy: harmonising the environment with the patient* (2nd ed.). Cambridge UK: Cambridge University Press.

Uher R, Zwicker A (2017). Etiology in psychiatry: embracing the reality of poly-gene-environmental causation of mental illness. *World Psychiat.*, 16, 121–129.

Ullsperger, JM, Nikolas, MA (2017). A meta-analytic review of the association between pubertal timing and psychopathology in adolescence: are there sex differences in risk? *Psychol. Bull.*, 143, 903–938.

Vaillant GE, Western RJ (2001). Healthy aging among inner-city men. *Int. J. Psychogeriatr.*, 13, 425–437.

Vaillant GE (2012). *Triumphs of experience: the men of the Harvard grant study*. Cambridge, MA: Harvard University Press.

Van der Kolk, BA (2014). *The body keeps the score*. New York: Viking.

Wade, M, Fox, NA, Zeanah, C, Nelson, CA (2019). Long-term effects of institutional rearing, foster care, and brain activity on memory and executive functioning. *PNAS*, 116, 1808–1813.

Wadsworth, M (2010). The origins and innovatory nature of the 1946 British national birth cohort study. *Long. Life Cours. Stud.*, 1, 121–136.

Wadsworth, M (2014). Focussing and funding a birth cohort study over 20 years: the British 1946 national birth cohort study from 16 to 36 years. *Long. Life Cours. Stud.*, 5, 79–92.

Wakefield, JC (2007). The concept of mental disorder: diagnostic implications of the harmful dysfunction analysis. *World Psychiat.*, 6, 149–156.

Wakefield, JC (2012). Should prolonged grief be reclassified as a mental disorder in DSM-5?: reconsidering the empirical and conceptual arguments for complicated grief disorder. *J. Nerv. Mental Dis.*, 200, 499–511.

Wampold, B, Imel, ZE (2015). *The great psychotherapy debate: the evidence for what makes psychotherapy work.* New York: Routledge.

Wang, J, Geng, L (2019). Effects of socioeconomic status on physical and psychological health: lifestyle as a mediator. *Inter. J. Environ. Res. Pub. Health*, 16, 281–291.

Watson, D, Stanton, K, Khoo, S, Ellickson-Larew, E et al (2019). Extraversion and psychopathology: a multilevel hierarchical review. *J. Res. Pers.*, 81, 1–10.

Werner, EE, Smith, RS (1992). *Overcoming the odds: high risk children from birth to adulthood.* New York: Cornell University Press.

Weiner, B. (2012). An attribution theory of motivation. In PA Van Lange, AW Kruglanski, & ET Higgins (Eds.), *Handbook of theories of social psychology: volume 1* (Vol. 1, pp. 135–155. Sage Publications Ltd.) https://www.doi.org/10.4135/9781446249215.n8.

Weinstein, TA, Capitanio, JP, Gosling S (2008). Personality in animals. In OR John, RW Rubins, LA Pervin (Eds.), *Handbook of personality* (3rd ed., pp. 328–350). New York: Guilford.

Wertz, J, Caspi, A, Ambler, A, Moffitt, TE et al (2020). Borderline symptoms at age 12 signal risk for poor outcomes during the transition to adulthood: findings from a genetically sensitive longitudinal cohort study. *J. Am. Acad. Child Adolesc. Psychiat.*, 59, 1165–1117.

Weaver, I, Cervoni, N, Champagne, F et al. (2004). Epigenetic programming by maternal behavior. *Nat. Neurosci.*, 7, 847–854.

Whitaker, R (2002). *Mad in America.* New York: Perseus.

Whittaker, R (2010). *Anatomy of an epidemic: magic bullets, psychiatric drugs, and the astonishing rise of mental illness in America.* New York: Crown.

Widiger T (2011). Personality and psychopathology. *World Psychiat.*, 10, 103–106.

Widiger, T (2017). *The Oxford handbook of the five-factor model.* New York: Oxford University Press.

Widiger, T, Oltmanns, JR (2017). Neuroticism is a fundamental domain of personality with enormous public health implications. *World Psychiat.*, 16, 144–145.

Widiger, TA, Sellbom, M, Chmielewski, M, Clark, L et al. (2019). Personality in a hierarchical model of psychopathology *Clin. Psychol. Sci.*, 2, 77–92.

Widom, CS (1989). The cycle of violence. *Sci.*, 244, 160–166.

Widom, CS (1999). Posttraumatic stress disorder in abused and neglected children grown up. *Am. J. Psychiat.*, 156, 1223–1229.

Widom, CS, Cjaza, C, Paris, J (2009). A prospective investigation of borderline personality disorder in abused and neglected children followed up into adulthood. *J. Personal. Disord.*, 23, 433–446.

Winick, M, Meyer, KK, Harris, RC (1975). Malnutrition and environmental enrichment by early adoption. *Science*, 190(4220), 1173–1175.

Winnicott, DW (1958). *Collected papers.* London: Tavistock.

Wong, CC, Caspi, A, Williams, B, Craig, IW, Houts, R, Ambler, A, Moffitt, TE, Mill, J (2010). A longitudinal study of epigenetic variation in twins. *Epigenet.*, 5, 516–526.

World Health Organization. (2018). *International classification of diseases* (11th rev.). Geneva, Switzerland, online.

Yarrow, MR, Campbell, JD, Burton, RV (1970). Recollections of childhood: a study of the retrospective method. *Mono. Soc. Res. Child Dev.*, p. 138. Chicago: University of Chicago Press.

References

Yehuda, R. (2002). Post-traumatic stress disorder. *N. Engl. J. Med.*, 346, 108–114.

Yehuda, R, Hoge, C, Mcfarlane, A, Vermetten, E, et al. (2015). Post-traumatic stress disorder. *Nat. Rev. Dis. Prim.*, 1, 15057. doi:10.1038/nrdp.2015.57.

Yehuda, R, McFarlane, AC (1995). Conflict between current knowledge. In R Yehuda, C Hoge, A Mcfarlane, E Vermetten et al. (2015). Post-traumatic stress disorder. *Nat. Rev. Dis. Prim.*, 15057. 10.1038/nrdp.2015.57.

Yehuda, R, Lerner A (2018). Intergenerational transmission of trauma effects: putative role of epigenetic mechanisms. *World Psychiat.*, 17, 243–257.

Zanarini, MC (2018). *In the fullness of time*. New York: Oxford University Press.

Zanarini, MC, Horwood, J, Wolke, D, Grant, BF (2011). Prevalence of DSM-IV borderline personality disorder in two community samples: 6,330 English 11-year-olds and 34,653 american adults. *J. Pers. Disord.*, 25, 607–619.

Zarbo, C, Tasca, GA, Cattafi, F, Compare, A (2016). Integrative psychotherapy works. *Front. Psychol.*, 6 10.3389/fpsyg.2015.02021.

Zarbo, V, Trai, GA, Cattafi, F (2015). Integrative psychotherapy works. *Front. Psychol.*, 6. doi:10.3389/fpsyg.2015.0202.

Zhang, L, Zhang, D, Sun, Y (2019). Adverse childhood experiences and early pubertal timing among girls: a meta-analysis. *Internat. J. Environ. Res. Pub. Heal.*, 16, 2887. 10.3390/ijerph16162887.

Zimmerman, M (2012). Why hierarchical dimensional approaches to classification will fail to transform diagnosis in psychiatry. *World Psychia.*, 20, 70–72.

Zimmerman, M., Rothschild, L., Chelminski, I. (2005). The prevalence of DSM-IV personality disorders in psychiatric outpatients. *American J Psychiatry*, 162, 1911–1918.

Zipfel, S, Giel, KE, Bulik, CM, Hay, P, Schmidt, U. (2015). Anorexia nervosa: aetiology, assessment, and treatment. *Lancet Psychiat.*, 2(12), 1099–1111. doi:10.1016/S2215-0366(15)00356-9. Epub 2015 Oct 27. PMID: 26514083.

Zwicker A, Denovan-Wright, EM, Uher R (2018). Gene–environment interplay in the etiology of psychosis. *Psychol. Med.*, 48, 1925–1936.

Index

Note: Italicized page numbers refer to figures.

absorption 28
Achenbach, T.M. 19, 21–22
Achenbach System of Empirically Based Assessment (ASBEA) *19*
ADHD *see* attention–deficit hyperactivity disorder (ADHD)
adult antisocial behavior 19
adversity: in childhood 60–66; cumulative 66–67; in evolutionary context 69–70; impact on childhood 59–60
affiliation 26, 34
aggressive negative affect 26
agreeableness 28–30, 32–34
Albany–Saratoga study 74–75
ALSPAC *see* Avon Longitudinal Study of Parents and Children (ALSPAC)
Alternative Model of Personality Disorders (AMPD) 2–23, 20, 33, 35, *35*
AMPD *see* Alternative Model of Personality Disorders (AMPD)
anankastia 33
anorexia nervosa 14
antidepressants 49, 50, 101, 118, 121
antineurotics 118
antisocial personality disorder 33
anxiety disorders 19, 29, 40, 54, 118
ASBEA *see* Achenbach System of Empirically Based Assessment (ASBEA)
Assary, E. 59
attachment theory 115
attention–deficit hyperactivity disorder (ADHD) 12, 87, 119
attribution theory 102
autism spectrum disorder 12
availability bias 10, 103

Avon Longitudinal Study of Parents and Children (ALSPAC) 84

Barkham, M. 105
base rate fallacy 95–96
behavioral disorders 19, 84
behavioral inhibition 27
behavior genetics 39–42, 57, 61, 83; and environment 42–45; laws of 41
Belsky, J. 27, 69, 75, 76, 87
bias: availability 10, 103; confirmation 10; recall bias problem 99–100; temperamental 25
Big Five factors 28–30
biological psychiatry 48, 49, 58, 104; nature–nurture interactions and 107–108
biopsychosocial model (BPS) 1, 2, 4, 6, 16, 21, 53, 67, 90–91, 108, 120, 121
bipolar disorders 12–14, 34, 38, 116
bipolar-I disorder 110
bipolarity 11, 119, 120
"bipolar spectrum" disorders 12
birth cohort studies 83; of children 84–85; resilience in children 75–76
Bolton, D. 91
borderline personality disorder (BPD) 4, 14, 23, 33–35, 58, 84, 110, 119
Borsboom, D. 52, 53
Bowlby, J. 70, 115
BPD *see* borderline personality disorder (BPD)
BPS *see* biopsychosocial model (BPS)
brain imaging 48–49
British Broadcasting Corporation 113

British Columbia Twin Project 41
British National Longitudinal Study 75
Brune, M. 54
Burt, S.A. 44

Cahalan, S. 12
candidate genes 38
caseness 95–96
Caspi, A. 4, 30, 55, 79, 85, 86, 116
Cattell, R. 28
causality, problems with 93–103; base rate fallacy 95–96; caseness 95–96; clinical population vs. community population 98–99; correlation 97–98; fatal attractions to explanations and attributions 102–103; medical research studies 93–95; recall bias problem 99–100; risk factors 96–97; statistical significance vs. clinical significance 100–102
cautiousness 28
CBCL see Child Behavior Checklist (CBCL)
CBT see cognitive behavior therapy (CBT)
CCS see Children in the Community Study (CCS)
Charney, D.S. 80
chemical imbalance 49–50, 57
Chess, S. 25, 26, 112
Child Behavior Checklist (CBCL) 19, 117
childhood/children: adversity in 60–66; cumulative adversities 66–67; emotional neglect 67–68; emotion regulation 67–68; experience and adult functioning, relationship between 114; impact of adversity 59–60; institutionalized 76–78; longitudinal studies of 83–88; maltreatment 7, 60, 61, 68; and nature–nurture interactions 56–70; quality of parenting 61–62; resilience in 73–78; surviving an unhappy 79–81; trauma 59–60, 62–65, 87
childhood sexual abuse (CSA) 63, 64
Children in the Community Study (CCS) 83
Cicchetti, D. 86, 97
Clarke, A.D.P. 77
Clarke, A.M. 77
clinical depression 14, 86

clinical population vs. community population 98–99
Clustered Regularly Interspaced Short Palindromic Repeats (CRISPR) 37
cognitive behavior therapy (CBT) 3, 58–59, 104–106, 109, 117, 118, 120; trauma-focused 106
cognitive schemas 58
Cohen, J. 74, 83, 94, 101
comorbidity 14, 19–22, 32, 34, 116, 117
complexity theory 123–125
complication or scar model 30
conduct disorder 19, 27, 79, 83, 84, 87, 88, 114, 119
confirmation bias 10
conscientiousness 28, 29, 32–34
Constraint 26, 28
co-occurrence 21
correlation 7, 8, 22, 27, 44, 49, 57, 59, 63, 64, 73, 88, 97–98, 115, 119
correlations between G and E (rGE): active 82; evocative 83
CRISPR see Clustered Regularly Interspaced Short Palindromic Repeats (CRISPR)
CSA see childhood sexual abuse (CSA)
cystic fibrosis 38

Darwinian principle of natural selection 54
DBT see dialectical behavior therapy (DBT)
depression 19, 40, 50, 111; clinical 14, 86; major 12–14, 29, 110, 118; melancholic 11, 34
detachment 19, 33
developmental psychopathology 9, 27, 43, 44, 59, 102, 113, 121–124; implications for models of 114–115
Diagnostic and Statistical Manual of Mental Disorders (DSM) 13, 15, 17, 20, 21, 36, 54, 96, 110, 117; Alternative Model of Personality Disorders 22–23; personality disorders 22, 33, 34; RDoC model of psychopathology 15–16
Diagnostic and Statistical Manual of Mental Disorders, IIIrd edition *(DSM-III)* 62, 107–108
Diagnostic and Statistical Manual of Mental Disorders 5th edition *(DSM-5)* 1, 5, 10, 13, 20; neuroscience 53
dialectical behavior therapy (DBT) 58, 111, 117, 119

differential susceptibility to the environment 44, 59
dimensional models for treatment: future of 22–23; implications of 116–120
disagreeableness 28
disillusionment 105
disinhibition 19, 33
dissociality 33
dissocial personality 33
distress vs. disorder 95
divorce 65–66, 74, 75, 100, 113
dizygotic (DZ) twins 40, 41, 88
DSM see Diagnostic and Statistical Manual of Mental Disorders (DSM)
DSM-III see Diagnostic and Statistical Manual of Mental Disorders, IIIrd edition (DSM-III)
DSM-5 see Diagnostic and Statistical Manual of Mental Disorders 5th edition (DSM-5)
Dunedin Multidisciplinary Health and Development Study 85–88
Dupre, J. 46
DZ see dizygotic (DZ) twins

Eagelman, D. 43
early intervention and prevention, implications of research for 112–114
eating disorders 32, 40, 108
educational attainment 42
effortful control 26
emergence 51–52, 90, 123
emotional dysregulation 4, 7, 54, 58
emotional neglect 7, 45, 60, 61, 67–68, 74, 76, 97
emotional stability 28
emotion regulation 7, 67–68
endophenotypes 38–39
Engel, G. 90
epigenetics 45–46
equifinality 97, 124
E-Risk study 75
evidence-based psychotherapy 3
evolutionary psychology 24
externalizing disorders 119
externalizing spectrum 19
extraversion 26, 28, 32
Eysenck, H. 28

factor analysis 13, 17, 20, 22, 26, 28, 31, 116

family breakdown, and childhood adversity 65–66
fatal attractions to explanations and attributions 102–103
Feigelman, W. 65
Fergusson, D.M. 85, 87
FFM see Five Factor Model (FFM)
Five Factor Model (FFM) 20, 23, 28–31, 33, 34, 35; gender differences 32
fMRI see functional magnetic imaging (fMRI)
Fonagy, P. 67
fragmentation 120
Frances, A. 1, 48, 121
Freud, S. 57, 68
functional magnetic imaging (fMRI) 49
fundamental attribution error 103

Galton, F. 28
G×E see gene–environment interactions (G×E)
gene–environment interactions (G×E) 2, 4, 5, 39, 59, 83, 110; types of 82–83
genetic determinism 56
genome 37–40
genome-wide association studies (GWAS) 37–39, 41, 76, 86–88, 124
Ghaemi, S.N. 90, 91
Gillett, G. 91
Goldberg, D. 118
goodness of fit 25, 45, 112, 122
Great Smoky Mountains Study 83
grief 10
GWAS see genome-wide association studies (GWAS)

Harden, K.P. 42
harmful dysfunction 1, 15
Harris, J.R. 44, 57, 115
Hawaii study 74, 76
heritability 27, 30, 37, 45, 56, 57, 61, 75, 77, 83, 390–42
Herman, J. 68
HEXACO model 28
Hierarchical Taxonomy of Psychopathology (HiTOP) 17–22, 18, 30, 33, 34, 35, 51, 54, 119; p-factor 17, 22, 31; super-spectra 19, 19–22
Hill, A.B. 94, 97
history 91–92

HiTOP *see* Hierarchical Taxonomy of Psychopathology (HiTOP)
Horwood, L.J. 87
Howard, D.M. 86–87, 105
Huxley, P. 118
hypermnesia 68

ICD *see* International Classification of Diseases (ICD)
ICD-10 *see* International Classification of Diseases 10th edition (ICD-10)
ICD-11 *see* International Classification of Diseases 11th edition (ICD-11)
impulsivity 26, 28, 32, 33, 35, 76, 78, 79, 84, 119, 122
Insel, T.R. 12–13, 17
institutionalized children 76–78
internalizing spectrum 19
International Classification of Diseases (ICD) 15, 17, 34
International Classification of Diseases 10th edition (ICD-10): dissocial personality 33
International Classification of Diseases 11th edition (ICD-11) 1, 5–6, 10, 20, 23; neuroscience 53; personality disorders 33, 34
introversion 28, 29, 32
intuition 28
Ioannidis, J. 53–54, 87
IQ 29, 41
Isle of Wight Study 73

Jang, K.L. 43, 44
Jung, C. 28

Kagan, J. 25, 27, 44, 45, 61, 67, 73
Kahnemann, D. 102
Kaufman, S.B. 45
Kendler, K. 40
Kern, M. 29
Kraepelin, E. 119
Krueger, R.F. 17
Kurosawa, A. 99

Larkin, P. 57
Leahy, B.L. 21
Lilienfeld, S.O. 49
Linehan, M.M. 58, 59, 107, 111
Littlefield, A.K. 31
Locke, J. 56
locus of control 103

longitudinal studies of children 83–88; birth cohort studies 84–85; Dunedin Multidisciplinary Health and Development Study 85–88; high-Risk samples 84
longitudinal studies of twins 88–89

major depression 12–14, 29, 110, 118
maltreatment 4; childhood 7, 60, 61, 68
marital conflict 62, 100
Mead, M. 56
Meaney, M. 45, 46
medical research studies causality 93–95
melancholic depression 11, 34
memory: recovered, myth of 68–69; research 68–69
Mencken, H.L. 8, 93
mental disorders 1–7, 10–13, 16, 17, 19, 20, 29–31, 34, 37–40, 48, 50, 52, 57, 58, 71, 96, 98, 104, 108, 110, 112, 116, 121, 122; adults 59–61, 63, 74; children 73; definition of 1, 15; diagnosis of 23; distress and 95; etiological model of 54; personality traits and 6, 21, 42; tendency of 22
"missing heritability" problem 39
Moffit, T. 55
Moffitt, T. 85
monozygotic (MZ) twins 40, 41
multifinality 97, 124
Myths of Childhood (Paris) 6–7
MZ *see* monozygotic (MZ) twins

National Comorbidity Survey 96
National Institute of Mental Health (NIMH) 6, 16, 48
National Longitudinal Survey of Adolescent to Adult Health 65
National Survey of Health and Development (NSHD) 85
nature–nurture interactions 2–4, 82–92, 104–107, 110, 115; and biological psychiatry 107–108; biopsychosocial model 90–91; childhood and 56–70; in clinical practice 8–9; gene–environment interplay 82–83; longitudinal studies of children 83–88; longitudinal studies of twins 88–89; personality and 6–8; psychology and history 91–92; social risk factors for psychopathology 89–90

negative affect 19, 33; aggressive 26; non-aggressive 26
Negative Emotional Temperament 26, 28
Neibuhr, R. 111
NEO Personality Inventory Revised (NEO-PI-R) 29
NEO-PI-R *see* NEO Personality Inventory Revised (NEO-PI-R)
network theory 20, 54
neurodevelopmental impairment 40
neuroplasticity 52
neuroscience 2–4, 6, 8, 13, 21, 38, 47–55, 57, 58, 91, 105, 121; brain imaging 48–49; chemical imbalance 49–50; clinical application of 17, 89; cognitive 16; complexity of 53–54; current status of 47–48; emergence of 51–52; reductionism 50–51
neuroticism 28, 29, 31, 32
NIMH *see* National Institute of Mental Health (NIMH)
non-aggressive negative affect 26
NSHD *see* National Survey of Health and Development (NSHD)

obsessive–compulsive disorder 32
ODD *see* oppositional defiant disorder (ODD)
Oltmanns, J.R. 31
openness to experience 28, 30
oppositional defiant disorder (ODD) 19, 119
optimism 20, 80
orienting sensitivity 26

Parental Bonding Index 61
parenting: implications for 122; quality of 61–62, 122
Parker, G. 61
pathoplasty model 30
PDs *see* personality disorders (PD)
personality 1; definition of 24; dissocial 33; profiles 30–32; in psychotherapy, working with 109–111
personality disorders (PDs) 12, 22, 29, 32–36, *35*, 58, 106, 108, 117, 119
personality traits 6–8; measurement of 28–30
personalized medicine 37
p-factor 17, 22, 31, 34, 116–117
pharmacotherapy 108
physical violence 65
physiological psychology 47

Pinker, S. 56, 106
Plomin, R. 40–41, 44
Pluess, M. 87
polygenic risk score (PRS) 39, 42, 76
Positive Emotional Temperament 26, 28
post-traumatic growth 80
post-traumatic stress disorder (PTSD) 12, 19, 29, 62, 63
poverty, and childhood adversity 66
predisposition-stress model of psychopathology 21
PRS *see* polygenic risk score (PRS)
psychiatric diagnosis 10–12, 108
psychiatry 5; biological 48, 58, 107–108
psychoanalytic theory 115
psychodynamics 115
psychological development 43
psychological immune system 1
psychology 91–92; evolutionary 24; physiological 47; trait 24
psychometrics 13
psychopathology 3, 5, 8; biopsychosocial model of 1, 2, 4, 6, 16, 21, 53, 67, 90–91, 108, 120, 121; categories of 13–15; childhood and 57–59; definition of 1; developmental 9, 27, 43, 44, 59, 102, 113–115, 121–124; dimensions of 4–6, 13–15; Hierarchical Taxonomy of Psychopathology 17–22, *18*, *19*; normal *vs.* abnormal 10–13; predisposition-stress model of 21; RDoC model of 6, 15–17; social risk factors for 89–90
psychopathy 34
psychoses 119–120
psychotherapy: evidence-based 3; implications for 104–111; integration 109; working principle of 108–109; working with personality in 109–111
psychoticism 19–20, 28
PTSD *see* post-traumatic stress disorder (PTSD)

Quinton, D. 76, 78
Quirion, R. 12–13, 17

radical acceptance 111
"Rashomon" (film) 99
RDoC *see* Research Domain Criteria (RDoC) model of psychopathology
recall bias problem 99–100
reductionism 50–51
remarriage 66

Research Domain Criteria (RDoC) model of psychopathology 6, 15–17, 48
resilience 59, 71–81, 113; Albany–Saratoga study 74–75; birth cohort studies 75–76; in children 73–78; Hawaii study 74; individual differences in 72–73; institutionalized children 76–78; mechanisms of 78–79; nature of 71–72; surviving an unhappy childhood 79–81
rGE *see* correlations between G and E (rGE)
risk factors, and causality 96–97
Rosenhan, D. 11, 12
Rothbart, M. 26
Rutter, M. 8, 24, 40, 67, 73, 76–78, 80, 85

Satel, S. 49
schizophrenia 12–14, 34, 38, 40, 56, 110, 116, 119
self-esteem 65, 100, 112
self-organization 123–124
sensation 28
SEPI *see* Society for the Exploration of Psychotherapy Integration (SEPI)
serotonin reuptake inhibitors (SSRIs) 118
"Seven Up!" 113
"63 Up" 113
Smith, G.T. 17
Smith, M.L. 104
Smith, R.S. 78, 80
social capital 90
social class, and childhood adversity 66
social cohesion 79, 80
social disintegration 89
social risk factors for psychopathology 89–90
Society for the Exploration of Psychotherapy Integration (SEPI) 109
socioeconomic status 66, 73
Southwick, S.M. 80
spectrum or co-aggregation model 30
SSRIs *see* serotonin reuptake inhibitors (SSRIs)
standard social science model 106
statistical significance *vs.* clinical significance 100–102
super-spectra *19*, 19–22
surgency 26

Tabery, J. 86
Taleb, N. 93
talking therapy 3, 121, 122
Tellegen, A. 28
temperament 7, 8, 24–27, 62, 107, 111, 114, 122; anxious 79; aspects of 26; bias 25; in children 59; definition of 25; quality 78; types of 25, 26
Terman Life Course Study 29
TFCBT *see* trauma-focused CBT (TFCBT)
then-dominant psychodynamic model 3
theoretical models into clinical practice, integrating 120–122
theory of mind 55
Thomas, A. 25, 26, 112
thought disorder 19–20
Tinbergen, N. 24
Torgersen, S. 32
tragic vision 56
trait psychology 24
trauma 4, 6–8, 45, 71, 106; childhood 58–60, 62–65, 87
trauma-focused CBT (TFCBT) 106
Turkheimer, E. 41, 43
twins: dizygotic 88; longitudinal studies of 88–89; monozygotic 40, 41, 88

Utopian vision 56, 57

Vaillant, G.E. 78
Van der Kolk, B.A. 68
Virginia Twin Study of Adolescent Behavioral Development 40
vulnerability or predisposition model 30

Wakefield, J.C. 1, 15
Waldron, M.C. 43
Werner, E.E. 74, 78, 80
Widiger, T. 29, 30–32
Widom, C.S. 63
Winnicott, D. 61

Zanarini, M.C. 84
Zentner, M. 73
Zimmerman, M. 22, 23
Zwicker, A. 87

Printed in the United States
by Baker & Taylor Publisher Services